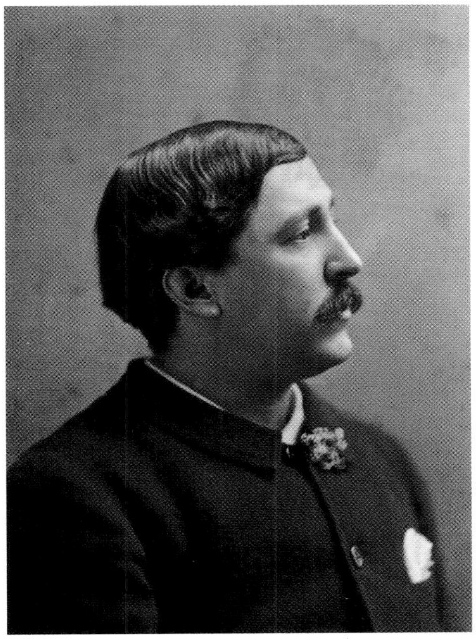

William Stott 1857–1900

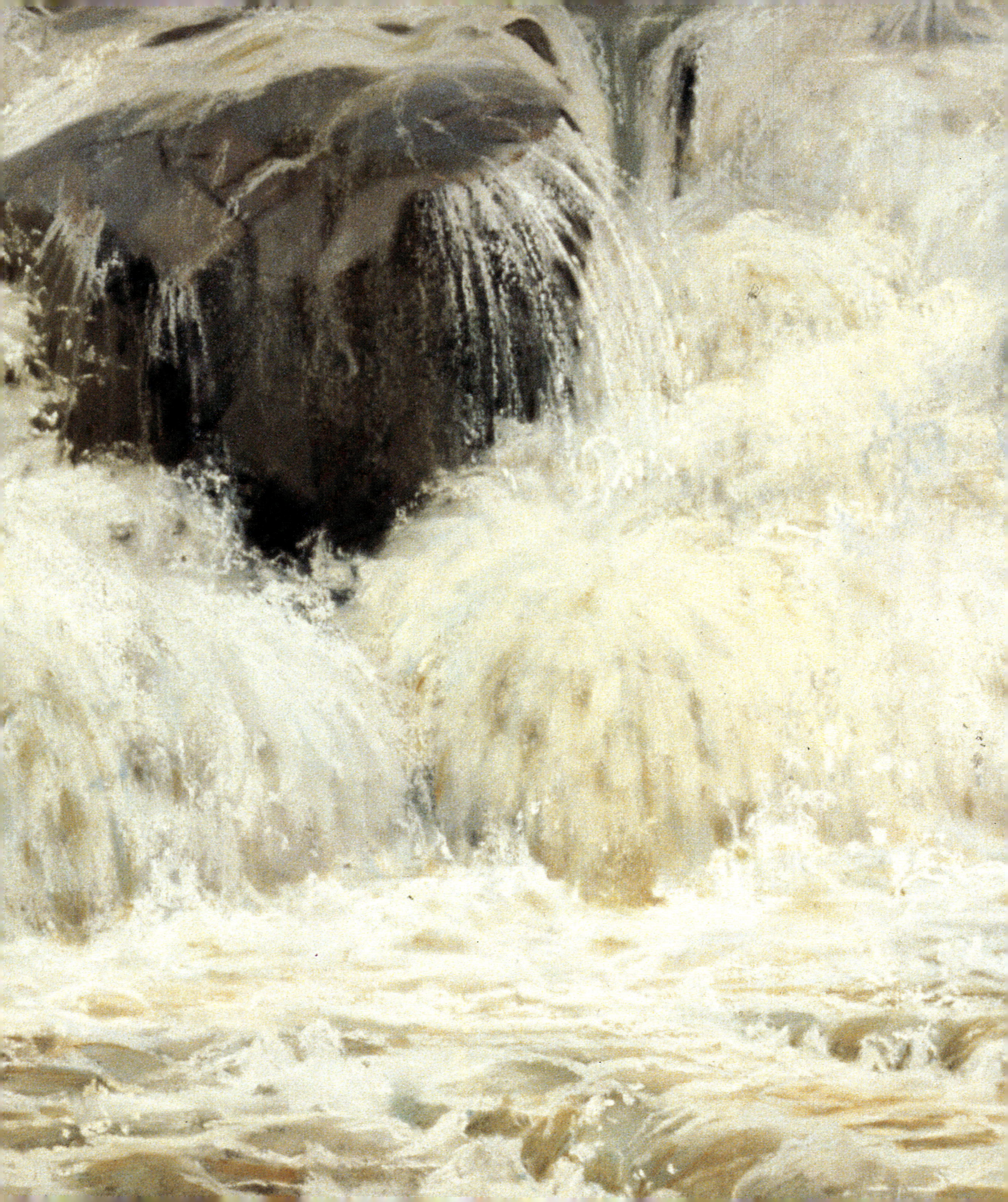

William Stott of Oldham 1857–1900 *"A Comet rushing to the Sun"*

ROGER BROWN

Paul Holberton publishing in association with Gallery Oldham

This book is dedicated to John and Muriel Brown

First published December 2003
by Paul Holberton publishing in association with Gallery Oldham
to accompany the exhibition *William Stott of Oldham* at Gallery Oldham
6 December 2003– 24 April 2004

GALLERY OLDHAM

OLDHAM
Education & Culture

ISBN (hardcover) 1 903470 21 8
(softcover) 1 903470 20 X

British Library Cataloguing in Publication Data
A catalogue record for this book is available from the British Library

Produced by Paul Holberton publishing
37 Snowsfields, London SE1 3SU
www.paul-holberton.net

Designed by Roger Davies daviesdesign@onetel.net.uk

Printed in Italy

Distributed in UK and Europe and the rest of the world by Greenhill Books
Distributed in USA and Canada by University of Washington Press
www.paul-holberton.net

Jacket/cover image William Stott, *Prince or Shepherd?*
(also known as *The Girl in a Meadow*), detail (cat. 8)
Back of jacket/ back of cover Theodore Robinson, *William Stott*, 1879 (fig. 1)

Contents

Foreword

Sheena Macfarlane
Head of Galleries, Museums and Arts
Oldham Metropolitan Borough Council

Gallery Oldham is proud to host the first major retrospective exhibition of the work of William Stott of Oldham. The exhibition, the first since the artist's death in 1900, and this accompanying biographical study of the man and his art, is in effect long overdue. Over the years there has been a steady interest in Stott, as both an artist and an Oldhamer, and his popularity is illustrated by the fact that he is represented in so many public and private collections across the country. Three of his works have recently toured internationally as part of the exhibition *Exposed: The Victorian Nude*, organized by Tate Britain. Gallery Oldham has nineteen of his works, spanning his artistic career, all of which are on show.

Although Stott's career was brief, he travelled widely, mixed with the famous artists of the day and became a notable and respected figure in the late nineteenth-century art world. Throughout his career he was a frequent visitor to his home town and retained links with the Lancashire art scene. Oldham is proud of Stott as he was of his roots, choosing to be known throughout his career as William Stott of Oldham to avoid confusion with a Rochdale contemporary. This exhibition celebrates an eminent artist and a local worthy.

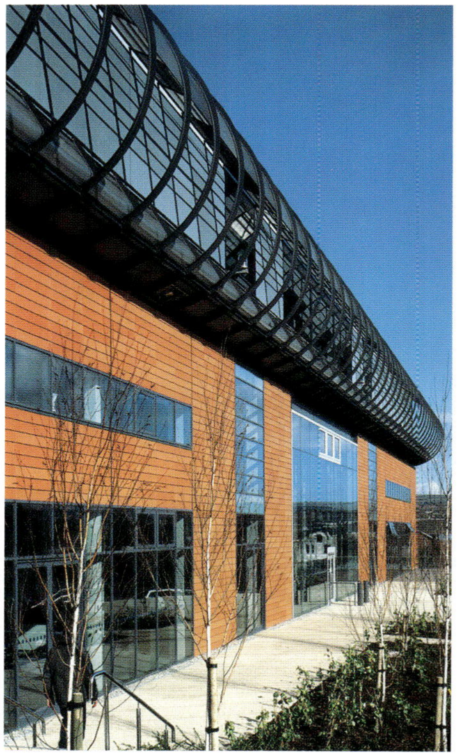

Gallery Oldham has been fortunate to be able to collaborate with Roger Brown, who has been researching the life and work of William Stott for many years. His knowledge and personal contacts with private collectors have helped to make this a comprehensive and insightful exhibition. Over half the works on show, many of which have never been seen in public before, are from private collectors, and we are grateful to them for their generosity in loaning their pictures. Thanks must also go to the many public galleries who have loaned works for the exhibition. We are also grateful for financial support towards this publication and the exhibition from Mr David Bellis, The Granada Foundation, the Marc Fitch Fund and The Paul Mellon Centre for Studies in British Art.

Acknowledgements

Roger Brown

One of the most rewarding aspects of the research I have carried out into the work of William Stott over the past few years has been the number of new friendships I have forged with art historians, museum and gallery staff, private owners and lovers of nineteenth-century art both in the United Kingdom and abroad. Everyone's enthusiasm, encouragement and willingness to assist have been overwhelming and kept me focused on my goal of a long-overdue retrospective exhibition of William Stott's work.

To begin with I want to acknowledge the help given to me by Christiana Payne and the late Jeanne Sheehy, my supervisors at Oxford Brookes University, whose wisdom and experience ensured that my research was set on firm foundations. I must also thank Anna Gruetzner Robins for providing invaluable information, and latterly Kenneth McConkey for his enthusiasm for the project and sharing with me his unrivalled knowledge of the period.

Special thanks must go to Trevor Coombs, former Keeper of Art at Oldham Art Gallery, who generously handed over to me his notes and preliminary research on William Stott. Also, I am indebted to Julia Willcox, who I have not met, but whose unpublished Honours degree dissertation on William Stott for St Andrews University in 1989 opened up a number avenues of investigation for me to pursue.

William Stott's only son had no children, so there are no direct descendants, but his family is numerous, with many branches. Those I have contacted have been extremely kind and supportive of the exhibition. Indeed 'word of mouth' among the family is how a number of pictures were located. I thank them all for welcoming me into their homes and for their generosity in lending to me documents and papers related to William Stott's life. Special thanks are due to Peter and Dinah Stott, who not only provided encouragement but superb hospitality and a bed for the night if needed! Mme Claire Leray from Grez-sur-Loing provided me with information on the artists' colony there, as well as warm friendship and conviviality on my visits to the village. David Pickup and Peter van Zeller from Ravenglass provided local knowledge in the identification of Stott's landscapes of the surrounding countryside.

Very sincere thanks must go to the staff of Gallery Oldham for putting up with me worrying and pestering them over the last five years, and in particular the Exhibitions Co-ordinator, Peter Fox, who I have enjoyed working with on this exhibition. My thanks must go also to the numerous museum and gallery curators, archivists, conservators and members of the art trade who have helped towards the realisation of this project: they include Jill Addleson, Barbara Angelicus, Janet Boston, Richard Burns, Kirsty Devine, Sheila Dewsbury, John Dunn, Caroline Durand-Ruel Godfroy, Yvonne Hardman, Ingrid Huber, Adrian Jenkins, Jennifer Jones, Joachim Kaak, Elaine Kilmurray, Moira Lindsay, Jennifer Melville, Lynda Mcleod, Edward Morris, Mark Pomeroy, Peyton Skipwith, Janice Slater, Helen Smailes, Ira Spanierman, Sheila Stoddard, Penny Thompson, Carolyn Walker and Clara Young. I would like to thank Paul Holberton and Roger Davies for guiding me through the traumas of my first publication and producing a catalogue which is a worthy tribute to William Stott.

My greatest debt is to my wife, Diana, for her unfailing support and encouragement, which made everything continue to seem possible.

Preface

Roger Brown

My interest in William Stott (1857–1900) stems from seeing three pictures by this artist in the *Impressionism in Britain* exhibition at the Barbican Art Gallery in the spring of 1995. As well as appreciating his work, I was intrigued by the fact that he was referred to as Stott 'of Oldham', whereas his contemporary Edward Stott (1859–1918) was never 'of Rochdale'. With my interest awakened, I was surprised when, a few weeks later at the *Landscapes of France: Impressionism and its Rivals* exhibition at the Hayward Gallery, the only English artist represented was William Stott of Oldham, with a magnificent Salon picture of 1882, *The Ferry* (cat. 10). On examining other catalogues of nineteenth-century British art I found that works by William Stott appeared regularly in a variety of genres. My interest in this English artist, who became a hero of the Paris Salon in the 1880s, befriended Whistler and was highly acclaimed on the Continent, was now fully stimulated, and I resolved to research his life and work. This publication, which is based on the dissertation I submitted for a Masters degree in the History of British Art, will analyse his stylistic development and re-appraise William Stott's contribution to British art in the late nineteenth century.

No monograph on Stott has been written since he died in 1900. The only two articles given over to his work are much quoted, but not particularly impartial or accurate. They are Alice Corkran's piece in the *Scottish Art Review* of 1889 and R.A.M. Stevenson's article in *The Studio* of 1894. The only exhibition to be devoted to his work, since a small retrospective in 1911, has been at The Fine Art Society in London in 1976, when he had to share the stage with his contemporary Edward Stott. Apart from two letters to the Press and two reported speeches, at the outset of my research no other evidence existed of William Stott's views on the role of the artist or of his own aesthetic values. Because of the lack of knowledge and information that existed about Stott, I felt it was valid to adopt a chronological approach to his development as an artist, in order to contextualize his work with that of his contemporaries, and to trace the influences on his stylistic progression. The approach was largely based on first-hand examination of his works in both public and private collections, of contemporary exhibition catalogues and reviews, obituaries, and the memoirs and papers of artists he came into contact with.

During the course of my research some exciting 'discoveries' were made, not least Stott's notebook covering the first twelve years of his artistic life – which I have consulted constantly, and which has helped to clarify the provenance and dating of a considerable number of pictures. In addition, certain pictures previously thought to have been lost have come to light, perhaps most excitingly *Idlers* (cat. 65), his 1896 Royal Academy exhibit, and *Alice White playing the Violin* (cat. 21), both of which are in private collections, but also others that were languishing in the vaults of public galleries. With the help of Professor Kenneth McConkey, Stott's 1883 Paris Salon picture, *The Kissing Ring* (fig. 24), was traced to Durban Art Gallery, South Africa. Sadly, lack of funds has meant that it has not been possible to bring the painting over for this exhibition. Some important letters from Stott to John Forbes White, the art critic and collector, came to light, which fortunately confirmed assumptions already made about the extent of Stott's associates in the artistic community in Paris. Very recently, two more letters, from Stott to the animal painter John MacAllan Swan R.A., have been found, which shed light on his method of working and his state of mind in his latter years. Finally, a previously unknown portrait of Stott has surfaced in New York (fig. 1). It is a small sketch by the American

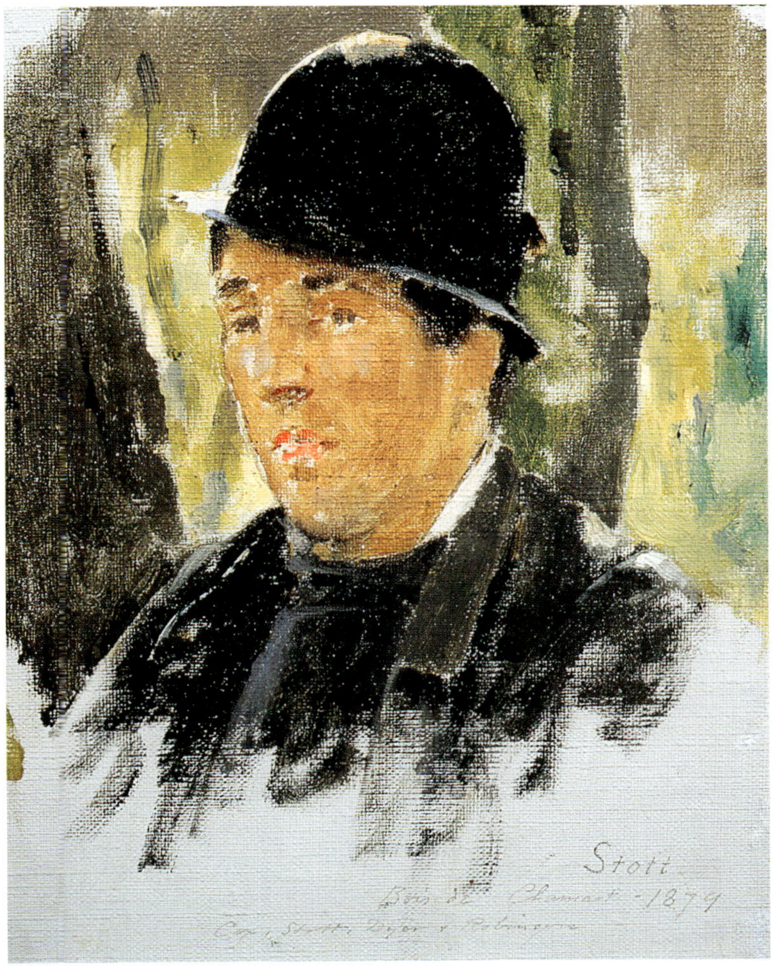

Fig. 1 Theodore Robinson (1852–1896)
William Stott, Bois de Clamart, near Paris, 1879
Oil on canvas, 22.5 x 18.4 cm
Courtesy of the Spanierman Gallery, New York

Theodore Robinson, a student companion at Jean-Léon Gérôme's studio, and bears testimony to Stott's involvement with the international community of artists in Paris.

William Stott arrived into the febrile world of Parisian art at a critical time in the development of Western art. The Impressionist exhibitions were in full swing and the Symbolist movement was gaining currency. He quickly absorbed the modern trends in naturalist art, being at first attracted, like many of his compatriots, to the work of Jules Bastien-Lepage and the *juste milieu* artists of the Third Republic. He gained early success at the Paris Salon, being medalled in 1882 for *The Bathing Place* (fig. 17), which marked him out as a leading member of the British and American community at Grez-sur-Loing and of the European *avant-garde*. For a time he was regarded on the Continent as one of the more progressive British painters, and was invited to exhibit at secessionist groups such as Les XX in Brussels, and also in Munich. However, with his poetic and romantic temperament, he became dissatisfied with 'commonplace realism' and moved towards Aestheticism, becoming a follower of Whistler until his picture *The Birth of Venus* (cat. 55), portraying Whistler's mistress, Maud Franklin, became a *cause célèbre* between the two men. In his latter years he moved to a form of decorative Symbolism for his exhibition pictures, with a clear influence from Puvis de Chavannes, but also with a reference to the Pre-Raphaelites and the English Aesthetic Movement. However, in his recreational work in and around his home at Ravenglass in Cumbria and on his increasingly frequent sea-trips he remained faithful to the Whistlerian aesthetic, finding beauty in the simple motifs provided by the patterns of the landscape and the changing moods of the sea.

Stott kept a base in Paris for a number of years and this factor, together with his fateful association with Whistler, mitigated against his wholehearted acceptance by the English art establishment. His last years seem to have been taken up with finding a formula to satisfy not only his own intellectual needs but also the demands of the Royal Academy. He found a degree of recognition, but his eclecticism and willingness to experiment made it difficult for the critics to understand his work - although they never doubted his sincerity. He died prematurely at the age of forty-two, and we shall not know whether he would have eventually found acceptance in the hallowed halls of the Royal Academy, but there is no doubt he deserves to be re-considered and re-evaluated as a significant figure in British art during the last quarter of the nineteenth century.

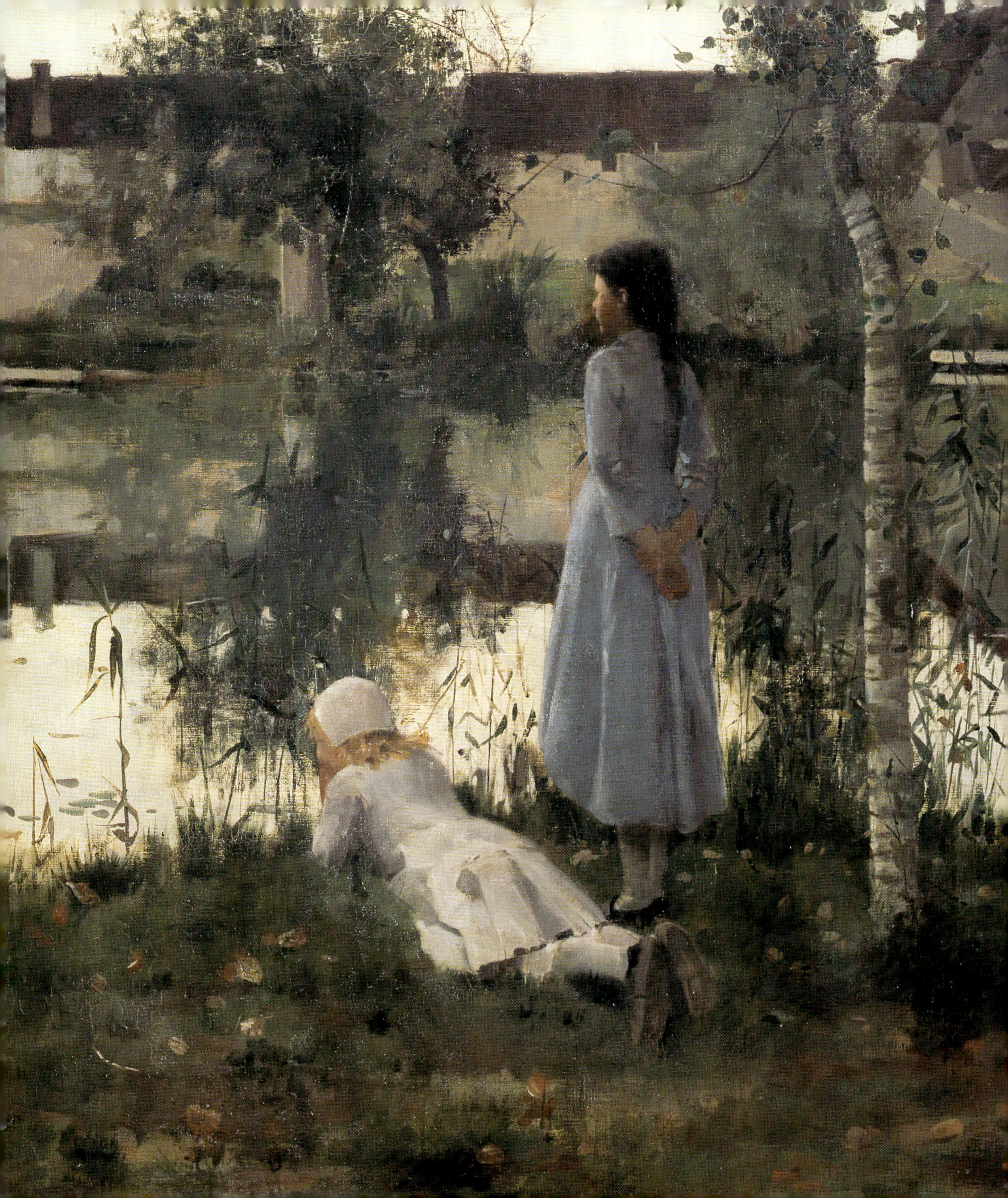

I
A Comet rushing to the Sun

"A young Lancashire painter, Mr William Stott ... has had great success at the Salon this year ... and the jury has just awarded him a medal. Medals are less willingly awarded to foreigners than even to Frenchmen, and therefore the honour is of double value. The success is only more interesting because Mr Stott represents a new departure in landscape. He is profoundly original."
The Manchester Guardian, 9 June 1882

In his sympathetic essay on William Stott in *The Studio* of October 1894 the art critic R.A.M. Stevenson wrote: "William Stott of Oldham sprang into being as an artist with the rapidity of a comet rushing to the sun .... I met him in 1879 when he landed in France without any training except the English stippling in chalk which he was bound to forget at the Beaux Arts."[1] In fact Stevenson is inaccurate on two counts. We now know from the artist's notebook[2] and an examination of the Salon records[3] that William Stott arrived in France in 1878 and that he was already a proficient artist of landscapes, which displayed a sensitivity to tone, atmosphere and colour that was to stay with him throughout his short artistic life. However, we can agree with Stevenson that, by any standards, Stott's progress and success after his arrival in France was meteoric. Having exhibited a number of small watercolours at the Salon each year from 1878, he then had two oil paintings accepted in 1881, both being bought by the same distinguished collector, and in 1882, at the age of twenty-four, he was highly acclaimed for two outstanding works, one of which was awarded a third-class medal.

The young William Stott was fortunate in two respects. First, on 20 November 1857, he was born into a family of well-to-do, although by no means wealthy, cotton spinners who owned Osborne Mill, at Busk near Oldham, Lancashire. He had three elder brothers who were already in the family business, so Abraham Stott, his father, looked favourably on William's expressed desire to become a painter and encouraged and subsidized his student years by buying many of his early watercolours, as did his brothers. We are told by the art critic Alice Corkran in her article on Stott in the *Scottish Arts Review* of 1889 that the young William Stott had a temperament that was "... eager, mobile, delicately impressionable. Such a temperament unfitted him for a business career, and made him peculiarly sensitive to the surrounding ugliness and depressing idealess routine. In his heart he longed to be a painter."[4] Just how Corkran knew this is not entirely clear, unless it was from Stott himself, as she was in correspondence with him for her article and quotes him at length later in the piece.

William Stott's second stroke of good fortune was to have an excellent teacher available at the Oldham School of Art, who also represented an appropriate role model. John Houghton Hague was an artist of some considerable merit, who had studied in Paris and was also the son of a mill owner.[5] In 1872 he had spent four months at Pont Aven in Brittany before returning to teach at Oldham School of Art (fig. 3) until its closure in 1878. In his work he became a chronicler of life in and around Oldham with genre pictures of cottage interiors and portraits of local 'characters' and of picturesque landscapes (fig. 6). His holiday book for 1878 records a visit to Morecombe and Heysham on the Lancashire coast and adds, "Will Stott of Oldham with one, learning to paint".[6] Released from the claustrophobic grime and gloom of industrial Oldham (figs. 2, 4), the young Stott found a response in the countryside and coastal areas that was to trigger his poetic and sensitive nature. Initially he worked mainly in watercolour, sketching local beauty spots in the north of England and on the Lancashire and Cumbrian coasts. The first entry in his notebook is a watercolour sketch, *Harry Taylor's House, Ravenglass* (untraced). The ancient settlement of Ravenglass, between the bleak sand dunes facing the the Irish Sea and the Cumbrian Fells, was to be to him, as Ville d'Avray became to Corot and Damvillers was to Bastien-Lepage, a place to which he

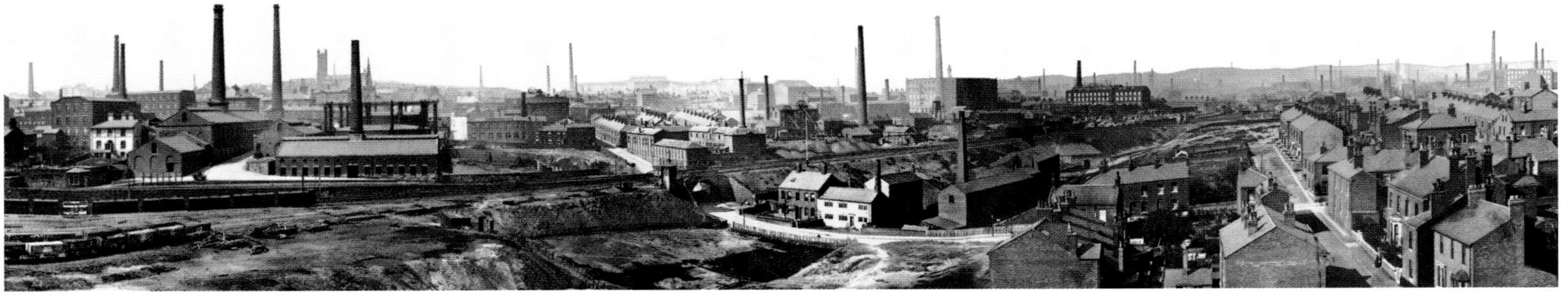

Fig. 2 Oldham, *ca.* 1879
Detail from Knott's Panorama of Oldham
Oldham Local Studies and Archives

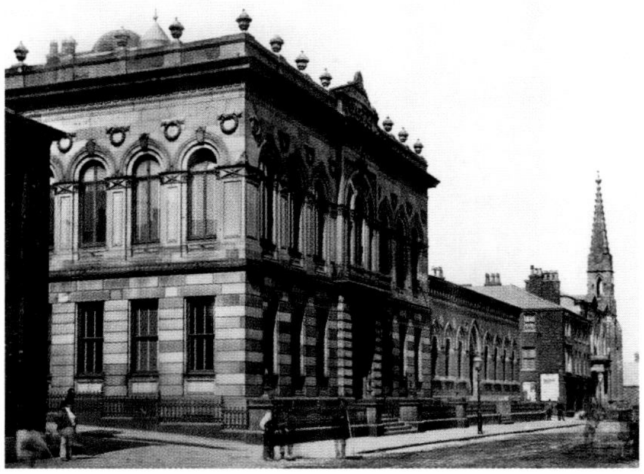

Fig. 3 The Lyceum and Art School, Union Street, Oldham, *ca.*. 1870
Oldham Local Studies and Archives

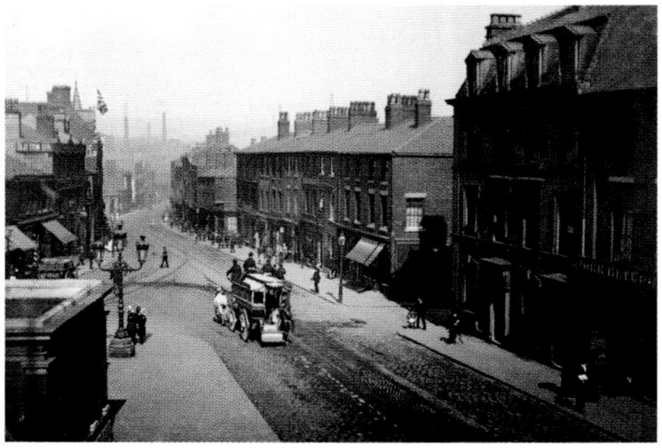

Fig. 4 Union Street and Star Inn Corner, Oldham, *ca.* 1880
Oldham Local Studies and Archives

returned again and again to find solace and inspiration and where many of his major works were conceived and completed. On his return from France he rented a house and studio there, which he maintained until his premature death in 1900, and he was sketching the wind-swept dunes and gorse-flecked pastures up to his last days.

Stott's student watercolours and '*pochades*' show an innate sense for place and atmosphere that was to be a feature of all his landscape work. The earliest known extant picture by William Stott is a small watercolour entitled *Chaplain's Porch, Haddon Hall* (cat. 1), which was completed in 1876 when he was still a student in Oldham. It shows a strong Dutch influence reminiscent of the interiors of Pieter van Hooch and Jan Vermeer, but also illustrates a confident understanding of perspective and the use of *chiaroscuro*. The Dutch derivation is apparent also in his landscape work of this period. The monochromatic tones of *River in Flood* (cat. 2) and *Boat at Low Tide* (cat. 3) are very suggestive of the work of the Hague School, a group of Dutch artists, including Jozef Israels (fig. 5), who were active in The Hague between 1860 and 1900 and whose landscapes became very popular with collectors in Britain.[7] Their work was, in turn, derived from the French Barbizon School of the mid-nineteenth century, who had defied classical conventions and pursued landscape painting for its own sake (fig. 7). Stott's *Woodgathering* (cat. 4), painted in the Bois de Clamart, near Paris, in 1878, is very 'Barbizonesque' in its earthy colours and sombre stillness. In this work the slender trees on the right provide a vertical axis as a compositional support which extends beyond the frame of the picture – a device favoured by both the Hague School and later Barbizon painters, and which reflects the increasing influence of photography on landscape painting. In *River in Flood, Boat at Low Tide* and *Woodgathering* the young William Stott shows, in his restricted use of colour, the simplicity of his motif and the importance he gives to the sky, that he had absorbed the current trends in naturalist art, and in particular those espoused by the painters of the Hague School. But even at this formative stage it is also possible to detect a sympathy with the Ruskinian belief that truth is more than mere imitation, but has reference both to material things and to "emotions, impressions and thoughts".[8] It would be wrong, therefore, to suggest, as Stevenson does, that Stott was a mere tyro when he arrived in Paris. Clearly he had already absorbed important lessons, been exposed to certain influences and, in addition, had considerable experience of *plein-air* painting in England.

Most aspiring artists in the last quarter of the nineteenth century considered time on the Continent essential to 'round off' their training and Paris was still seen as the centre

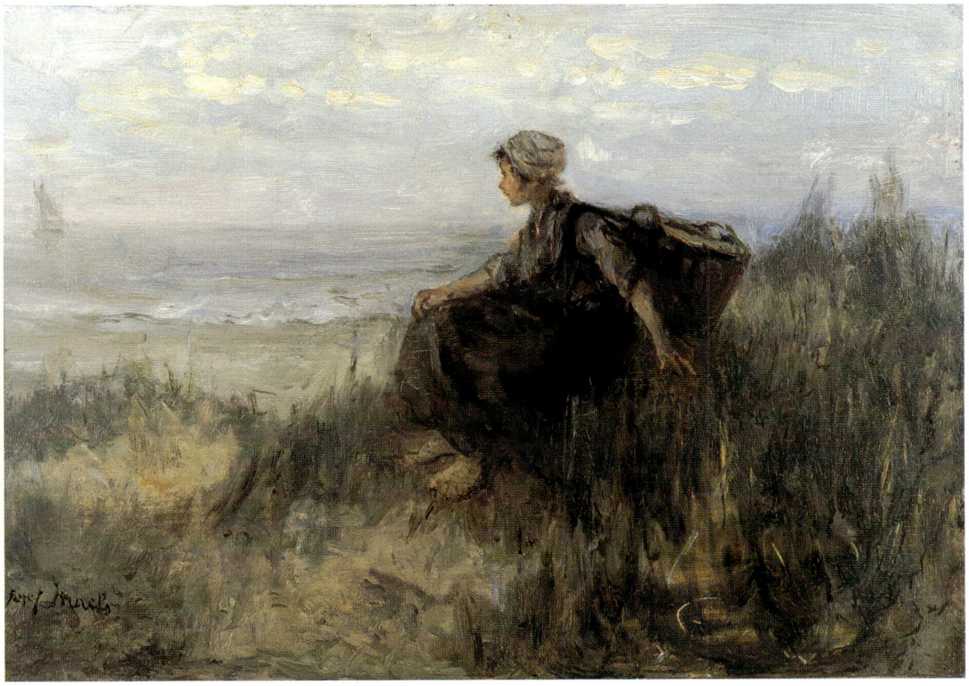

Fig. 5 Jozef Israels (1824–1911)
On the Dunes, ca. 1880
Oil on canvas
Courtesy of Bonham's, London

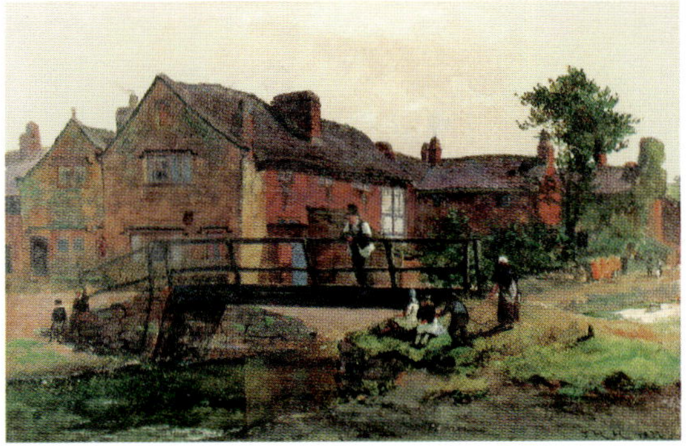

Fig. 6 John Houghton Hague (1831–1934)
Chadderton Fold, near Oldham, 1882
Oil on canvas, 73.5 x 111 cm
Gallery Oldham

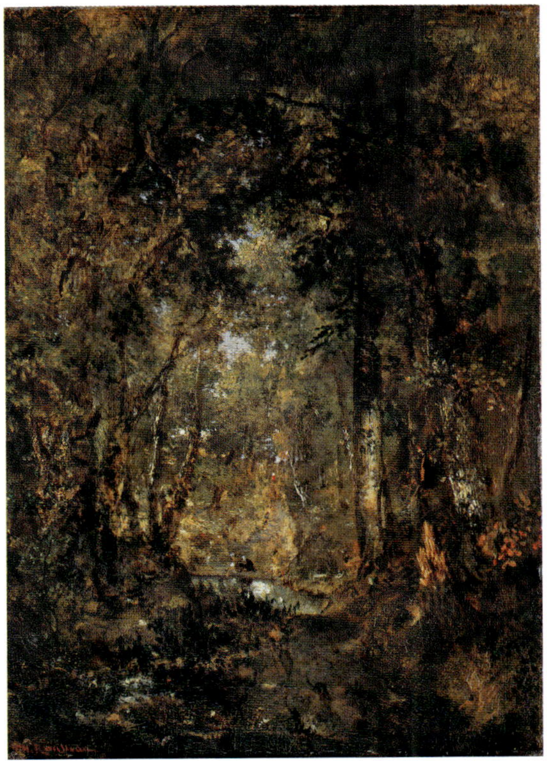

Fig. 7 Théodore Rousseau (1812–1867)
In the Wood at Fontainebleau, ca. 1860
Oil on panel, 40.5 x 30 cm
Hamburger Kunsthalle, Hamburg

of the artistic world. Paris offered a choice of distinguished teachers at the free, state-run Ecole des Beaux-Arts as well as numerous independent studios and many fine galleries and collections to study. By contrast, art education in Britain in the second half of the nineteeth century did not favour the fine artist. From 1847 it had been in the grip of the 'South Kensington system', emanating from the National Art Training School in London, which each year tested conformity to established principles.[9] For those wishing to progress from the provincial schools the choice was limited. The Royal Academy Schools in London were considered conventional and uninspiring and the more progressive Slade School, which had recently been founded (1871), was fee-paying and limited to one hundred students. For all these reasons, coupled to the fact that students from outside London often found it cheaper to live abroad, it is not surprising that many students from the provincial schools of art by-passed London altogether.[10] So, William Stott set out for Paris, with an introduction to the painter/sculptor Jean-Léon Gérôme,[11] to pit himself against the brightest and best of his generation.

Stott arrived in Paris at a time which later proved to be a watershed in the development of modern art. Paris was undoubtedly still the capital of the art world, but in the late 1870s and early 1880s it was in ferment. The classicists and Romantics still held sway in the Salon and in academic circles, but the Realism of Courbet and Manet was beginning to make its intellectual mark and divide the critics. The Impressionist exhibitions were in full swing,[12] albeit still on the fringe of critical acceptability, but offering an attractive alternative to susceptible young artists. Through the work of Puvis

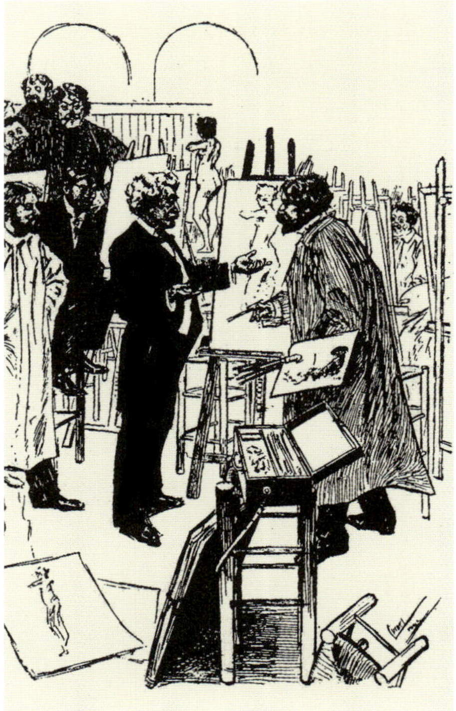

Fig. 8 *Jean-Léon Gérôme teaching in his atelier*
Caricature by Eduard Cucuel, 1899

de Chavannes, Gustave Moreau and Paul Gauguin, the incipient Symbolist movement was gaining ground and, although this was not apparent at the time, was to be the movement that became most influential to the development of twentieth-century art. It was into this maelstrom of artistic cross-currents that William Stott was plunged when he arrived in Paris in 1878. The young Lancastrian was confident and ambitious, but also impressionable, with a certain provincial naivety which he was never to shake off entirely. However, he rapidly became absorbed into the artistic milieu of the Ecole, the ateliers and the café life of Paris and quickly made friendships, some of which were to be important to him for the rest of his days. James Paterson, one of a group of Scottish artists studying in Paris at that time, later recalled the cameraderie that existed between the English, Scottish, Irish and American students: "What times we had there, finding our meals at a little cabman's restaurant where among the habitués were Hawkins, a bibulous American, William Stott of Oldham, an able artist and voluminous talker and others".[13] The only portrait we have of Stott (fig. 1) comes from this period: it was sketched in the Bois de Clamart in 1879 by the American artist Theodore Robinson, who was just finishing his training under Gérôme, and who later befriended Monet and became a leading American Impressionist.[14]

Despite the new-found friendships and the endless talk and the gaiety of the Parisian scene, life was tough for the young *aspirant* in the ateliers at that time and none was more strict and austere than that of Gérôme. The painter and sculptor Jean-Léon Gérôme (1824–1904) was a pupil of Delaroche and Gleyre, and had inherited their highly finished academic style. His history paintings and oriental scenes (fig. 9) had won him great popularity and he had become the champion of the academic tradition, opposing progressive trends in art and in particular the influence of the Impressionists. According to the memoirs of the English painter John Shirley Fox, he was "... like his work, neat correct and impeccable. Upright as a dart, his spare figure and clear cut features arrested the attention and his manner, abrupt, sharp and incisive, marked him out as a ruler among men. Of the most scrupulous punctuality, intolerant of anybody lacking in energy or smartness, he was in many ways an ideal master."[15] In spite of his severe manner and high standards Gérôme was popular among his students, to whom he often showed much kindness and concern for their development. Although still an upholder of traditional values and methods, by this time he had become a mellower, more understanding teacher (fig. 8). Kenyon Cox, one of Stott's companions in the Bois de Clamart, writing in *Century Magazine* in 1886, refuted the notion that Gérôme was rigid in his methods of instruction, and that his pupils became, almost of necessity, his imitators. He said, "His criticism was always of results, and never ... of method".[16] Gérôme's biographer, Moreau-Vauthier, recounts that the master urged his students "... to work assiduously, to study nature scrupulously, especially in drawing, in composing sketches, and not to get down to painting a picture until after they had their trade in hand as perfectly as possible, and always to look for the truth".[17] It is certainly advice which William Stott seems to have taken to heart and practised throughout his career.

The young Stott appears to have thrived in the atmosphere of Gérôme's atelier. Alice Corkran reports that he soon "... won distinction as a fine draughtsman in a school where to 'draw' is considered the highest merit of an artist. His work attracted the attention of

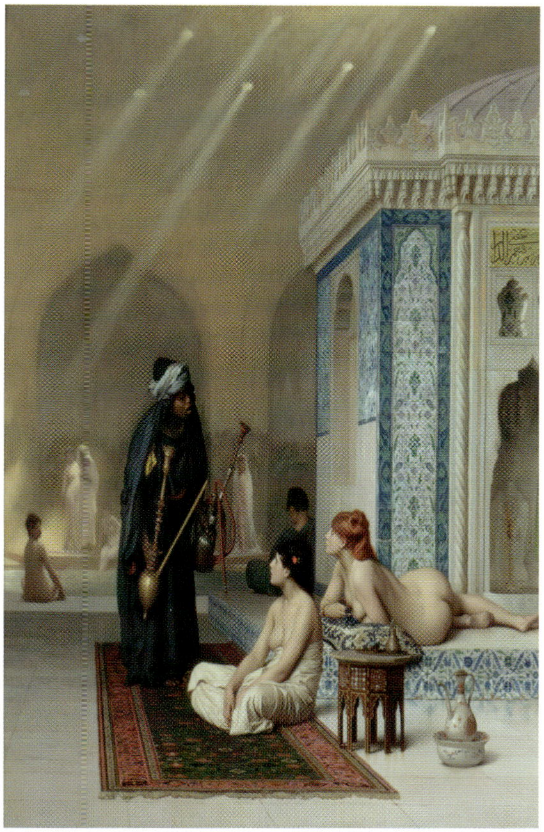

Fig. 9 Jean-Léon Gérôme (1824–1904)
Pool in a Harem, ca. 1876
Oil on canvas
Hermitage, St Petersburg

Gérôme who, most reticent and most caustic of professors, praised and encouraged him."[18] Indeed Gérôme sent Stott for a few months to the studio of his life-long friend Léon Bonnat (1833–1922), a practice he reserved for only his most able students. There is no doubt that the period spent with Gérôme provided Stott with a solid artistic foundation, and throughout the course of his career he remained committed to the formal academic principles of sound draughtsmanship and a realistic depiction of nature. But temperamentally young Stott and his master were poles apart. Stott was a passionate and poetic young man impatient to make his mark and seek after his own 'truth', or, as Alice Corkran put it a few years later, "... there was a profound difference in the manner and spirit of the apprehension of art between the young student and the academical seniors around him. He was above all things an Impressionist; always on the alert for new problems of colour, of line, of effect; impatient of the trammels of tradition; intensely alive in the present."[19] Corkran is using the term 'Impressionist' here not in the meaning that we understand it today, as a member of a particular school of art, but in the broader sense that it was used by art critics in the last quarter of the nineteenth century – to describe young *avant-garde* artists who did not conform to the academic conventions of the Salon, or the Academy, but who sought freedom and 'truth' through individual originality. William Stott was never invited to exhibit at any of the Impressionist group exhibitions held in Paris during the years he was there. He was always more of a Realist than an Impressionist. He was not interested in spontaneity or bright colours; he was more concerned with attention to detail and atmosphere and tonal values.

However, there was a middle way and it was down this path that the young Stott went with almost immediate success. The *juste milieu* artists of the Third Republic represented the acceptable face of Impressionism. The establishment did not approve of what it considered to be the 'unfinished' paintings of the Impressionists. The *juste milieu* group represented a compromise between modernism and traditionalism by adopting some of the informal techniques of the Impressionists, perhaps leaving part of the picture loosely finished, or using texture to suggest spatial depth, while at the same time they gave their forms an underlying structure. The art historian Albert Boime has said that the impact of the *juste milieu* group should not be underestimated: "... they gratified the public taste for modernism combined with traditionalism by modifying the disquieting features of Impressionism and rejecting the polished technique of the academic painters. The public could appreciate the Impressionists' doctrine of light and colour when it was made more palatable by more solid draughtsmanship."[20]

The leading figure in this group was Jules Bastien-Lepage (1848–1884), and to many English, Irish, Scottish and American artists he became something of an idol. Having failed to win the Prix de Rome in 1875 as expected, he returned home to Damvillers in north-east France and began to paint the people of his village. Unlike the peasants of Jean-François Millet, who were iconic figures used 'to symbolize a human condition', Bastien's peasants are real characters, engaged in real tasks at a specific moment in time. He achieved an almost photographic realism and immediacy by working *en plein air* and by his handling of the paint on the canvas. He quickly became a role model for aspiring young painters, and Walter Shaw-Sparrow in his biography of John Lavery describes how a group consisting of John Lavery, Alexander Roche, Tom Millie Dow, William Kennedy,

William Stott and other British and American students used to meet in a little café near the Luxembourg Gardens, where "... ardour and tobacco were burned freely before the shrines of Puvis de Chavannes and Jules Bastien-Lepage. Between these two extremes the talk went to and fro on some evenings, but as a rule, the favourite topics were Bastien-Lepage and *plein-air*."[21] In fact both these painters were to have an influence on Stott. In his latter years he moved towards the more overt symbolism and mannered style of Puvis de Chavannes (1824–1898), but it was in his immediate response to Bastien-Lepage that he made his name and reputation at the Salon.

Stott had exhibited several small watercolours at the Salon from 1878 to 1880, mainly coastal views in the north of England and at Concarneau. It was during these years that Bastien-Lepage's success at the Salon was being consolidated with *The Haymakers* (1877; fig. 10), *Potato-gatherers* (1879) and *Joan of Arc listening to the Voices* (1879; fig. 38, p. 58). For Stott these pictures would have been a revelation and an inspiration. It may have been one of the American painters – Theodore Robinson or Alexander Harrison, both fellow pupils of Gérôme – who introduced Stott to the delights of Grez-sur-Loing, where an international colony of artists had been in residence since the mid 1870s (fig. 11). It is possible, too, that R.A.M. Stevenson, who met Stott in Paris in 1879, recommended the attractions of the village, as he had been visiting Grez since 1875 with his cousin R.L. Stevenson and artists such as Frank O'Meara and W.H. Low.[22] The picturesque village, with its somewhat melancholy mood, clearly triggered a chord in the young Stott's psyche, as it did for many other artists, and he began painting works in the manner of Bastien-Lepage which were an instant success at the Salon and were soon to attract a following of young admirers. Stott's rapid assimulation of Bastien-Lepage's technique does seem remarkable given that in the space of twelve months he went from producing a few seaside sketches to – in 1880 at Grez – completing three large exhibition paintings in oil, *Girl Knitting* (*La Tricoteuse*), *Daydream (Rêve de Midi)* and *Shepherd or Prince? (Prince ou Berger?*; subsequently known as *Girl in a Meadow*; cat. 8). Stott was one of the first of his group of companions to achieve success at the Salon, in 1881 with *Girl Knitting* and *Daydream*, both works being bought out of the Salon by the same collector, M. Ramon Subercaseaux, the Chilian ambassador in Paris, an enthusiastic collector and amateur artist who had accompanied John Singer Sargent on painting trips to Venice. At the same Salon Sargent's portrait of Mme Subercaseaux was awarded a second-class medal.

The fact that such a high-profile figure as Subercaseaux bought both Stott's Salon paintings indicates what a strong impression they must have made, and the purchase not only boosted Stott's stock among his fellow artists, but also led to invitations to exhibit at the more progressive galleries in both Paris and London. It seems that Sargent, whom Stott had possibly befriended at Concarneau in 1879, was definitely promoting the young man at this stage. He had himself bought one of Stott's Concarneau sketches, which was shown later in 1881 at Le Cercle des Arts Liberaux, one of the 'fringe' groups in Paris. At this show Sargent exhibited two Venetian interiors and other exhibitors included Monet, Degas, Renoir and Rodin. Later in the same year Stott was invited to exhibit in London at the Grosvenor Gallery, which had been founded in 1877 as a venue for Academy outsiders and the Continental *avant-garde*. In 1880 a retrospective exhibition of the work of Bastien-Lepage had been held there, so it was fitting that in 1881 Stott sent to the

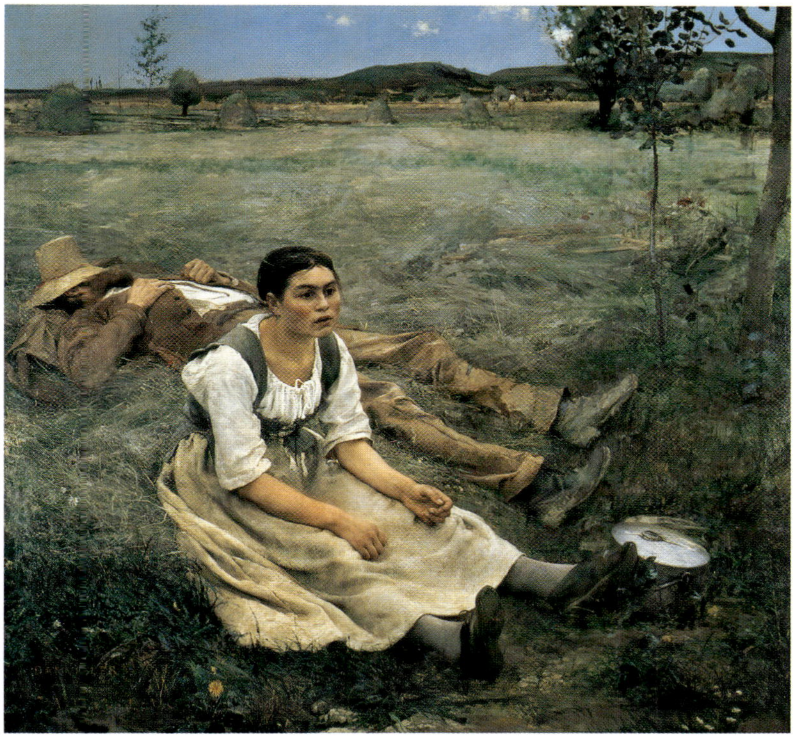

Fig. 10 Jules Bastien-Lepage (1848–1884)
The Haymakers, 1877
Oil on canvas, 180 × 195 cm
Musée d'Orsay, Paris

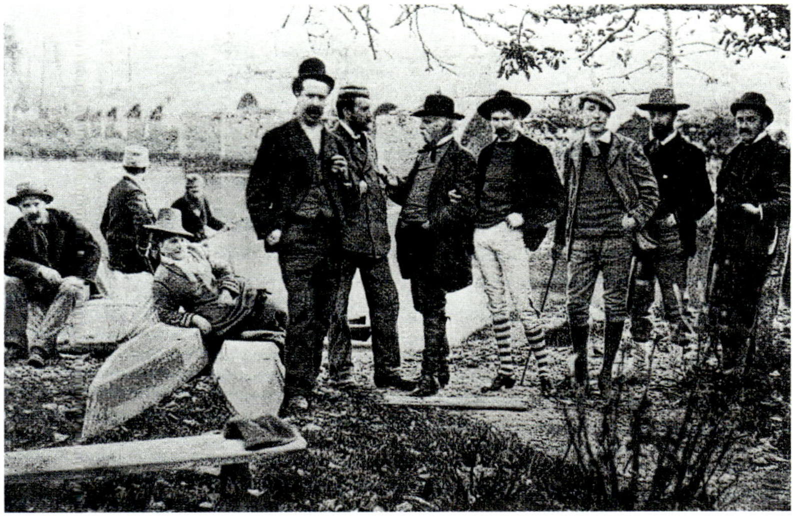

Fig. 11 Artists at Grez-sur-Loing, *ca.* 1878
(R.A.M. Stevenson in the striped socks and
Frank O'Meara with the pipe and stick)
Anonymous photograph illustrated in Will Low,
A Chronicle of Friendships, 1908

winter exhibition *Prince or Shepherd?*, his canvas which most closely imitates the style and technique of Bastien-Lepage. There can be no doubt that Stott's two Salon pictures of 1881 were also inspired by Bastien-Lepage, although, having been sold into a private collection, they do not seem to have been exhibited in public again and they remain untraced today. We do know that both works contained single figures integrated into a naturalist landscape with a prevailing enigmatic mood. We have a faded sepia print of *Girl Knitting*, but more helpful is Alice Corkran's vivid description of the picture: "It is a river scene: a corner filled with a tangle of water-side blossoms, bordered with straight-stemmed silver birch trees, through the foliage of which rains the sunlight. A young peasant girl walks through this sun-spotted world, knitting as she walks. She is part of the freshness and pleasantness, a note in the impression of sunlight and flower, of cool water and of the innocent active life of nature."[23] We have some idea of what *Daydream* looked like from a crude line-engraving in *Le Catalogue illustré du Salon* for 1881, which shows a single figure of a peasant girl seated on a grassy bank beside a track. From this superficial image one might conjecture that some inspiration was derived from Bastien's *The Haymakers*. As to technique we can only guess, but as both the 1881 Salon pictures were painted in the same year as *Prince or Shepherd?* it is probably safe to assume that the handling was very similar.

Prince or Shepherd? shows the closest affinity to Bastien-Lepage of all Stott's works. A single figure is placed prominently in the foreground and a tree which extends beyond the frame of the canvas acts as a vertical axis to give compositional support, as in Bastien's *Poor Little Warbler (Pauvre Fauvette*; fig. 12) and *Joan of Arc listening to the Voices* (fig. 38, p. 58). The horizon is placed high, creating the effect in the viewer's mind of a direct encounter with the figure. Stott also adopts his mentor's technique of indicating perspective by a change of handling rather than by any pictorial indication of recession. To achieve a photographic realism the central figure is first finely delineated and then cut across by changes in brushstroke. The foreground is sharply defined in heavy impasto and appears as a layer on an already completed canvas. Broad, square brushstrokes model the middle distance and a softer, less defined brushwork indicates the far distance. Thus spatial transition is provided through the handling of the paint on the canvas.

Prince or Shepherd? was exhibited at the Grosvenor Gallery in 1881, where it was bought by a French collector. Like its two

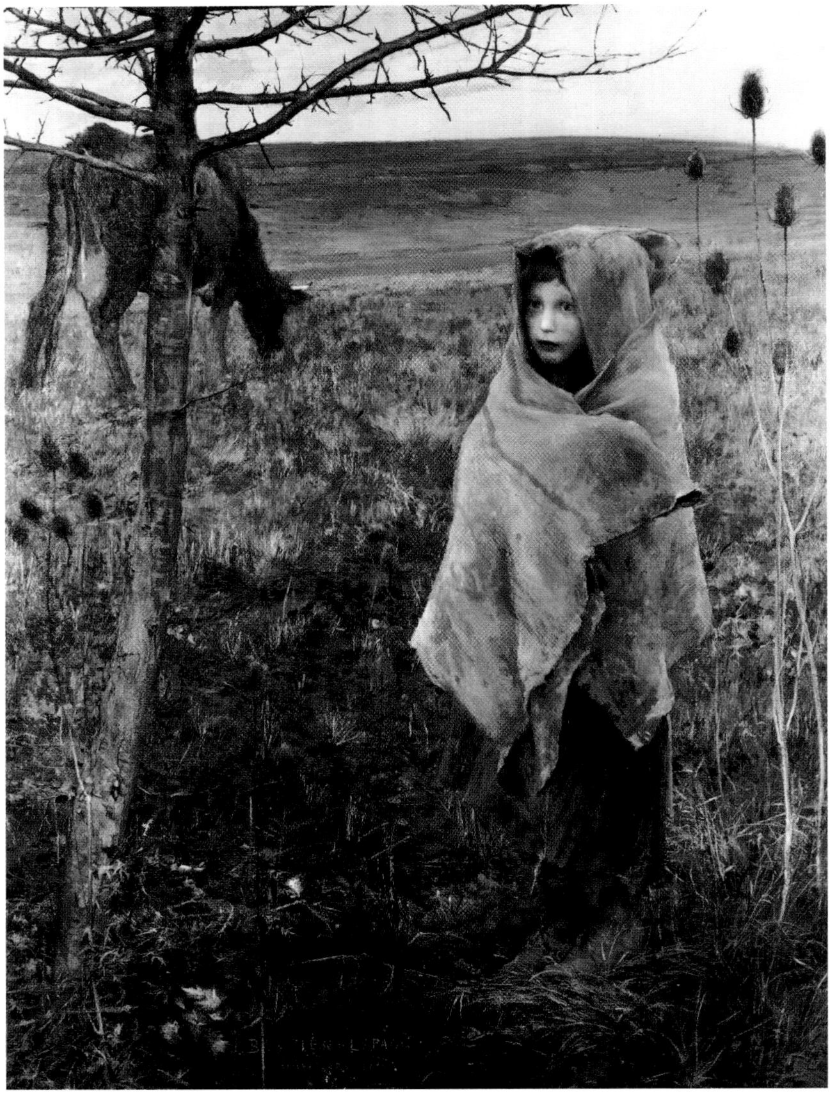

Fig. 12 Jules Bastien-Lepage (1848–1884)
Poor Little Warbler (*Pauvre Fauvette*), 1881
Oil on canvas, 162.5 x 125.7 cm
Glasgow Art Gallery and Museum

companions it disappeared from public view but fortuitously reappeared in 1928, when it was bought by an English collector at an auction in Vichy, France, after which it was given the title by which it has since been known, *Girl in a Meadow*. Stott's title for the picture, *Prince ou berger?* (Prince or Shepherd?), presumably alludes to the daydream of the young girl and is typical of the *rêve de bonheur* works popular with artists at Grez-sur-Loing. There is no doubt that at this stage Stott was still experimenting and still absorbing the different influences around him. Indeed there is evidence that he may have been 'flirting' with Impressionism, as a later picture in 1880, *October Morning* (cat. 9), perhaps the closest he gets to an 'Impressionist' style, is reminiscent of views by Sisley and Pissarro of the Paris road at Louveciennes (see fig. 39, p. 61). Interestingly, Stott referred to the picture as a "sketch", which explains the unfinished nature and looseness of some of the brushwork. However, it is an important picture in Stott's stylistic development. Julian Campbell in *The Irish Impressionists* has called it "a quintessential *plein-air* painting of the period".[24] Although some of the devices of Bastien-Lepage are

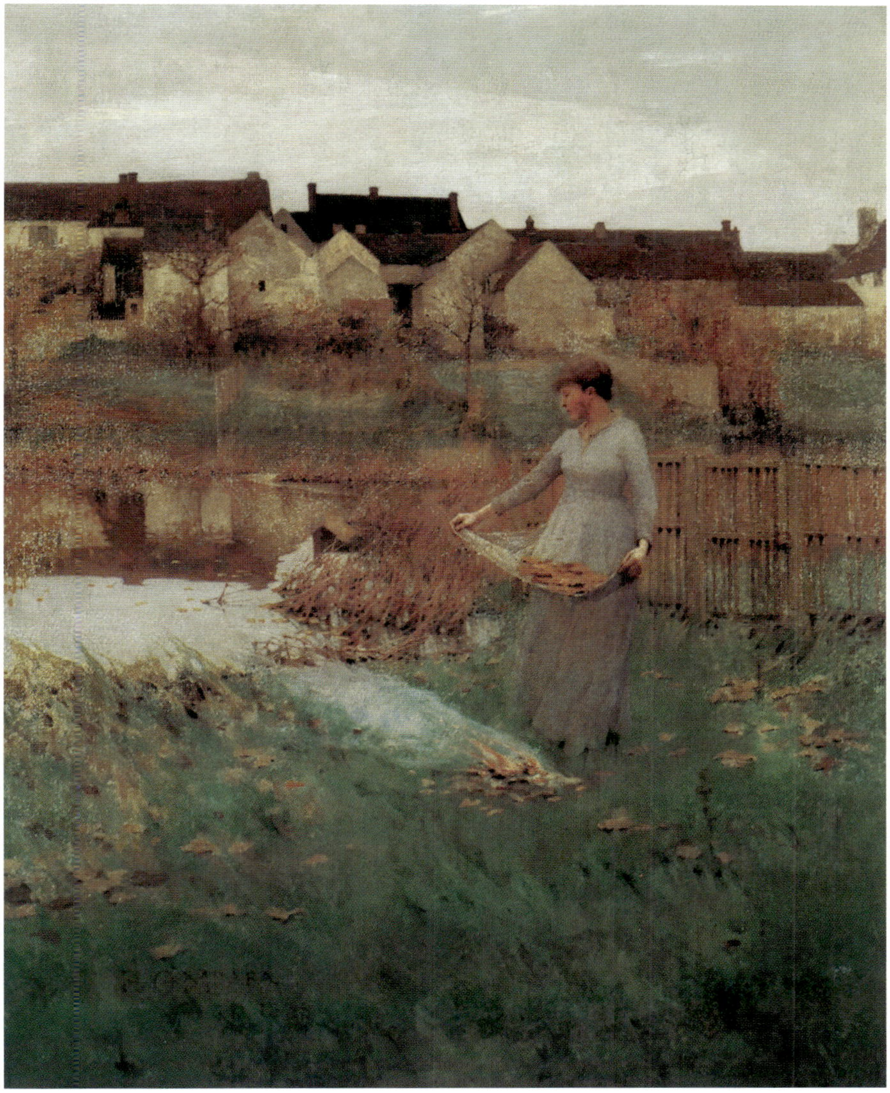

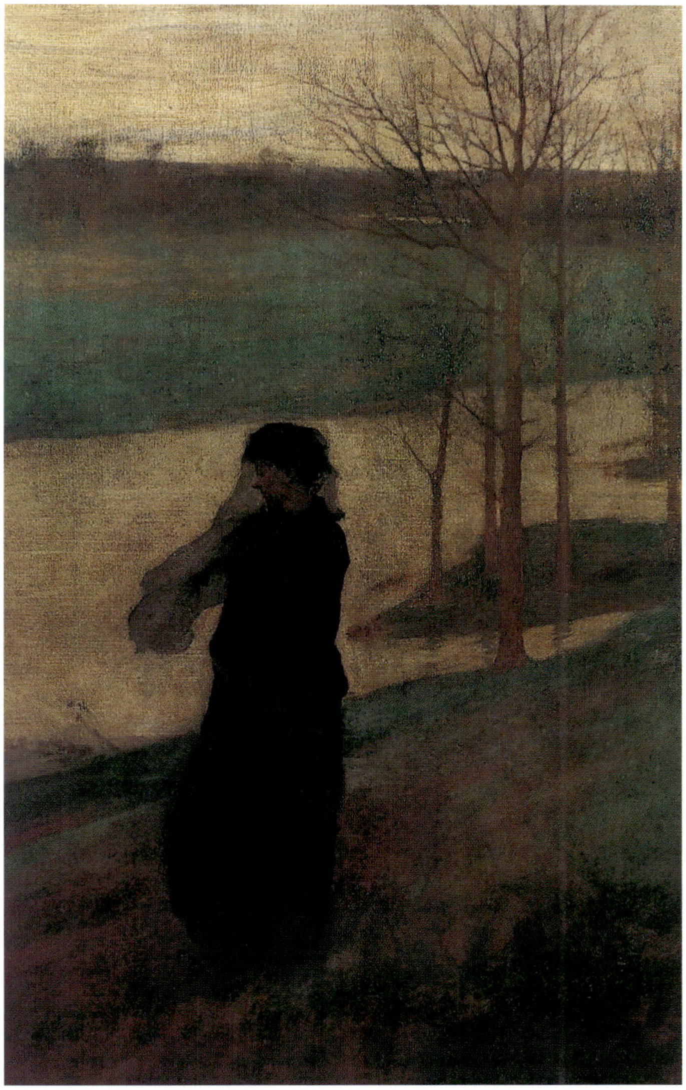

still present – the high horizon, the frieze of wintry trees extending beyond the frame – there is no central figure and the perspective is wider and more distant than is the norm with Bastien. But, despite the affinity with the 'Impressionists' that can be detected in *October Morning*, it is more likely that, having spent the summer months at Grez, Stott was falling under yet another influence, that of Frank O'Meara (1853–1888), an Irish painter and Grez habitué who rapidly became a close friend and painting companion.[25]

O'Meara was a seminal figure in late nineteenth-century art, but his talent was constrained by his capricious Celtic temperament. The "irresistible Frank O'Meara", as John Singer Sargent called him,[26] was a painter's painter. Indeed one obituarist wrote in 1888: "... O'Meara was recognized as one who had set out in the 'new movement', which is now so wide in its influence – the movement towards the treatment of landscape with special regard to atmospheric planes, the various tones thus searched out lending themselves to a strongly realistic, yet beautifully decorative treatment ..." (figs. 13 and 14).[27] Stott's friendship with O'Meara provided the catalyst for a shift of style to a more

Fig. 13 Frank O'Meara (1853–1888)
Towards Night and Winter, 1885
Oil on canvas, 150 x 127 cm
The Hugh Lane Municipal Art Gallery, Dublin

Fig. 14 Frank O'Meara
The Widow, 1882
Oil on canvas, 150 x 100 cm
The Hugh Lane Municipal Art Gallery, Dublin

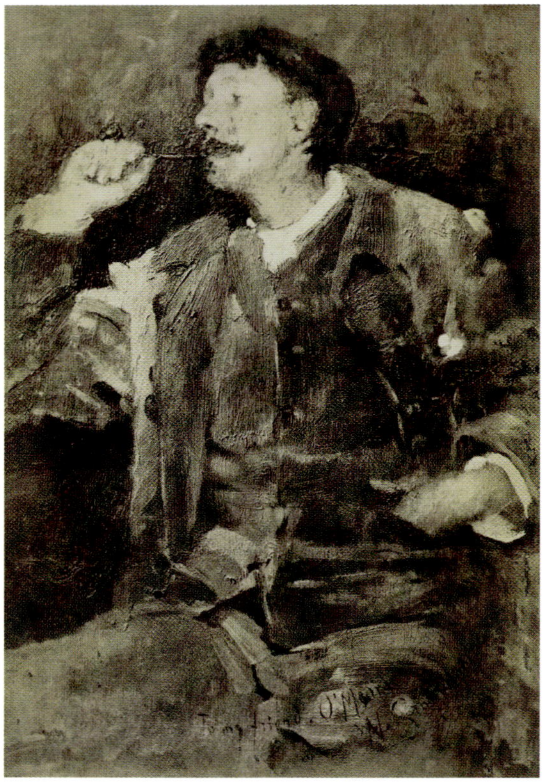

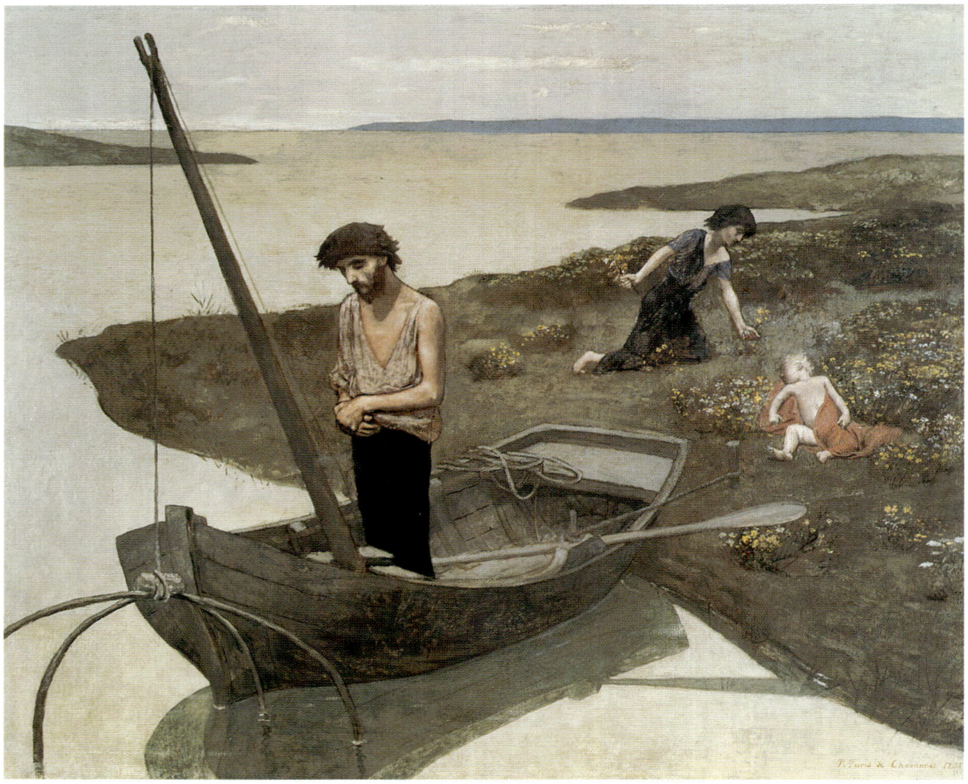

Fig. 15 (above left) William Stott of Oldham
Frank O'Meara, 1881
Oil on canvas
Untraced

Fig. 16 (above right) Puvis de Chavannes (1824–1898)
The Poor Fisherman (*Le Pauvre Pêcheur*), 1881
Oil on canvas, 155.5 × 192 cm
Musée d'Orsay, Paris

poetic naturalism, which combined truth with a decorative treatment. In O'Meara he found an artistic soulmate and in 1881 at Grez he painted a vibrant portrait of his friend, which he presented to him (fig. 15). The introspective mood in O'Meara's work, which links him with *fin-de-siècle* Symbolism, seemed also to strike a chord with Stott. Once again Stott was quick to distil and refine another artist's work and methodology, and his superior technical ability, together with his further success at the 1882 Salon, placed him on a pedestal as far as his fellow painters were concerned. Stott's debt to O'Meara at this formative stage in his development is amply acknowledged by R.A.M. Stevenson in his 1894 article: "Mr Stott's personal view of art ripened at Grez ... and among the young men whom Mr Stott found striving to express the exquisite delicacy of the still stream, with its tall bending poplars and shimmering river growths, the most remarkable perhaps was the late Frank O'Meara .... To the expression of this scenery Mr Stott brought a mind of more practical energy, a completer training, and also a robuster constitution. He rapidly built up a style which contained the elements of this natural poetry and the results of previous study under Gérôme in Paris."[28]

Stott's 1882 Salon pictures, *The Ferry* (*Le Passeur*; cat. 10) and *The Bathing Place* (*La Baignade*; fig. 17),[29] which were painted at Grez in the summer of 1881, were quite different from those of the previous year. The conformity with the *juste milieu* conventions of finish and form is still apparent, but gone is the slavish obeisance to Bastien-Lepage, and what we see emerging is a more personal and passionate response to nature and mankind's place within it. As Corkran in the *Scottish Art Review* put it, "... the basis of Mr Stott's art is founded in the belief that human nature is but a note in nature,

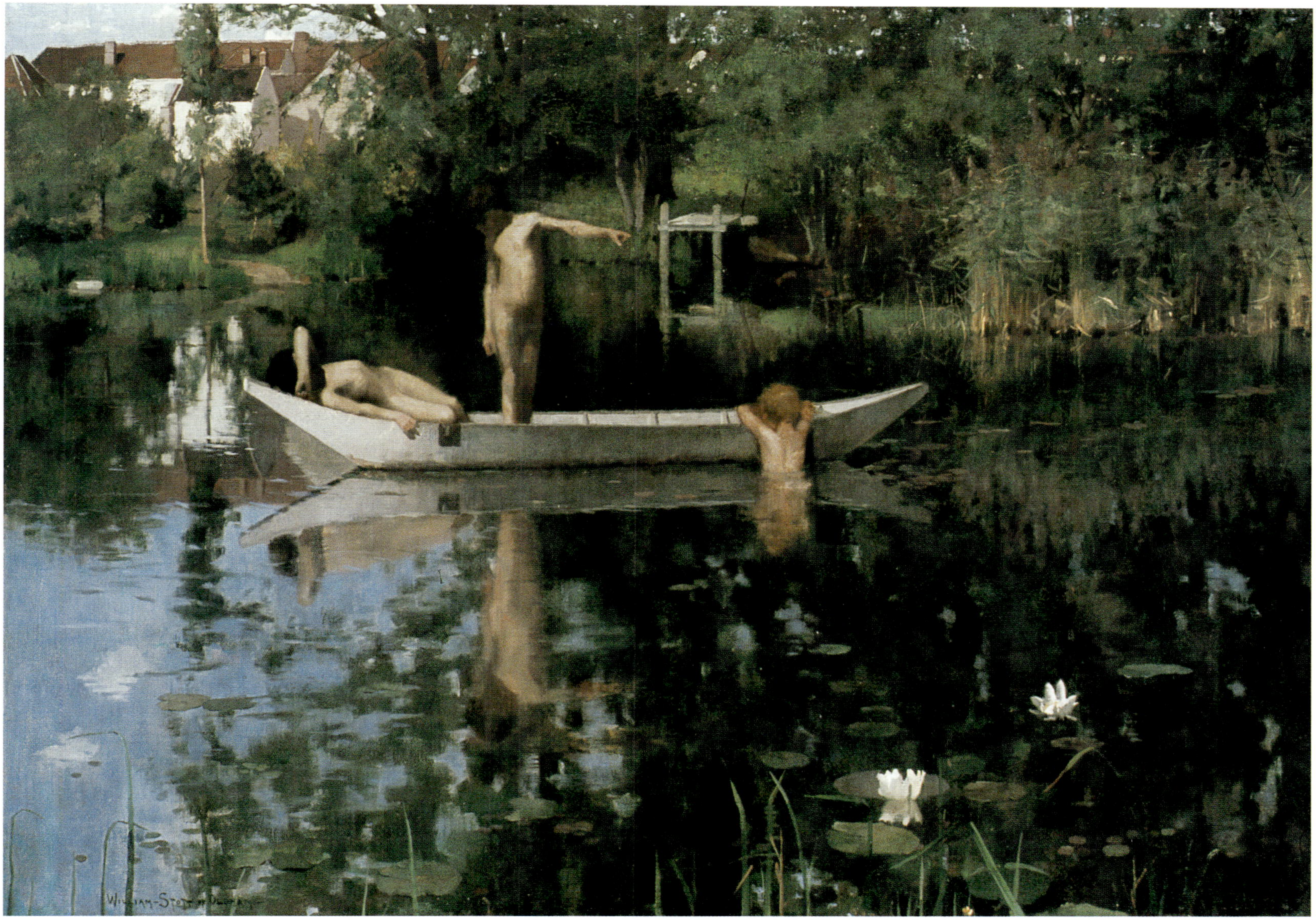

Fig. 17 William Stott of Oldham
The Bathing Place (La Baignade), 1881
Oil on canvas, 137.5 × 200.5 cm
Neue Pinakothek, Munich

Fig. 19 John Lavery (1856–1941)
The Passing Salute: The Bridge at Grez, 1883
Oil on canvas, 76.2 × 182.8 cm
Private collection

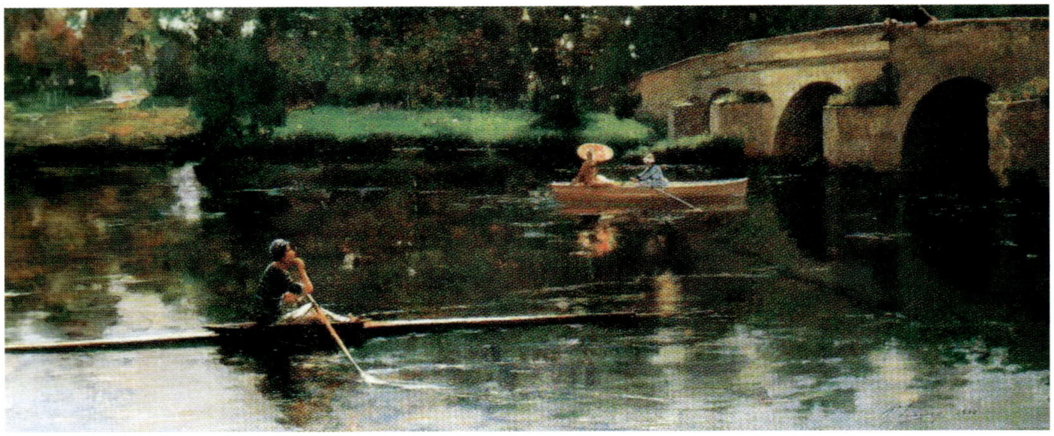

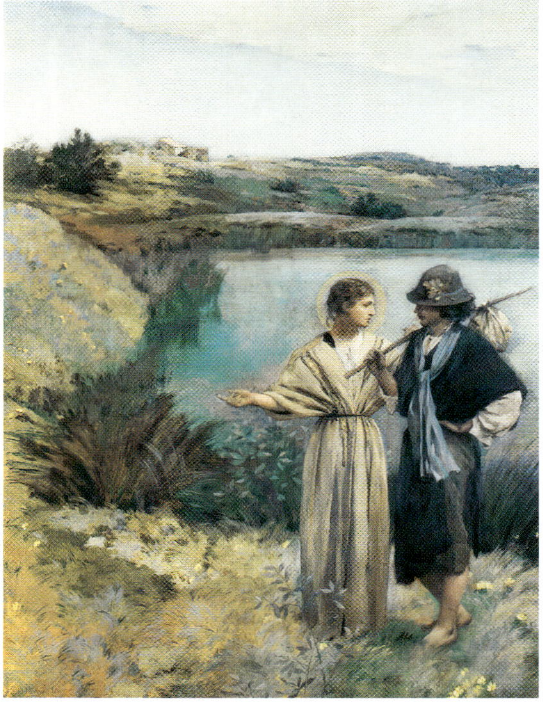

Fig. 18 Jean-Charles Cazin (1841–1901)
Tobias and the Angel, 1880
Oil on canvas, 186 × 142 cm
Musée des Beaux-Arts, Lille

and is unintelligible, but as a part of the general harmony".[30] In *The Ferry* and *The Bathing Place* Stott breaks away from the single-figure compositions favoured by Bastien-Lepage and his new companion Frank O'Meara. The emphasis is still on solitary contemplation and pastoral simplicity, but the more poetic and decorative treatment seems to represent a fusion of styles, which suggests the influence of Puvis de Chavannes and the 'tonalist' naturalism of Jean-Charles Cazin (1841–1901), both artists admired by O'Meara. At the 1881 Salon Puvis de Chavannes had shown *The Poor Fisherman* (*Le Pauvre Pêcheur*; fig. 16), which, with its enigmatic mood and its theme of 'metaphysical isolation and melancholy', was to be so influential with the emerging modern movement. In *The Ferry* the simplicity of form in the cubic buildings and the planar organization of space also reflects the style of Puvis, as well as Stott's own profound feeling for form.

Jean-Charles Cazin was well known for his melancholic biblical subjects set among sand dunes. He had won a first-class medal at the 1880 Salon with *Tobias and the Angel* (fig. 18). Although highly popular at the turn of the century his influence has been neglected of late; but recently Gabriel Weisberg has written, "He was a painter whose works meshed with the French Symbolist movement and whose landscapes created elusive poetic moods".[31] This poetic mood and the cool harmonies of pale green and grey which dominate *The Ferry* and *The Bathing Place* would also seem to evoke echoes of Corot's pastoral idylls.

The Ferry was an important picture in the development of *plein-airisme*, moving away from a studied naturalism towards a more open format with its latent symbolism and horizontal design set out in parallel planes. The picture inspired John Lavery during his time at Grez in such works as *On the Loing: An Afternoon Chat*, *A Passing Salute: The Bridge at Grez* (fig. 19) and a later work, *The Tennis Party* (fig. 20), which clearly shows a debt to Stott with its horizontal layout and its restricted grey/green tonality. Lavery acknowledged this debt when writing some years later, "... Harrison the American, Stott the English, and O'Meara the Irish, have much influenced me, above all the last, during the three or four seasons that I spent at Gres [*sic*]".[32]

At the 1882 Salon Stott had gained widespread attention with *The Ferry* and *The Bathing Place*, the latter being awarded a third-class medal. This great honour for the young English artist resulted in him becoming a 'hero figure' among his compatriots.

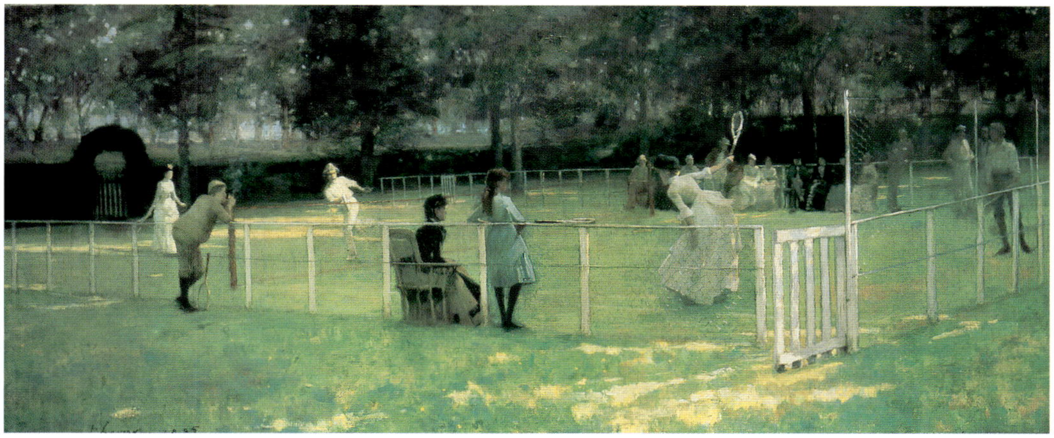

Fig. 20 John Lavery
The Tennis Party, 1885
Oil on canvas, 76.2 x 183 cm
Aberdeen Art Gallery and Museum

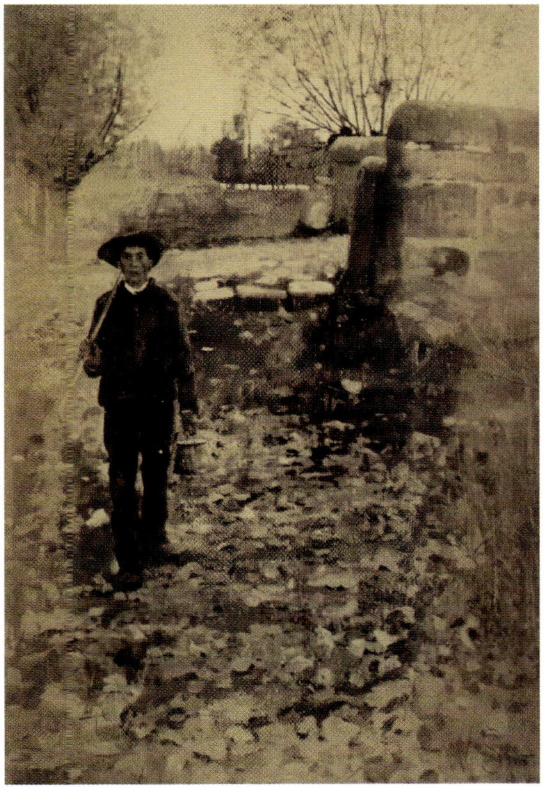

Fig. 21 William Stott of Oldham
Return from Fishing (Retour de Pêche), 1881
Watercolour, 81.2 x 55.8 cm
Untraced

However, although he was lionized by his fellow painters, the critics in France and England were divided over Stott's work. One Parisian reviewer said of his work at the Salon, "Eccentricity is often confused with originality. That is why M. Stott, who does have some talent, is taken for an original painter".[33] But Antonin Proust praised Stott as one of a number of artists who had succeeded in achieving "solidity" in their paintings by combining colour relationships with tonal values.[34] The London critics were just as ambivalent when *The Ferry* and *The Bathing Place* were shown in July 1882 at the Fine Art Society's exhibition of 'Paintings by British and American Artists from the Paris Salon'. There were only fourteen works shown, including *Rêverie* by O'Meara (fig. 41, p. 62), *El Jaleo* and a portrait of Carolus-Duran by Sargent, and works by Alexander Harrison, Kenyon Cox and others. Stott's work attracted a considerable amount of attention, according to the *Art Journal* critic, who, commenting on his individual style in landscape expression, acknowledged that "the desired impression, repose, has been admirably caught", but added, "with the sacrifice, it is true, of many details which would vex the soul of the majority of English landscape painters".[35] Further back-handed praise came from the *Magazine of Art*, which did not consider *The Ferry* as individual because of the obvious French influence: "Mr Stott's two landscapes, *The Ferry* and *The Bathers*, are fresh and pleasant in sentiment, and of uncommon merit in respect of workmanship and treatment of nature. Mr Stott (who is a pupil of Gérôme) has been taken, however, with the manner of Bastien-Lepage, and is less original and inventive than dexterous and intelligent."[36]

To put these reviews into context one must remember the almost xenophobic mistrust and jealousy that existed in the English art establishment over all things French. The Royal Academy felt under the threat of foreign invasion as young artists returned inspired and influenced by French modes and manners in painting and, above all, in the early 1880s, the work of Bastien-Lepage. On a more rational level the concern was about national identity and originality. Even the normally francophile art critic George Moore reflected this anxiety when he wrote: "Stott and Sargent are clever fellows enough; I like Stott the best. If they had remained at home and hadn't been taught, they might have developed a personal art, but the trail of the serpent is over all they do .... Stott's getting over it by degrees."[37] It was therefore a strange quirk of fate that it was in 1882, the year

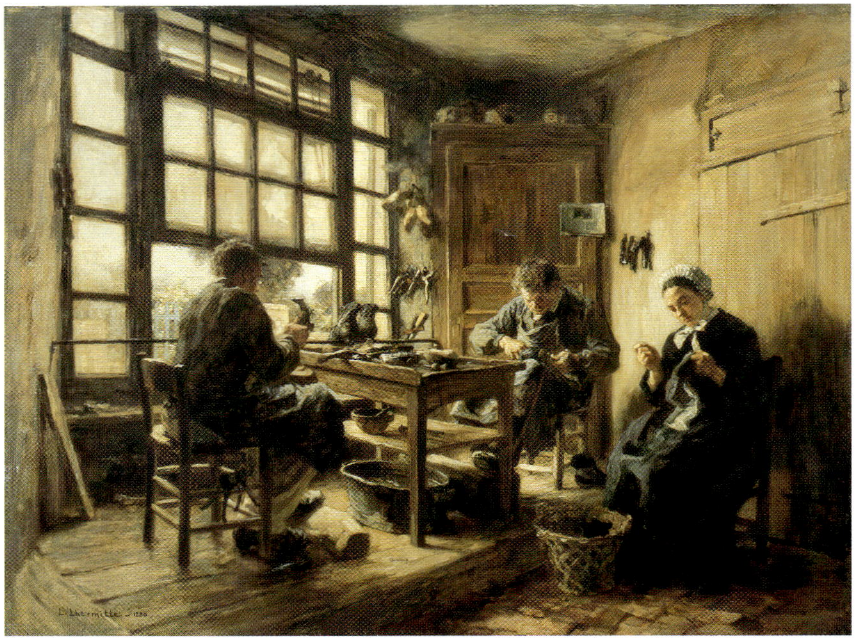

Fig. 22 Léon Lhermitte (1844–1925)
The Cobblers, 1880
Oil on canvas, 53 × 66 cm
Private collection

of his triumph at the Paris Salon, that Stott had his first picture shown at the Royal Academy in London, *Return from Fishing* (*Retour de Pêche*; untraced; fig. 21). It was to be another nine years before the Academy again displayed a work by William Stott. In that time he had become a leading member of the European *avant-garde* and for a time a 'follower' of James McNeill Whistler, which is perhaps why he was to be passed over by the English art establishment for so long.

Stott returned home to Oldham in June 1882 to marry Christina Mary Bradbury, a local doctor's daughter. Much of the honeymoon seems to have been spent painting in Scotland, first at the home of Tom Millie Dow's parents at Dysart and later at Seaton Cottage, Aberdeen, the home of the collector and art critic John Forbes White, who had bought *The Ferry*, and had commissioned a portrait of his daughter from Stott (cat. 21). Forbes White was a great admirer of Rembrandt and Velázquez and indeed wrote the entries for the *Encyclopaedia Britannica* on both these artists. Stott's portrait of his friend the painter Tom Millie Dow (cat. 13), completed in Paris in the spring of 1882, with its realistic intensity and use of a dark background, displays an understanding of both these masters. It is also worth noting that, at the time of Stott's stay, Forbes White had a number of Corots in his collection. Corot, with his subdued tonality and atmospheric depiction of nature, was a painter much admired by the Grez artists. To have such a knowledgeable patron must have been an inspiration and encouragement to Stott at this time, and the weeks he spent with Forbes White were remembered with much joy. He wrote later to the family: "Do you know that the six weeks with you at Seaton Cottage are quite the prettiest six weeks of my life – will they ever come again? They must. I cannot, will not, believe that such Eldorado days are gone for ever."[38]

From Scotland Stott returned with his wife to Ravenglass in Cumberland, where he rented a house and studio, and where much of his most important work was to be accomplished until his death eighteen years later. In the autumn and winter of 1882 he worked on three major canvases which were to be exhibited in Paris. Two of these works were to show a further shift in technique and stylistic approach, but the third, *Grandfather's Workshop (L'Atelier du grand-père*; fig. 23) was a *tour de force* in photographic realism and can perhaps be seen as an homage to the French Realist painter Léon Lhermitte (1844–1925), who specialized in scenes of workaday life (fig. 22). Stott would have met Lhermitte on their visits to Grez and clearly struck up a firm friendship. In May 1885 he records in his notebook visiting the Lhermitte home at Mont-St-Père, where he presented a pastel drawing of Léon's eldest son to the family. Lhermitte had trained under Lecoq de Boisbaudran and Stott may have gained from him a knowledge of Lecoq's theory of memory training, which he believed heightened an artist's perception and imagination.

Grandfather's Workshop, which was exhibited at the Salon of 1883, shows a carpenter's

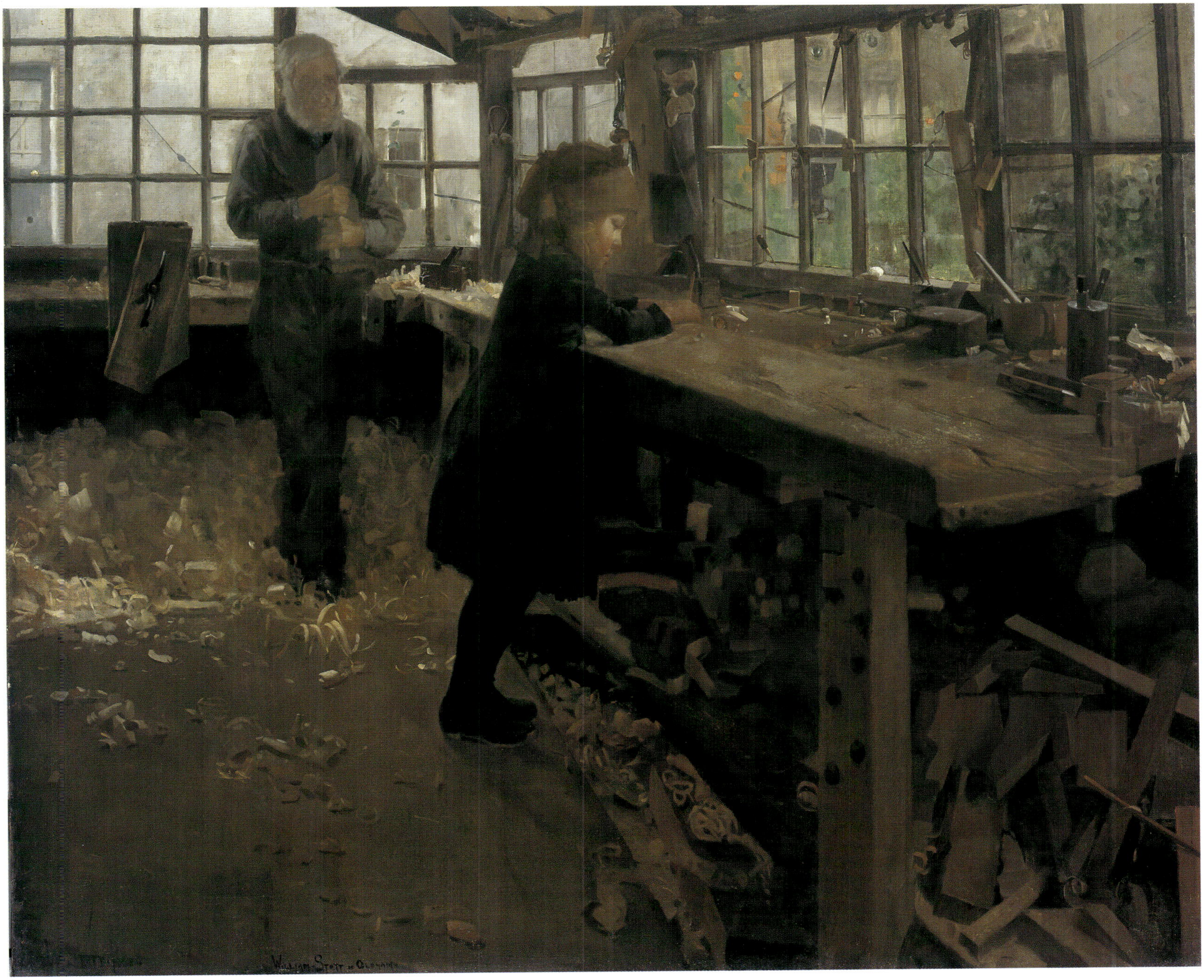

Fig. 23 William Stott of Oldham
Grandfather's Workshop (*L'Atelier du grand-père*) , 1882
Oil on canvas, 123.5 × 149.5 cm
Neue Pinakothek, Munich

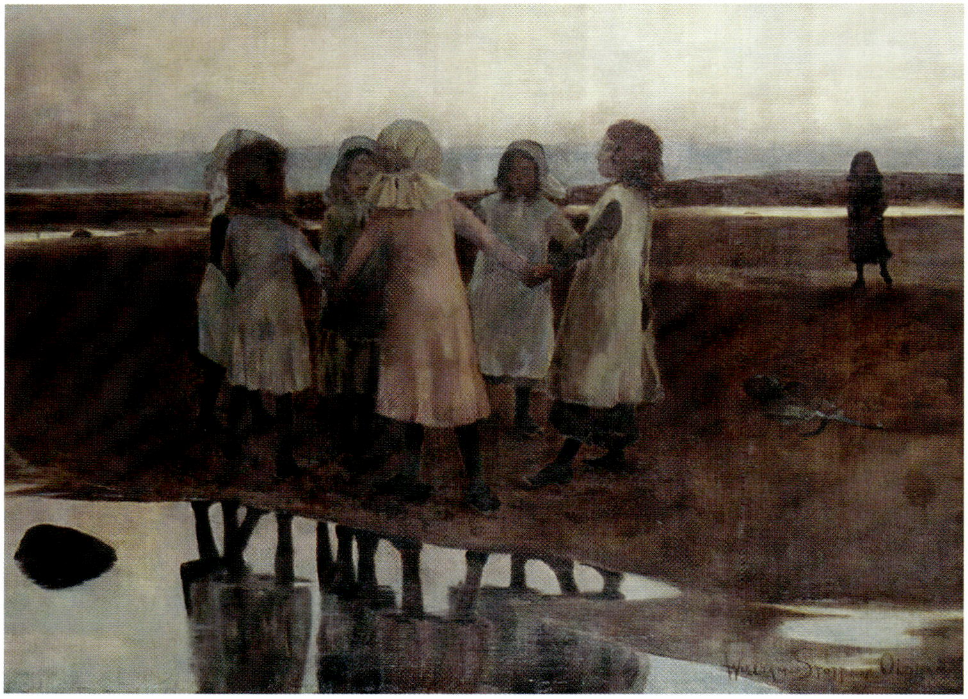

Fig. 24 William Stott of Oldham
The Kissing Ring (Ronde d'Enfants), 1882
Oil on canvas, 114.2 x 150 cm
Durban Art Gallery, South Africa

workshop with a young girl working at a bench while her grandfather stands pensive in the background, as if nostalgic for the innocence of youth. In its painstaking detail the picture has a Pre-Raphaelite quality. It also has an overt symbolism on the theme of youth and the passing of time, a topic that was only hinted at in Stott's Salon pictures of the previous year. This preoccupation with life's cycle is also implicit in his two other exhibition pictures executed at Ravenglass in the autumn of 1882, *The Two Sisters* (*Les Deux Sœurs;* cat. 14) and *The Kissing Ring* (*Ronde d'enfants*; fig. 24). However, in these paintings the mood and style changes. Both reflect the meditative and melancholy quality of so much of Frank O'Meara's work. *The Two Sisters* is painted in a one-tone grey light and the overcast atmosphere is reflected in the demeanour of the children, so that they appear to be totally congruent with their environment. Technically, the forms have been flattened and simplified as in a woodblock print, which perhaps suggests an appreciation of Japanese art, but is also in the style of O'Meara, who applied his paint thinly and sparingly. Stott may also have been influenced by Puvis de Chavannes's *Poor Fisherman* (fig. 16, p. 20), which is also striking for its simplicity, its large flat areas of colour and its geometry, and has a similarly enigmatic and disturbing effect. *The Kissing Ring* also has a mysterious and primitive feel about it. The village girls do not dash about like carefree children but appear to gyrate in the solemnity of some pagan rite in the chilly twilight of a winter afternoon. Alice Corkran wrote of it: "*The Kissing Ring* is another picture very low in tone. Twilight is falling over the seashore .... The critics have protested at the gravity of the children. Romping little ones would have been an intrusion on the scene, they would have destroyed the magical secret of the departing day. These rhythmically moving children ... seem to be the essences of the surrounding twilight, part of the repose, of the vague all-prevalent satisfaction that is yet akin to melancholy, as far removed from joy as it is from sorrow."[39] The perceptive Corkran clearly appreciates what Stott is trying to achieve, but critics at the time were not so understanding. When it was exhibited at the Society of British Artists in 1886 the *Art Journal* commented, "Mr Stott's *Kissing Ring* is an adequate example of a particular class of modern work, but lacks tenderness and real beauty".[40]

In spite of this less than rapturous welcome by the critics at home, on the Continent Stott was perceived as one of the most radical and promising English painters of his day. On both sides of the Channel, where battles between the establishment and the *avant-garde* raged incessantly, Stott was seen to belong to the modernist camp. In terms of conservative taste in the 1880s his work was regarded as daring and provocative. In London there was a greater polarity between academicians and modernists than in Paris. But the Grosvenor Gallery offered a kind of 'Salon des Refusés'[41] to British and Continental *avant-garde* artists, and the formation of the New English Art Club in 1886 provided a venue for 'francophile' British artists who had trained in Paris, as did the Society of British Artists under Whistler's short 'reign'. In addition other independent galleries such as the Dudley, Dowdeswell's, the Fine Art Society and Goupil offered a platform for progressive British artists and a showcase for the Impressionists and Symbolists from France and beyond. William Stott was to exhibit at all these venues during the 1880s. In Paris, owing largely to the Gallic compromise of the *juste milieu*, there was not the same polarization, and it was possible for artists to exhibit at the independent clubs and still gain acceptance at the Salon.

Although William Stott longed for recognition by the art establishment at home, for the time being he was content to be hero-worshipped by the more progressive among his contemporaries. Stott was particularly idolized by the Scottish Impressionist group which became known as the 'Glasgow Boys', having formed friendships with John Lavery, Alexander Roche, William Kennedy, James Paterson and Tom Millie Dow while in Paris and at Grez. He exhibited regularly at the Glasgow Institute from 1883. In that year *The Bathing Place* was shown alongside Bastien-Lepage's *The Beggar* (Ny Carlsberg Glyptotek, Copenhagen).

Stott was now firmly associated with the European *avant-garde*. In December 1882 he was invited to show at the inaugural exhibition of the Société Internationale de Peintres et Sculpteurs at the newly opened Galerie Georges Petit on the rue de Sèze. He sent *The Two Sisters* and *Portrait of Tom Millie Dow*, which was the first public showing for both pictures. The exhibition included works by twenty-two young *juste milieu* artists (sometimes nicknamed '*Les Jeunes*'). They included Bastien-Lepage, Béraud, Boldini, Cazin, Duez, Liebermann and Sargent. The critic Paul Mantz wrote, "As soon as you walk into the gallery on the rue de Sèze, you realise that you are dealing with honest ultra-subtle people who are at pains to say unexpected things".[42]

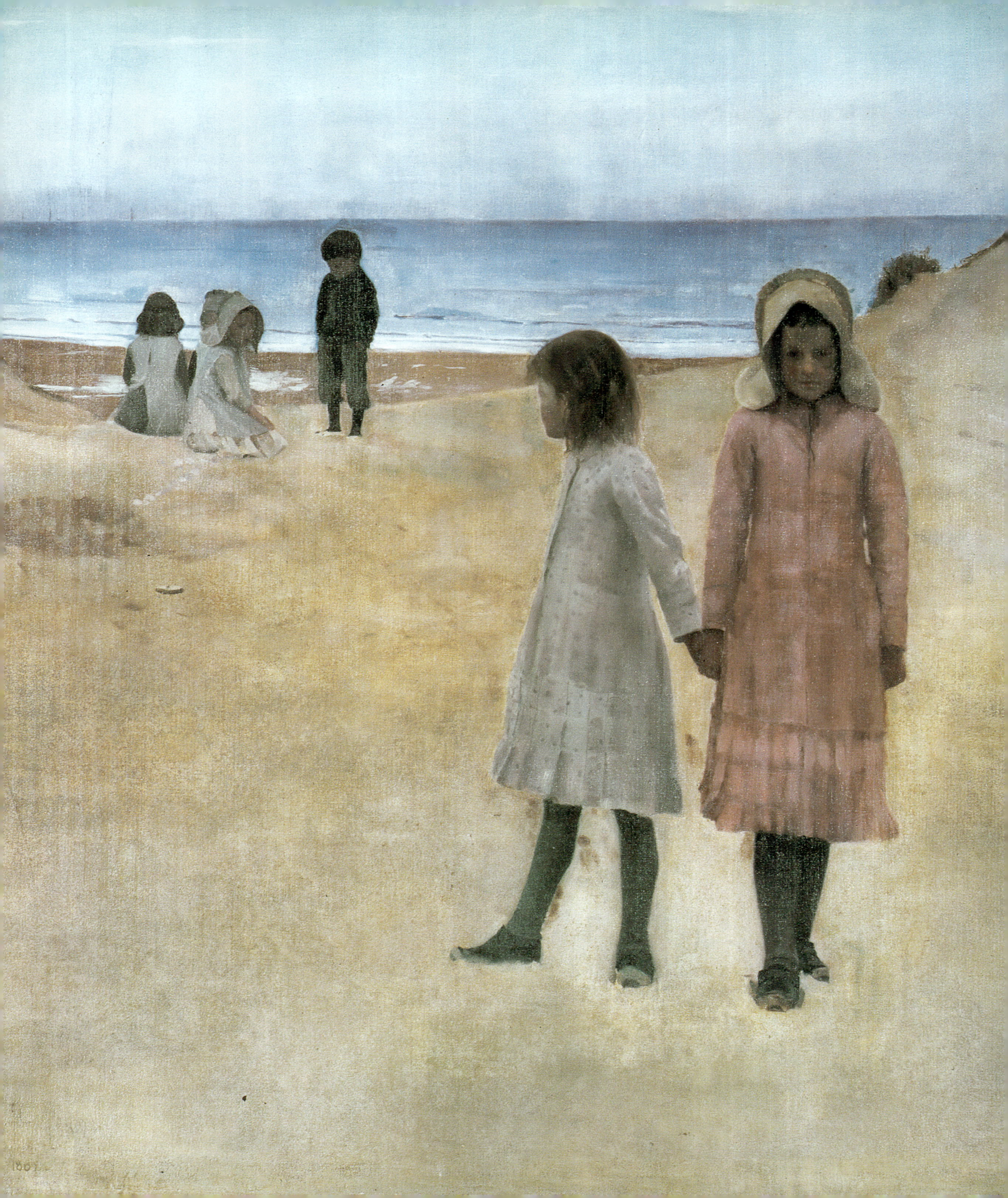

2
In the Steps of the Master

"We were true followers. We had such a reverence for the Master that, highly as we esteemed Velasquez and Rembrandt, we looked upon them as mere drivellers compared with him, and of course we placed him far above Raphael. The only master with whom we could compare our own was Hokusai the Japanese painter"[43]
Mortimer Menpes,
Whistler as I Knew Him, 1904

The year 1883 represents something of a watershed in Stott's artistic development. After the momentous events of the previous year – marriage, a medal at the Salon and the production of five major canvases – his notebook for 1883 records only a few minor studies. There seems little doubt that it was at this time that Stott was falling under the spell of the 'master magician' James McNeill Whistler (1834–1903). Exactly when Stott came under the influence of Whistler is not entirely clear. There are indications in his work before 1883 that Whistler's aesthetic was understood and endorsed by Stott even if it was received vicariously through painters such as Puvis de Chavannes and Cazin, who in turn were admired by Whistler. But Whistler's reputation and notoriety after the famous Ruskin libel case of 1878 would have been the talk of artistic circles. Whistler espoused the 'art for art's sake' aesthetic, a phrase adopted by the Aesthetic Movement from the French writer Theophile Gautier (1811–1872) and used to imply that art is a self-sufficient entity concerned solely with beauty and needing no moral or social justification. Whistler also promoted the analogy between music and painting made popular by the writings of Walter Pater (1839–1894), the English essayist and critic. Pater's essays were a leading influence on the Aesthetic Movement and his book *Studies in the History of the Renaissance* (1873) was acclaimed by Oscar Wilde as "the holy writ of beauty". In it his dictum "all art aspires towards a condition of music", although not original, gave credence to Whistler's aesthetic. Stott was clearly very influenced by Pater's writings and Neo-Platonist philosophy.[44] Pater's book *Marius the Epicurean* (1885) was written to illustrate the highest ideal of aesthetic life, and probably inspired Stott's late picture *Hide and Seek in the Garden of Epicurus* (cat. 67).

In his early naturalist work at Grez and Ravenglass Stott showed a desire to go beyond replicating nature, and was intent on creating atmospheric and tonal harmony in his pictures. With his poetic nature, and encouraged by his friend at Grez, Frank O'Meara, he became "poorly satisfied with the results of commonplace realism".[45] His training and temperament led him to reject the gimmickry and bourgeois urbanism of the Impressionists. An alternative, and to Stott much more attractive, route was offered by the Aesthetic Movement, with its emphasis on the parallels between music, poetry and painting. Aestheticism eliminated the traditional framework of reference in representational painting, emphasizing the values of paint, form and colour in themselves. Or, as Whistler was to put it in the most famous of his public statements, the *Ten O'Clock Lecture* delivered in 1885, "Nature contains the elements, in colour and form, of all pictures, as the keyboard contains the notes of all music".[46]

In the decade prior to 1878 Whistler (fig. 26) was one the central figures of the Aesthetic Movement in England. It was in 1882 that he arrived back in Paris from his self-imposed exile in Venice after the Ruskin trial. In France his reputation had suffered less from the trial than it had in England and to many he was still a hero. In 1882 Whistler exhibited at the Paris Salon for the first time in fifteen years.[47] As the event coincided with Stott being medalled for *The Bathing Place*, it is most probable that Whistler, who was in the process of recruiting followers, would have shown interest at this time in this 'rising star' among the English painters and that the two men would have met through mutual acquaintances. At the Salon of 1883 Whistler showed *Arrangement in Grey and Black: Portrait of the Painter's Mother* (fig. 25) and received a third-class medal.

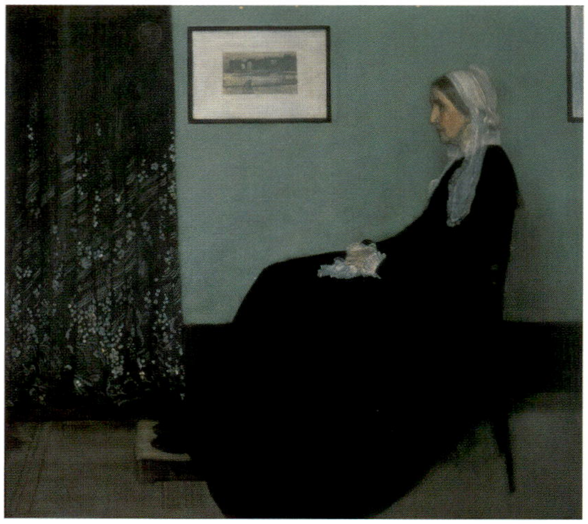

Fig. 25 James McNeill Whistler (1834–1903)
Arrangement in Grey and Black No. 1: Portrait of the Painter's Mother, 1871
Oil on canvas, 144.3 × 162.5 cm
Musée d'Orsay, Paris

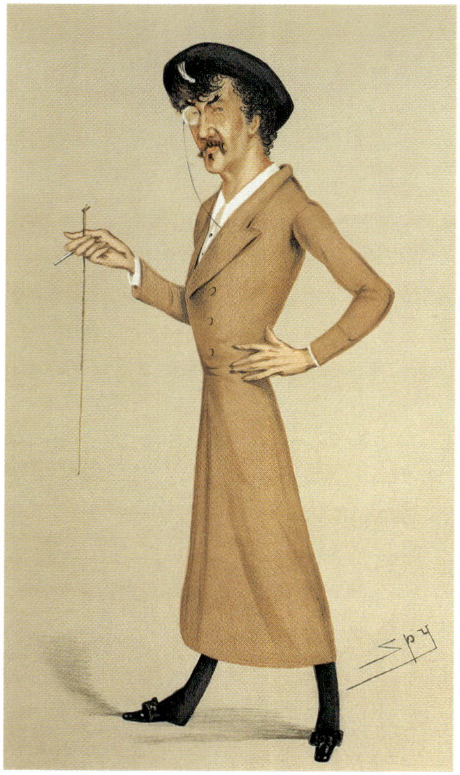

Fig. 26 'Spy' (Sir Leslie Ward)
A Symphony (caricature of James McNeill Whistler)
Lithograph for *Vanity Fair*, 12 January 1878
Private collection

Stott, who was back in Paris, had *The Kissing Ring* and *Grandfather's Workshop* exhibited that year. It may well be that it was at this time that Stott became a follower of the 'master', joining Mortimer Menpes and Walter Sickert, who the previous year had abandoned their training with Poynter and Legros to become Whistler's disciples. Evidence that Stott must have fallen in with Whistler around this time can be assumed from two sources. In September 1883 Octave Maus, the founder of the Belgian secessionist group 'Les XX', wrote an article entitled '*Le Modernisme de Frans Hals*' in *L'Art moderne*. Maus referred to a young 'Franco-American school' in which he included Whistler, Sargent, William Chase and William Stott. Such vagueness was attacked by a French correspondent, who rejected the connection between all these artists, adding that Stott was an Englishman, "who only dreams of Whistler".[48] Both Stott and Whistler were listed as English in the inaugural exhibition of Les XX in 1884. It is clear that Maus had looked for his artists among the English-American *avant-garde* colony in Paris. On what works Maus based his association of Stott with Frans Hals is not clear, unless it was taken as implied in Stott's already perceived link with Whistler, who was an avowed admirer of Hals and Velázquez. It is true that in his portraiture Stott used a more expressive brushwork and it is possible that Maus had seen the portrait of *Tom Millie Dow* (cat. 13) at the Galerie Georges Petit in Paris earlier that year. Or he may have seen *Alice White playing the Violin* (cat. 21), which was in Stott's Paris studio during the summer of 1883 and which Stott records Lhermitte declaring to be excellent, "especially in its freedom of handling".[49]

There is another reason to believe that 1883 was a defining moment in Stott's association with Whistler. At the Salon that year Whistler had shown *Portrait of the Painter's Mother* (fig. 25), and it cannot be coincidence that on returning home to Oldham in the autumn of 1883 Stott began work on his *Portrait of My Father and Mother* (cat. 17). The picture shows a strong affinity with Whistler's carefully composed and formated comment on his mother's character and domestic situation. The side view of the old gentleman, in black clothes, staring straight ahead, his hands resting in his lap, seems like an implied counterpoise to Whistler's *Mother*, who one almost expects to see sitting opposite him. The formal positioning of Stott's sitters and the furniture and accessories of his room reflect Whistler's care in composition, even if the overall effect lacks Whistler's simplicity and elegance. Once again, albeit in a domestic context, Stott is representing human beings in relation to the general harmony of their setting. We know that Whistler spent the spring and summer of 1883 in Paris, and it was then that he introduced Walter Sickert to his long-standing friend Edgar Degas. It may well have been at this time that Stott was also introduced to Degas, if indeed they were not already acquainted, perhaps through Degas's friend, and Stott's '*maître*', Jean-Léon Gérôme.[50] Certainly from 1883 onwards Stott started working in pastel, a preferred medium of Degas's, almost exclusively for *plein-air* landscape work and in preliminary sketches for exhibition pictures – and he proved to be a superb pastellist. Most of the thirty works he produced in 1884 were in pastel, ranging from portraits of his family which reflect the domesticity of some of Degas's work to small subjectless seascapes and nocturnes in the manner of both Degas's and Whistler's pastels of the 1860s and 1870s.[51]

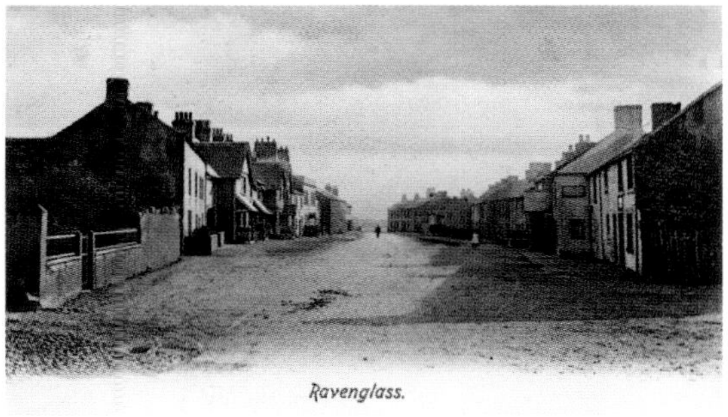

Fig. 27 Ravenglass, *ca.* 1890
Collection of Peter van Zeller

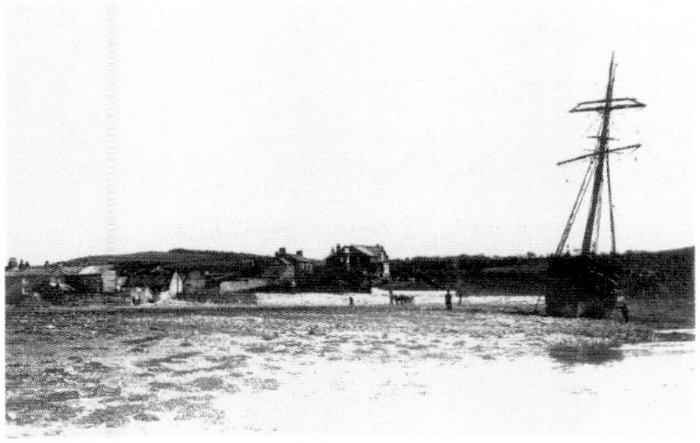

Fig. 28 Ravenglass, *ca.* 1914
Cumbrian Railways Association

There was a long-standing prejudice that pastel was an ephemeral medium. But technical improvements in the mid nineteenth century and the introduction of synthetic aniline dyes, which enabled a range of high-keyed colours, rekindled interest in the medium. To add impetus to the rehabilitation of pastel, Whistler had brought back a large number from Venice, which were exhibited at the Fine Art Society in 1881, and the first annual exposition of the Société des Pastellistes Français took place at the Galerie Georges Petit in 1882. The young William Stott would have been very aware of these developments and would have been eager to rise to another challenge. His sudden conversion to pastel from 1884 almost certainly also coincides with some sort of contact with Degas. As might be expected, Degas's finish was more 'impressionist' than Stott's. He preferred to leave individual strokes of colour clearly visible and used various layers of pastel individually fixed to the surface. Stott's finish, on the other hand, was so fine that it is sometimes difficult to identify the medium, and some of his pastels were wrongly catalogued as watercolours. However, both artists used gouache and pastel paste to give body and improve the binding qualities.

Stott's rapid mastery of pastel seems to illustrate yet again his ability to absorb new influences and techniques quickly. If we examine his domestic pastels, the debt to Degas can quite clearly be established. In the winter of 1883–84, at the same time that he was working on *Portrait of my Father and Mother* in Oldham, Stott drew a series of exquisite pastels of his wife. *The Artist's Wife* (cat. 15) seems to owe much to contact with Degas, but also has strong echoes, in the tilt of the head, the hands resting on the lap and the sombre dress, with Puvis de Chavannes' *Portrait of Madame M.C.* (fig. 42, p. 68), which was shown at the 1883 Salon and much admired by Stott.[52] In *CMS* [Christina Mary Stott] *reading by Gaslight* (cat. 16) and *By the Fireside* (cat. 20) Stott again succeeds in catching the atmosphere of sterile domesticity and the tension within his sitter. His small pastel *CMS at the Piano* (cat. 18) clearly reflects Whistler's painting of his half-sister Deborah at the piano (fig. 44, p. 72).

At Ravenglass (figs. 27, 28), in the summer of 1884, Stott worked on a series of seascapes and coastal views in pastel, which follow Whistler's simplicity and economy of expression almost to abstraction. Stott was to produce many such landscapes in the remaining years of his life, almost exclusively on the Cumberland coast. These figureless, subjectless scenes with titles such as *Sand, Sea and Sky* (cat. 23), *Choppy Sea* (cat. 32), *Turquoise Sea* (cat. 26) and *Sandhill* (cat. 25) are a celebration of Stott's belief in the beauty and symbolism in nature unsullied by the human presence or the limitations of narrative. More and more these small landscapes and seascapes seem to display a form of pantheism, where emotional and spiritual values are expressed through the moods of nature. Like Whistler, Stott was pushing further the boundaries of the apparently limited subject. However, these values were still not shared by the bulk of the art world in England. Corkran records one critic as saying, "... a streak of blue above and a streak of green below, constitutes the Stott formula for a work of genius".[53]

Increasingly Stott began working by moonlight at Ravenglass (cat. 82, 83), perhaps another gesture towards Whistler and his 'nocturnes', and a habit which was to lead him to draw by night in the Alps a few years later. *Moonrise* (untraced; fig. 29) was a success at the Salon of 1885 before being shown at the winter show of the Society of British

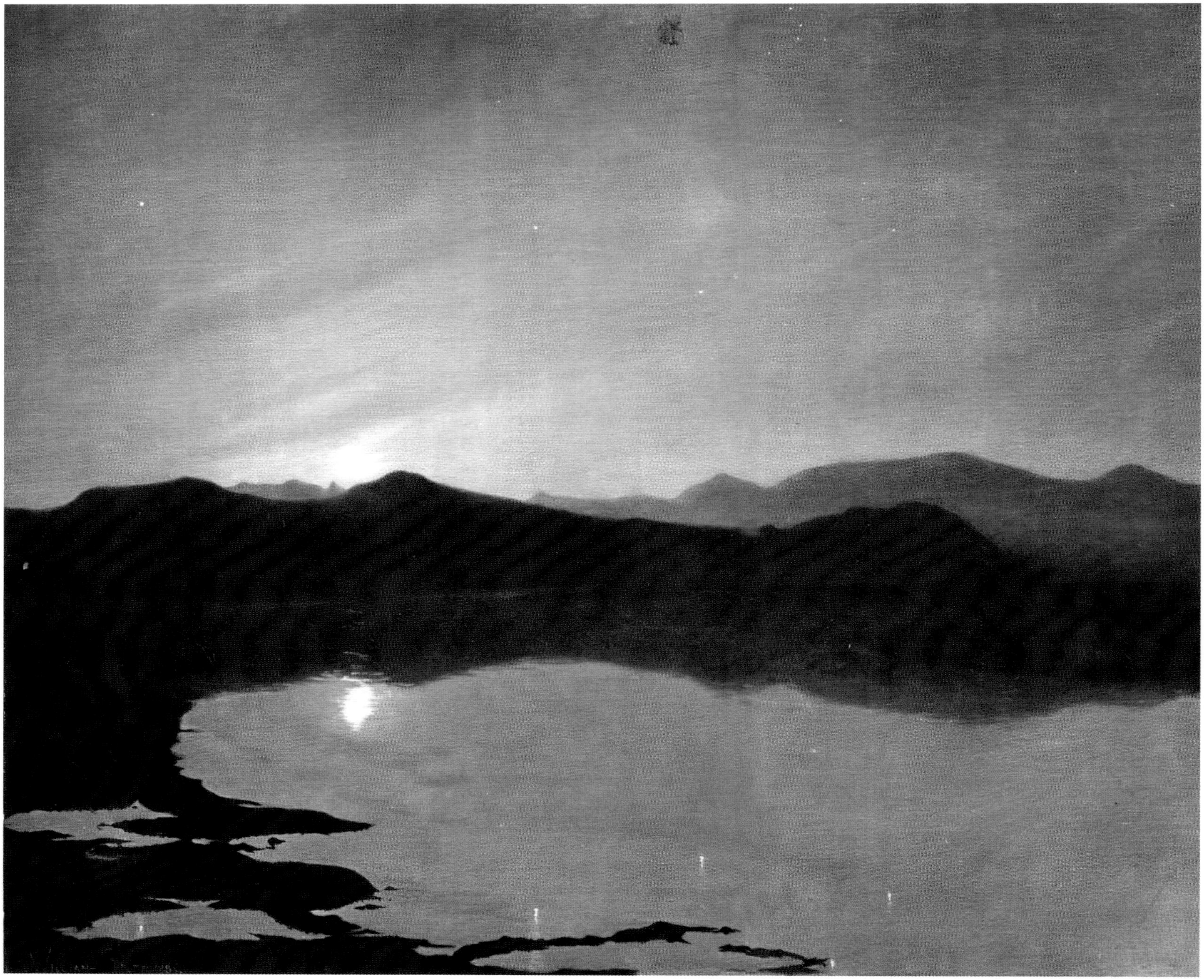

Fig. 29 William Stott of Oldham
Moonrise, 1885
Oil on canvas
Untraced

Artists the same year. Of *Moonrise* the faithful Corkran says, "The picture made upon me a deep impression. The lines of the hills echoing each other, as it were, in the pale clearness of the sky, affected me as music might."[54] She goes on to say that she cannot understand Stott's treatment at the hands of the critics and quotes a review commenting on *Moonrise* at the Society of Bristish Artists in 1885: "The picture is undoubtedly truthful. It embodies in the most exact fashion the general impression of a moonlight night. But most people want more for their money than a severely bare, bald representation of this kind."[55] Such criticism seems to have reverberations of the Ruskin versus Whistler trial of 1878, but Corkran claims it could not have been more wide of the mark. "Whatever else he is not, this painter is passionately painstaking. Every touch has its intention."[56]

When in England Stott was being drawn more and more into Whistler's entourage. Although one senses that Stott's somewhat prudish character never quite took to Whistler the man, with his flamboyance and air of decadence, there is no doubt he believed passionately in Whistler's aesthetic, and in the face of continued carping from the critics over his work he was increasingly pushed further into the Whistler camp. But he found, like all Whistler's acolytes, that he was losing his own individuality as he trod in the steps of the 'master'. This was a dangerous and debilitating ménage to become involved with, and Stott, in common with a number of other artists, discovered to his cost that, although the relationship was temporarily gratifying and uplifting, it had no future. After he was elected to the Society of British Artists in 1884, Whistler started packing it with his followers and Stott was duly invited to join in 1885. He opened his account at the SBA with *Portrait of My Father and Mother* and *Moonrise*. Although still retaining a Paris address and spending much of his year at Ravenglass, Stott had now acquired a house in North London so that he could enter fully into the artistic life of the metropolis and be close to the 'master' when in England. That the two men were very close at this point there is no doubt. Whistler's biographers Elizabeth and Joseph Pennell record that when Whistler was elected President of the Society of British Artists on 1 June 1886, "The comic papers were full of caricatures, the serious papers of astonishment .... Younger artists, William Stott of Oldham among them, rushed to his support."[57] A letter by Stott published in the *Court and Society Review* of July 1886 is the only statement we have of his ideas on art from this time. As might be expected, he extols the virtues of Whistler and sets out what his followers considered to be their aesthetic maxims, taken almost *verbatim* from Whistler's *Ten O'Clock Lecture*, delivered in the previous year. Replying to a previous contributor who claimed he could not understand Mr Whistler's work, Stott rather pompously opines: "I must tell our [contributor] that some twenty years ago this art of Mr Whistler's was no laughing matter on the Continent; that Whistler then took his place among their greatest artists, and has held it ever since; that today the only artist living amongst us seriously recognized by such painters as Puvis de Chavannes, Degas, Gérôme, etc., is Whistler; while the rest of our painters they ignore."[58] Stott's choice of artists to invoke in support of Whistler is enlightening. They are not French artists who were particularly popular or well-known among English collectors at that time, but clearly reflect the 'hero' figures to whom he himself felt indebted.

In August 1886 Whistler visited Stott at Ravenglass, which, in view of the distance from London, does seem to testify to a certain commitment in their relationship. Whistler had with him 'Mrs Whistler', or Maud Franklin, his long-standing mistress, shortly to become the *cause célèbre* that led to the break-up of the friendship between the two men. Stott drew a beautiful pastel portrait of Maud (fig. 30) in a rocking-chair, which does seem to reflect a degree of personal affection. It appears that Whistler cut short the visit, as he wrote later that he had returned from Cumberland "... where I have been staying with Stott of Oldham - until I had enough of that sort of fresh air!"[59] This phrase is

Fig. 30 William Stott of Oldham
Maud in a Rocking Chair, 1886
Pastel, 52 x 43.8 cm
Glasgow Museum and Art Gallery

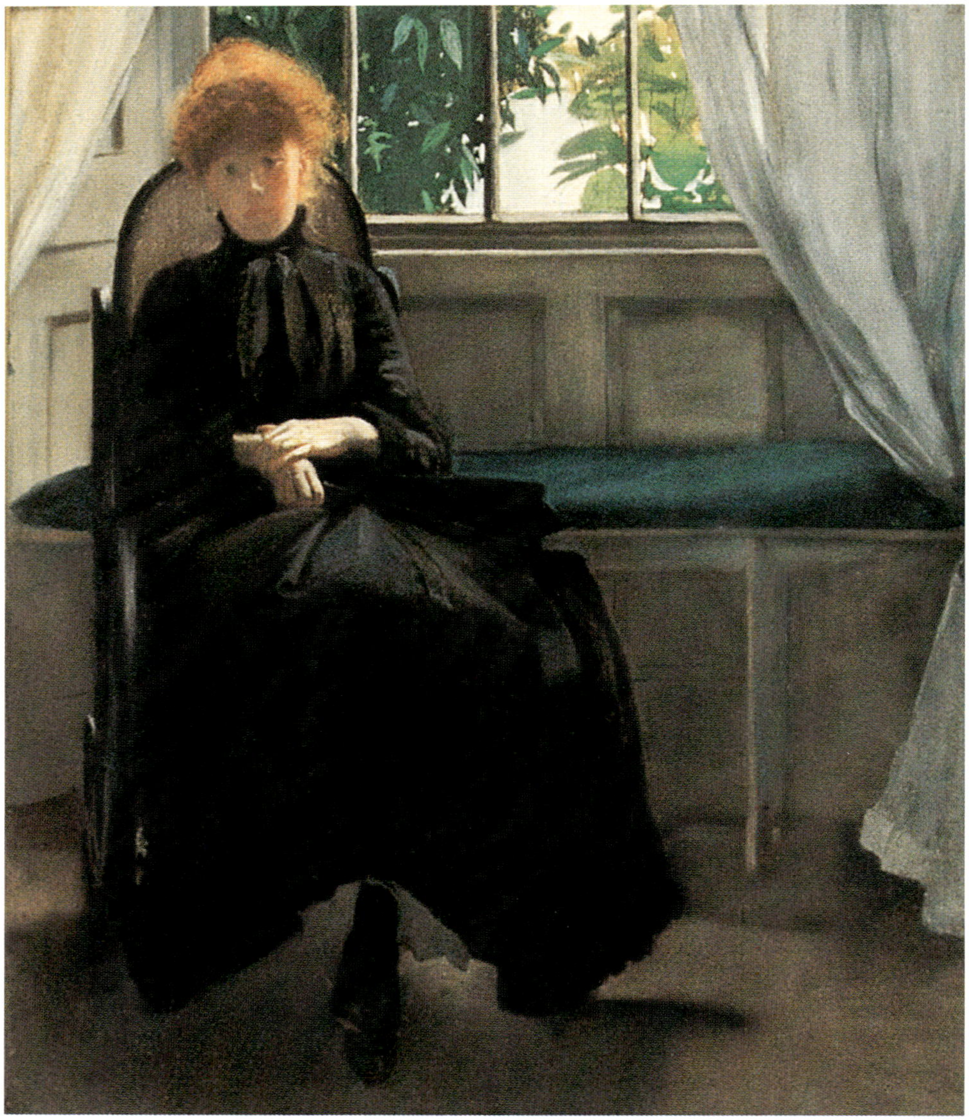

somewhat ambiguous and one wonders whether he considered Stott's manner too earnest and eager, qualities which Whistler would definitely have found tiresome. It may well have been about this time that Stott began to realise that he had to seek an independent path, away from the suffocating influence of Whistler, if he was to be recognized as a great painter in his own right. His notebook records as early as 1886 "Study of underwood for 'Nymph' (Oil)", "The Thicket" and "Pastel large first draught of 'Faerie Wood' (destroyed)", which seems to indicate that he was already contemplating a move away from the realist Aestheticism of Whistler to a more decorative and symbolic form of Aestheticism.

In November 1886 Stott showed four works at the SBA Winter Exhibition which were not well received by the critics. *Portrait of Miss White* was, according to the *Pall Mall Gazette*, "a clever, but unpleasing, whole length".[60] This picture was Stott's beloved *Alice*, of which, we know from his letters, he was particularly proud and which had been praised in France by Lhermitte, Sargent and Puvis de Chavannes, no less![61] Even more hurtful must have been the charges that it lacked originality. Unfortunately for Stott, the year before Whistler had shown his 1884 *Portrait of Senor Pablo de Sarasate* playing the violin. This led *The Standard*, when reviewing Stott's *Alice*, to quip, "Miss White of Aberdeen standing to play the favourite instrument of the moment - to name it would be superfluous."[62] This criticism is particularly unfair, as it ignores the fact that *Alice* was painted two years before Whistler's *Sarasate*, but illustrates how 'the followers' were always open to charges of plagiarism and found themselves in the shadow of their 'master'. As if the criticism of *Alice* were not enough, another canvas, *A Summer's Day* (cat. 49) was singled out for especial abuse: "Three dirty little street arabs are bathing on a mudbank of some airless, dingy Stygian shore ... a sort of hybrid Tom Thumb and living skeleton, stretches his limbs towards us in an attitude as obscene as this highly imaginative painter can conceive ...."[63] Stott had clearly invested a great deal in *A Summer's Day,* which he worked on at Ravenglass early in 1886 and sent off on 4 March to the Paris Salon, where it was first shown, before it would be mauled by the Press at the Society of British Artists' exhibition in November. In his 1894 article Stevenson says that it was "a favourite with its author",[64] largely on account of the amount of serious work and conscientious study that went into it. We know that the previous summer Stott had begun studies for it in both oil and pastel and also records several charcoal drawings of the boys (cat. 50–52). Altogether around twenty studies are recorded in his notebook and some, such as *Sandpools* (cat. 24), were later exhibited and sold as works of art in their own right. In composition *A Summer's Day* is a strange mixture between an academic exercise in figure drawing and a form of abstract realism, which, in sympathy with the values of Whistler, has no narrative and reflects the simplicity of Whistler's own beach scenes.[65] Stevenson tries to explain why the picture has an uncomfortable quality for the viewer. It seems that Stott has superimposed three photo-realistic studio figures on to a painterly background. As Stevenson says, "... the over-modelling of the figures ... seems too hard to suit the general feeling of the landscape. The modelling is too intimate for the width of view embraced, and so the figures appear cold, frozen, and over-studied as separate objects."[66] In short, Stott has compromised a true *plein-airisme* by placing a composition of three carefully drawn figures in a setting which, with its broad panorama, distorts the closeness of the figures so that the observer's view appears to be voyeuristic. It was a device used by Japanese print makers to give intimacy to the rituals of their figures and was to be taken up by Gauguin and later Symbolists.

A Summer's Day was to be the last 'realist' picture with figures Stott was to produce. The constant attacks from the London critics seemed to spur him to move further down the road of Aestheticism towards a more personal artistic vision. His notebook for 1887 appears to show a dramatic move into a world of decorative symbolism – the world of Keats, of Wagnerian legend and of Greek mythology.

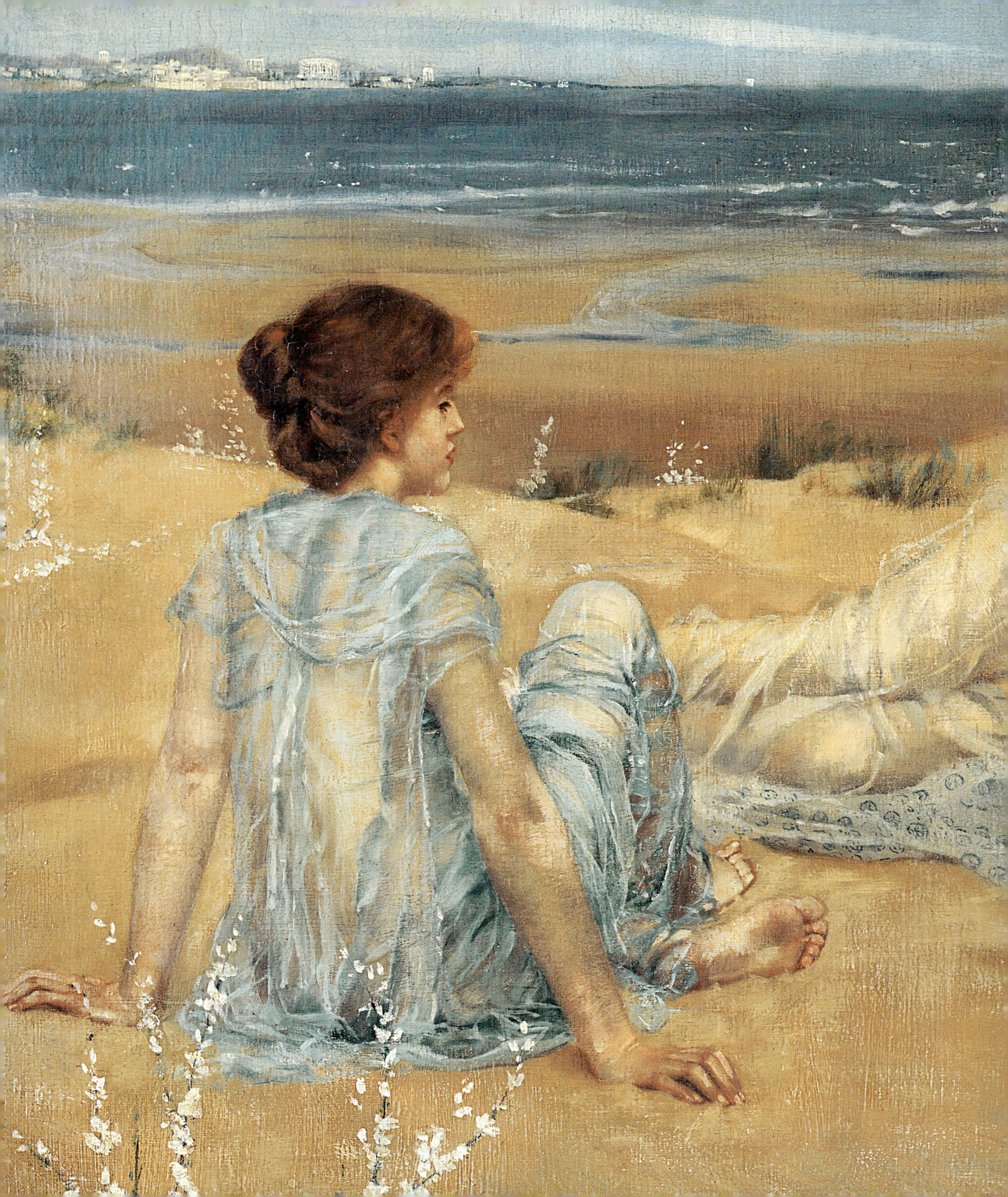

3
The Escape from Reality

"For Taffy was, or thought himself, a passionate realist in those days. He has changed, and now paints nothing but King Arthurs and Guineveres and Lancelots and Elaines, and floating Ladies of Shalott."[67]
George Du Maurier, *Trilby*, 1895

In 1887 Stott produced two major exhibition canvases, *The Nymph* (cat. 54)and *The Birth of Venus* or *Venus Born from the Sea-Foam* (cat. 55), both involving the nude female figure in a radical, not to say fateful, departure from his previous subject-matter. In addition his notebook for that year reads "First draught of Endymion"; "First draught of Diana"; "First draught of the Idlers". Although a latent symbolism has been noted in his early works at Grez, and his adoption of the 'art for art's sake' aesthetic has been documented, the change to a full-blooded Aestheticism in his search for absolute beauty still comes as a shock to us, if not to Stevenson, who says: "Let me hasten on to *The Nymph* and *Venus* which I consider stages as important in Mr Stott's later career as *The Bathers* in his earlier. During these five years Mr Stott has become less of a servant, more of a friend of nature. He dreams more; he decorates, he invents more."[68] The change of direction in 1887 was so complete that it must have been calculated. From now on Stott's spiritual values were to be submerged into a decorative and imaginary world and Whistlerian economy of expression to be replaced by a lush and lurid naturalism. Perhaps, particularly after the depressing reviews of 1886, Stott realised that his association with Whistler was doing him no good and by striking off in a counter direction, but remaining faithful to the Aesthetic Movement, he was establishing his own independence and individuality. It may well be also, given his still strong links with the Parisian art world, that he was aware that Edward Burne-Jones had become the English artist of the moment and that his popularity had given support to the emerging Symbolist movement in France.[69] Through his contact with Les XX in Belgium Stott would have appreciated the Symbolist direction in the work of Fernand Khnopff and Jean Delville. This group's founding principle was the promotion of the new in art, where art was understood in Wagnerian terms as encompassing the visual arts, literature and music. But Stott was now settled in England, and it was probably the English poets and precursors of the Aesthetic Movement in this country who most influenced him.

Writers such as Swinburne, Pater, Symons and Wilde and artists such as Rossetti, Burne-Jones, G.F. Watts and Albert Moore, although lacking any coherent manifesto, represented and articulated the Symbolist ideals in Britain. Stott's first work in his new exhibition genre was *The Nymph* (cat. 54), a large, richly decorative oil painting of a sleeping dryad in a woodland glade. It is a picture of the type that was commonplace at the time in the pages of the *Magazine of Art* or the *Art Journal* and, more importantly, on the walls of the Royal Academy under its President, Sir Frederic Leighton. It proved a popular choice for inclusion in national and foreign exhibitions in later years and indeed was included in the British section at the 1889 Exposition Universelle in Paris.[70]

The ever steadfast Stevenson praised *The Nymph* for its "potent colour" and its perfect balance "in the placing, handling and decorative adaptation of real nature."[71] But when it was shown at the Society of British Artists in the Spring of 1887 not all the critics were so taken. George Bernard Shaw in *The World* expressed his disapproval: "Mr William Stott exhibits a nymph; and she, basking in the sun on a couch formed by her own red hair, exhibits herself freely and not gracefully. The red hair is ill painted ...."[72] There is no doubt that Stott had difficulty in representing the naked female form, and comment on his limitations in this respect were to be a recurring theme in reviews of his work throughout the 1890s. It is strange that an artist praised for his figure drawing at the

Ecole des Beaux-Arts should have such difficulty. In *The Bathing Place* and *A Summer's Day* he had proved very adept and truthful in his depiction of the young male body. But whether through lack of practice or some hidden psychological barrier the female nudes of Stott's later work are rarely convincing, and often their awkwardness detracts from the beauty and precision of their setting.

Increasingly in Stott's career there seem to be parallels with Claude Lantier, the anti-hero in Emile Zola's novel *L'Œuvre*, who strove to produce a masterpiece that would be a landmark of contemporary painting, but could not give birth to the genius within him.[73] It seems that from 1887 onwards Stott quite clearly set his sights on the Royal Academy and was hoping to make the breakthrough to acceptance and recognition with a major work. If this was the case he was to be disappointed once more with his next exhibition canvas, *The Birth of Venus* (cat. 55), a monumental circular work six foot in diameter. The picture certainly caused a stir at the Society of British Artists in Suffolk Street, but not of the kind which Stott might have hoped for. Whether *Venus* was a deliberate attempt to upstage Whistler is not clear, but Stott felt that with this classical subject he was going to be noticed and clearly a great deal was invested in it. Stott considered the picture one of his finest achievements so far.[74] It is something of an irony that only a year after writing in the *Court and Society Review*, "Whistler ... has never asked interest for his art by the aid of classic anecdote or bedabbled his works with names fished out of Latin lexicons ...",[75] Stott embarked on a series of exhibition canvases with titles from mythology and legend. Again, it could be taken as a deliberate decision to disassociate himself from the work of Whistler and to 'set his cap' at the Royal Academy by falling in with the fashionable Aestheticism of the art establishment. However, *The Birth of Venus* was savaged by the critics. They liked the background, but detested the figure of Venus, for which Maud Franklin had posed nude. A typical comment was, "The head is cocked coquettishly on one side, and the eyes, which are evidently meant to be some what roguish, positively lear at the beholder. Mr. Wm Stott, in fact, instead of a goddess, has given us a red-haired Topsy."[76] George Bernard Shaw in *The World* was equally scathing: "... that a painter who sees nothing in a woman but an idiotic doll, sees too little whatever his school may be."[77] The unkindest comment of all came from *The Times*: "Candour compels us to say that his [Stott's] ambition exceeds his ability ...".[78]

The acceptance and positioning of *Venus* at the Society of British Artists had been managed by the hanging committee and Whistler, preoccupied with other affairs, did not see it until it became a public sensation. For once the 'master' was said to be speechless! It is difficult to know whether his embarrassment and infuriation arose because he had not known Maud was posing for Stott, or because his mistress was labelled by the Press as "an idiotic doll". Either way it spelt the end of the relationship between Stott and Whistler.

Whether for his health or to escape the London critics we do not know, but Stott spent much of the summer and autumn of 1888 in Switzerland. It was to be a time of solitude and reflection and resulted in some of his finest landscape work. Stott's notebook records over thirty pastels of varying sizes being produced during his stay in the Alps. Much of the work was *en plein air*, and he endured considerable hardship in the icy conditions. Corkran speaks of how Stott "encamped among the frozen altitudes of the

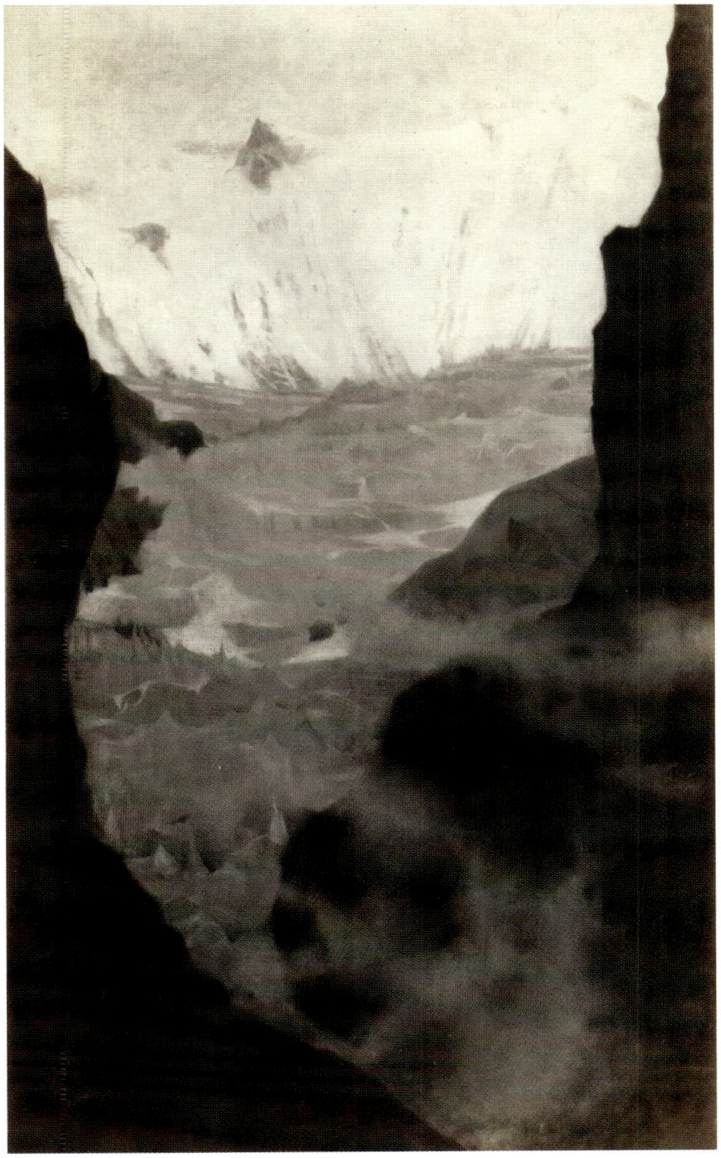

Fig. 31 William Stott of Oldham
Morning in the Alps
Pastel, untraced

Jungfrau and watched, through the night till dawn, the white world given over to the sway of the September moon."[79] A number of the pastel studies were worked up into major oils on his return home. These include works such as *The Alps by Night* (cat. 61), *The Eiger* (cat. 62), *Amethyst Cloud* (cat. 56) and *White Mountain* (cat. 59), all of which are now held in public collections in Britain, and the untraced *Morning in the Alps* (fig. 31). Stott's Alpine pastels offer a unique realisation of the mountain landscape. They are not just topographical views, but mystical evocations of atmosphere and above all mood. After his death most commentators agreed that they were unequalled and represented perhaps Stott's finest achievement. Stevenson says, "... these pictures are not for the Alpine climber who wishes to retrace his perilous route", rather they are "dreamy visions of delicate colour and exquisitely soft definition".[80] As with his seascapes, Stott in his mountainscapes achieves a poetic synthesis of Whistler's principles which almost reaches an abstract quality.

In November 1888 Stott returned to Ravenglass, where he worked on exhibition versions in oil of *Amethyst Cloud* and *White Mountain*, the latter being sent the following spring to Les XX in Brussels, where it was well received. On his return to England, Stott discovered that both he and Maud Franklin had been outwitted by Whistler. During Stott's absence abroad Whistler had arranged for Maud to stay with Stott's parents in Oldham on the pretext that she needed a period of convalescence. While she was there Whistler married Beatrice Godwin. Stott was outraged at Whistler's treatment of Maud and matters came to a head between the two men when Stott came across Whistler at the Hogarth Club in London on the evening of 3 January 1889. Stott challenged Whistler by accusing him of being a "liar and a coward". There was a scuffle in which Whistler kicked Stott. Both men had to apologize to the committee of the Hogarth Club and Whistler endeavoured to have Stott expelled. He wrote an indignant letter to the committee in which he requested "that some measures be taken to prevent a recurrence of such intolerable provocation and such monstrous insult".[81] In typically malicious fashion he 'leaked' his letter to the Press. The gossip columnists both in Britain and on the Continent had a field day, with headlines such as "Mr Whistler insulted .... Slaps and Kicks a Brother Artist".[82] Stott went immediately to Paris, and from there he wrote to the Press with his own version of the incident. Finding out where Stott had gone, Whistler lost no time in writing to their mutual acquaintances in Paris to malign and ridicule Stott. These letters give us an insight into Stott's involvement in artistic and aesthetic circles in Paris. To the Belgian painter Alfred Stevens he wrote, "Stott 'of Oldham' is dead! I gave him a couple of splendid slaps in the face and an elegant kick in the rear in the drawing-room of the Hogarth Club! all in the most perfect and distinguished manner possible! ... A masterpiece! You must tell the story on the boulevards."[83] He also wrote to Sargent, comte Robert de Montesquiou and Edgar Degas. Whistler's letter to Degas is particularly

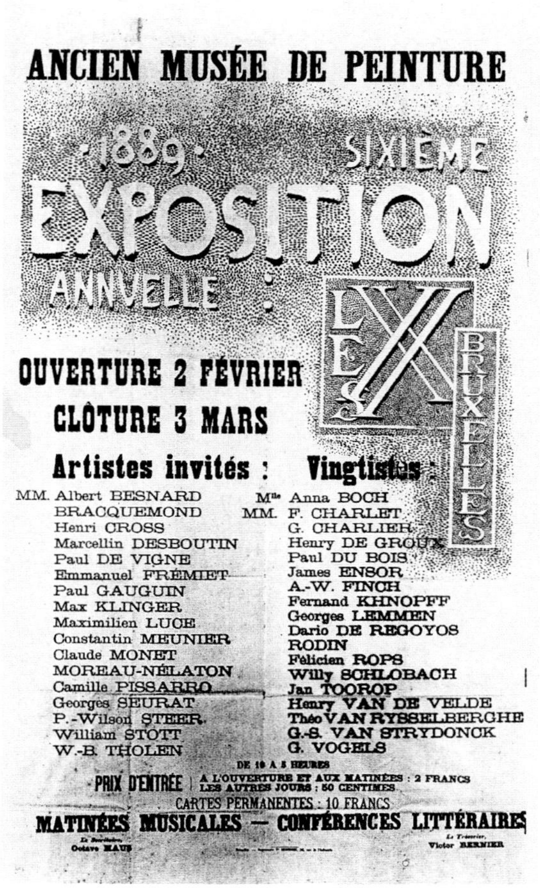

Fig. 32 Poster for the 1889 Salon des XX, Brussels
(Stott is among the artists named)
Archives de l'art contemporain, Brussels

interesting, as he seems to assume that Stott will have already visited Degas, which seems to testify to a close relationship between the two men: "I write to you, see enclosed, about the laughable news of the sad tale of William Stott of Oldham. Doubtless he has already been to see you, since his return, to explain that he is not ridiculous - for it seems he still has the impudence to do so."[84]

It is doubtful whether this *contretemps* had any lasting effect on Stott's work or development as an artist. By that time he was well on the way to establishing his own independent artistic identity and destiny. If anything it may have raised his stock among certain members of the English artistic establishment, who had no love for the bullying and bombastic Whistler. Indeed many of Whistler's friends considered his treatment of Maud had been intolerable. Walter Sickert remained loyal to Stott. Although still an admirer of Whistler's work he had for some time taken an independent path, and had refused to join the Society of British Artists in 1886. In fact in 1890 Sickert wrote to Whistler urging him to forgive Stott, as he feared that the 'master' would try to prevent his ex-follower from being elected as a member of the New English Art Club: "... his accession would strengthen the Club ... none of us has the right to drag the trail of a personal quarrel over the rest of his professional career in London".[85] In the event Stott was elected to the NEAC in 1890, but only exhibited once at the Club.[86] A number of his friends from his days at Grez were members – John Lavery, John Singer Sargent, Tom Millie Dow, James Paterson – but at this time the NEAC had come to be dominated by the 'London Impressionists', many of whom were ex-followers of Whistler, for example Paul Maitland, Theodore Roussel, Walter Sickert and Sydney Starr. Perhaps, with his sights now firmly set on the Royal Academy, Stott sensed the danger of being snared again into a clique with a collective label. He had fought and suffered to gain an independent standing and he clearly intended to maintain that position and in artistic terms to be his own man.

After the fracas with Whistler in January, 1889 was a busy year for William Stott. For many artists it might be seen as the pinnacle of success to be invited to exhibit at Les XX in February, while at the same time having a one-man exhibition at Durand-Ruel in Paris and having a large canvas selected for the British Section at the Exposition Universelle in the same city in May. But all these accolades and indicators of success were on foreign soil. Stott still longed for acceptance among his own at home. He sent to Les XX *The White Mountain* (cat. 59) along with one of his Swiss pastels, *Blue Glacier*, and two portraits in pastel, *Maud* (fig. 30)and *By the Fireside* (cat. 20). Among his fellow *artistes invités* were Monet, Pissarro, Moreau, Gauguin and Seurat, the only other English artist being Philip Wilson Steer (fig. 32). It was the second and last time that Stott contributed to Les XX. At Durand-Ruel Stott showed sixty works, which included twenty-three pastels and three watercolours. It was a truly retrospective display of ten years of endeavour, from his early Salon successes, such as *The Ferry* and *The Bathing Place*, through his family portraits and Alpine pastels to *The Nymph*, *Endymion* (fig. 33) and the infamous *Birth of Venus*. Reviews for the show were mixed, with many critics not sure what to make of such an eclectic output. Alice Corkran's article in *The Scottish Art Review* coincided with the Durand-Ruel show, which, in her opinion, confirmed that William Stott was "unrivalled as a poet-painter".[87]

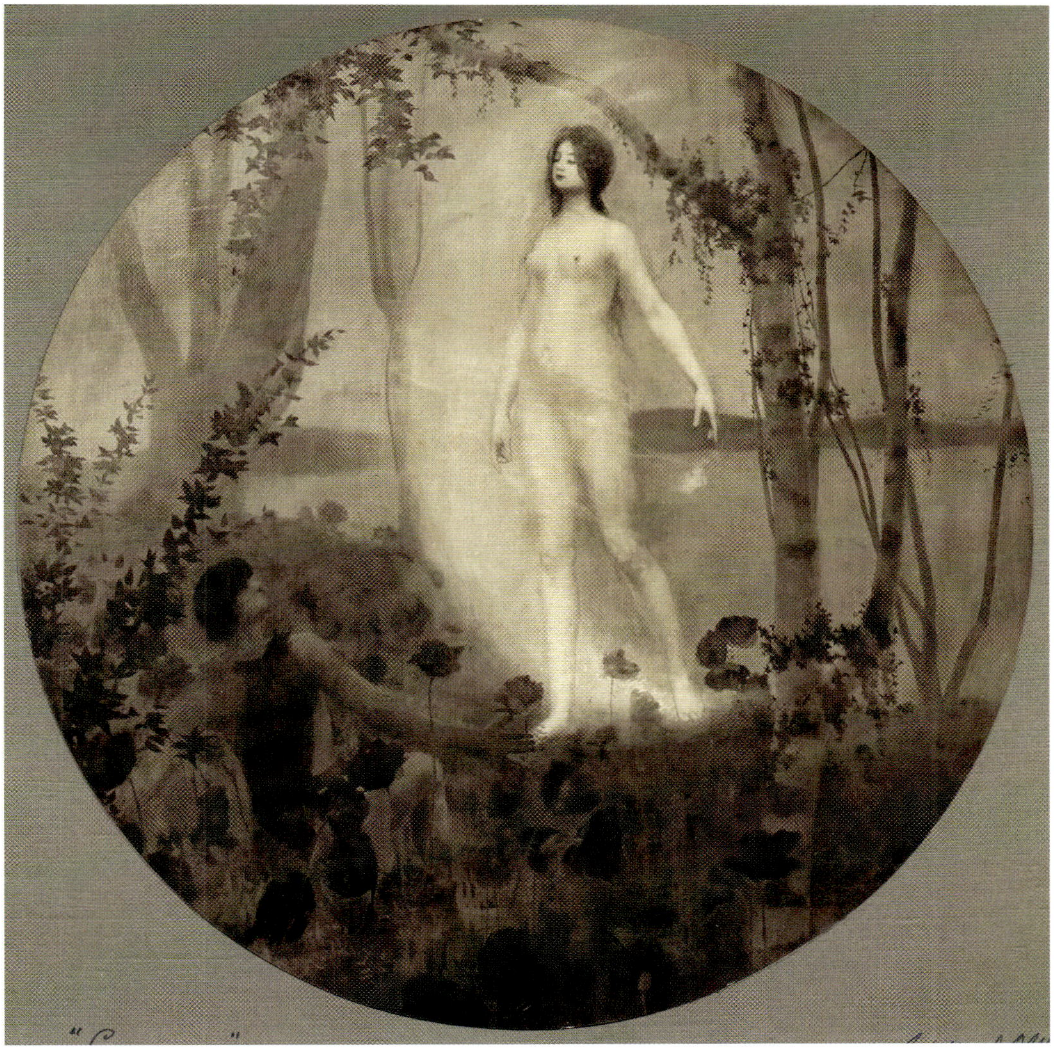

Fig. 33 William Stott of Oldham
Endymion, 1888
Oil on canvas, 162.5 x162.5 cm (tondo)
Untraced

As he began to spend more time in England Stott became increasingly involved with the artistic life of the provinces, mainly in the northern cities and in Scotland, where he still had a loyal following. As well as in Glasgow, he began exhibiting regularly at Liverpool, where he was on the Hanging Committee in 1892 (fig. 34),[88] and at Manchester, Leeds and Birmingham. He was always faithful to his home town of Oldham, sending works on a regular basis to the Spring Exhibition, which he was invited to open in 1893. In the metropolis he continued to exhibit at the more progressive exhibition venues, such as the Grosvenor, the Grafton and the New Gallery. Stott's pictures were in demand for loan exhibitions both at home and abroad. *The Birth of Venus* for example, was shown at Ghent (1889), Munich (1891), Vienna (1894), Prague (1895) and Venice (1897) and at no less than seven different venues in Britain during his lifetime. On the back of his relationship with the 'Glasgow Boys' Stott found considerable popularity in Munich. In 1890 Adolphus Paulus of the Munich Art Society visited Glasgow and was impressed with the Glasgow painters' work, which demonstrated that painting in a naturalistic manner need not be done at the expense of colour. He

Fig. 34 The Hanging Committee at the 1892 Liverpool Autumn Exhibition, including William Stott of Oldham (centre), Stanhope Forbes (far right) and P.H. Rathbone, Chairman of the Committee (seated next to Forbes)

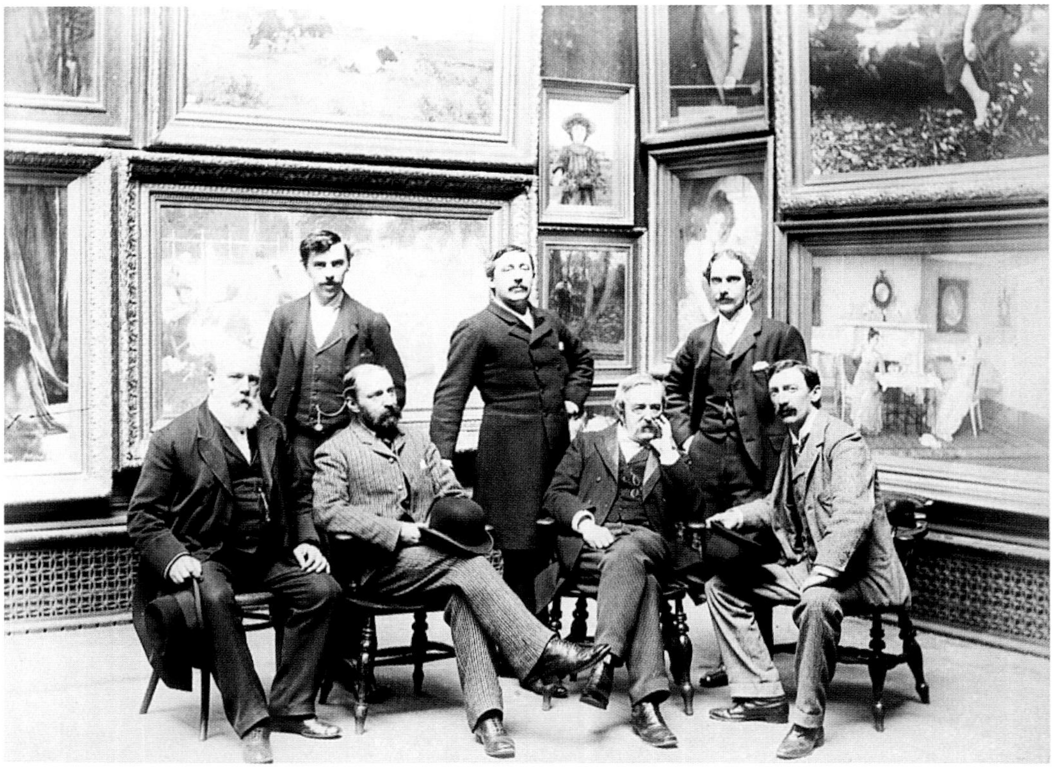

immediately agreed to show their works in Munich, and Stott, who was exhibiting in Glasgow at that time, was also invited to exhibit. He achieved immediate success, receiving medals in 1891 for *The Bathing Place* (fig. 17) and in 1892 for *Grandfather's Workshop* (fig. 23), which were bought, at the time, by the Bavarian government for the state collection now in the Neue Pinakothek, Munich.

Stott's success abroad and in the provincial galleries must have had some effect in whittling away at the art establishment as embodied in the Royal Academy. It is somewhat ironic that ten years after being medalled at the Paris Salon and only months before being bought by a foreign government, *The Bathing Place* was belatedly accepted for the 1891 exhibition at the Royal Academy. Two years later *The Ferry* was also accepted by the Academy. It is strange that these two pictures, which launched Stott on his career in 1882, although out of kilter with his current aims and ideals, should now provide the breakthrough he needed into the priviledged precincts of the Royal Academy.

Throughout the 1890s Stott produced a series of large exhibition canvases based on medieval legend and classical mythology. The first picture in 'Academy' style accepted by Burlington House was *The Awakening of the Spirit of the Rose* (fig. 35), in 1894. This employs the same iconography as *The Nymph*, using the popular formula of a classically draped figure in a floral setting much favoured by private collectors and public galleries at the time. *The Awakening of the Spirit of the Rose* concentrates on the decorative features and there is little overt symbolism. Clearly, Stott was not concerned with the literary Symbolism of Aubrey Beardsley or Gustave Moreau, whose line drawings and paintings were inspired by the poems of Charles Baudelaire and Edgar Allan Poe and theories of

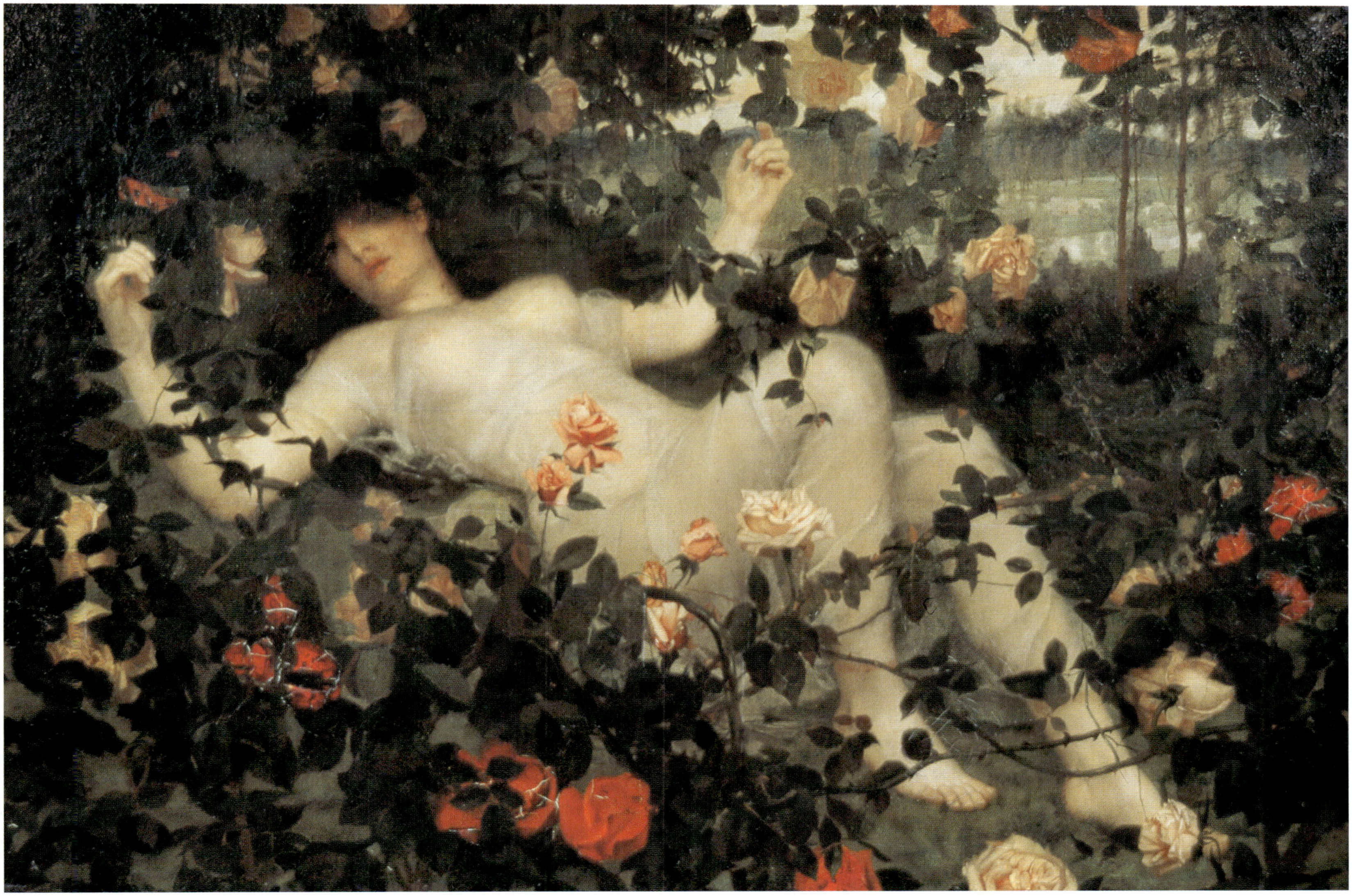

Fig. 35 William Stott of Oldham
The Awakening of the Spirit of the Rose, ca. 1893
Oil on canvas, 94.6 x 142.2 cm
Manchester City Art Galleries

the decadence of man. Where there is symbolism in Stott's paintings of the 1890s, rather than the 'black' symbolism of the Decadents, it is a form of 'white' symbolism which allies him to Puvis de Chavannes and in particular Maurice Denis, the French painter and theorist. Denis was a leading member of the Nabis, a group of French painters whose work was inspired by Gauguin's use of colour and rhythmic pattern and who held their first exhibition in Paris in 1892. Alice Corkran wrote that Stott rebelled against any attempt to "intellectualize art, in his passionate assertion that art must appeal by beauty only to that which is sensuous and simple within us",[89] but she was writing in 1889, and in the last ten years of his life it does seem that Stott attempted to introduce an intellectual and didactic element into his oeuvre by linking paintings to poetry and by his choice of classical and mythological subject-matter. It was in his landscapes that he kept faith with Whistlerian principles and achieved "a spiritual beauty of which the physical is but the emblem and token".[90] Increasingly, in what were to be Stott's last years, there seem to be three strands running through his work. There are the figureless elemental

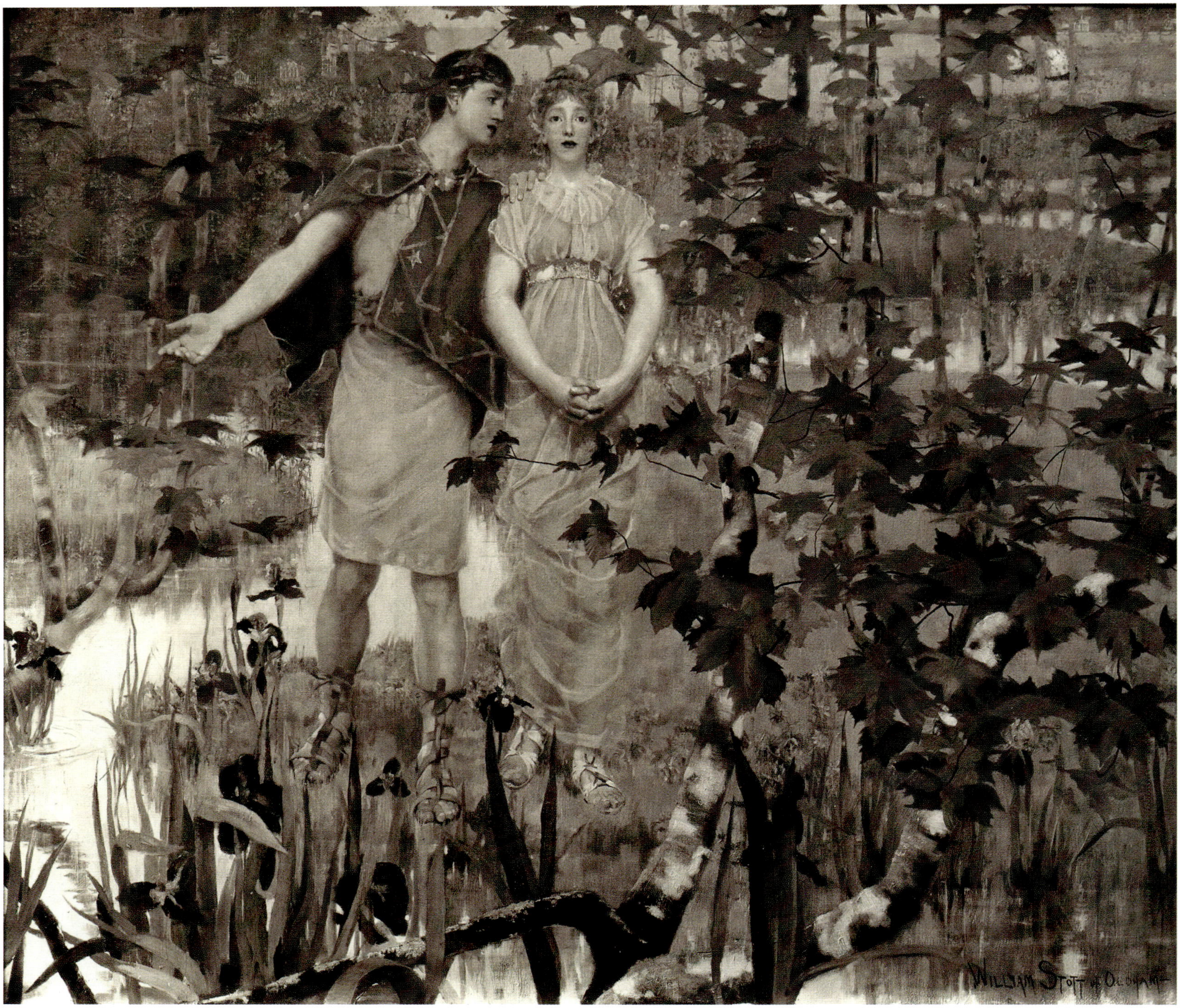

Fig. 36 William Stott of Oldham
The Happy Valley, 1896
Oil on canvas, 125 × 150 cm
Untraced

landscapes where nature is reduced to its simple grandeur. Then there are the essentially decorative works unashamedly aiming for the Royal Academy, in which colours are intense and the poetry emphatic. But other works, such as *The Fairie Wood* (cat. 66), *The Happy Valley* (fig. 36) and *Hide and Seek in the Garden of Epicurus* (cat. 67) display a greater degree of symbolism, in a search for the innocence and simplicity of an imaginary bygone age, and link Stott to Neo-Platonist ideas of beauty.

In 1894 *Fairie Wood* was exhibited at the Royal Academy, the subject-matter reflecting the popularity at the time of themes from Malory's *Morte d'Arthur* and Spencer's *Faerie Queen* among Academy painters such as Frank Dicksee, Evelyn de Morgan, Walter Crane and J.W. Waterhouse. *Fairie Wood* also bears a strong resemblence to Altdorfer's *St George* (fig. 50, p. 110), which was in Munich and which Stott might have seen if he had followed his pictures there in 1891 and 1892. Alongside *Fairie Wood* at the Academy of 1894 was *The Awakening of the Spirit of the Rose*, both pictures competing for attention with their meticulous replication of nature in the leaves and flowers. In these later pictures Stott continues his mission to harmonize man with nature. One commentator speaking of *Hide and Seek* in 1901 said: "... the figures are carried, as figures, just as far as he can go with them. They are drawn and elaborated like any work on a gem, and every leaf in the composition has its due relation to them, as they have their relation, both of form and colour to every leaf. It was magnificent as a conception, but in my judgement, it was hardly realisable. It had never been tried before ... with the fullness and completeness with which Stott saw it in his dreams."[91]

With his continued emphasis in the 1890s on medieval and literary themes and his commitment to painting with complete fidelity to nature, it seems that Stott was referencing back to the Pre-Raphaelites. The Pre-Raphaelites, divorced from moralizing and religious overtones, remained a driving inspiration for the Aesthetic Movement in England and through the work of Burne-Jones were an influence on the Symbolist movement on the Continent. Stott had never really lost the respect for form and finish instilled into him by Gérôme and in his later years, in his search for absolute beauty in the natural world, also shows an affinity with the ideals of John Ruskin, the champion of the Pre-Raphaelites. In *Modern Painters* Ruskin wrote, "Go to nature in all singleness of heart ... rejecting nothing, selecting nothing and scorning nothing; believing all things to be right and good, and rejoicing always in the truth".[92] This is a credo that William Stott would have been very comfortable with in the last decade of his short life. It has been said that the Pre-Raphaelites were "unquestionably the Victorian heirs of the Romantic Movement",[93] and there is no doubt that Stott was a romantic at heart. The change in Stott's palette from the subtle, soft harmonizing tonalities that he worked with in France to the bright, clear and intense colours of the1890s also reflects Ruskin's belief that such colours were the visible symbol of purity and the sacredness of beauty. What is more, around 1891 Stott joined the Ruskin-inspired Art Worker's Guild, of which he was still a subscribing member at his death, and he exhibited with the Exhibition Society, the Guild's splinter group, at the New Gallery.[94] The inspiration behind the Society was William Morris, who identified with Ruskin's ideas in art and with his socialism. Morris's ambition was to make the decorative arts functional, noble and beautiful, as well as accessible to all the people. We do not know Stott's political views, but he certainly seemed to align himself to Morris's ideals in a speech he made in 1893, when opening the Oldham Spring Art Exhibition: "... art, like the others of music and poetry, is the property of all the world, from the highest to the lowest".[95]

In this speech Stott displays a typically Victorian attitude to self-improvement through art, poetry and music. He also goes to considerable lengths to justify the role of the artist in society: "... the business of the artist is ... while his fellow worker is busy at the anvil or the loom, to collect together and bring home these beautiful things in life, so that when the one comes home weary from the toil of his body, he shall have these things to refresh his brain and so beguile away his weariness".[96] He goes on to say that the artist's existence is as exacting and demanding as that of the engineer or city merchant. Stott then expounds on the analogy of art with music, which indicates that, although he had broken with Whistler the man, he had not parted company with his aesthetic ideals. Speaking of people who say they do not understand pictures, or art, he says: "This, I must confess, remains to me an enigma; for surely, most of the things we enjoy we do not necessarily understand .... In music I myself understand not even the rudiments, and yet I have no greater pleasure in the world than to listen to 'Tristram and Iseult' or the moonlight sonata – a pleasure quite as great to me as looking at the finest picture."[97] In another speech, to the Manchester Arts Club in February 1898, Stott gives us another rare insight into the influences on his later work. The speech was entitled 'A Retrospect of Art', and after paying predictable tributes to Van Eyck, Titian, Velázquez, Dürer (whose *Self-portrait* he seems to have seen in Munich) and Holbein, *The Manchester Guardian* report states, "Mr Stott next spoke of Botticelli, whose work he compared to that of Chaucer".[98] After expressing admiration for Botticelli's imagination and romance, Stott went on to say: "I have personally had as much delight in looking at Botticelli's pictures as I have had in the pondering over the poems of Keats, and when I tell you that the reading of Keats has been one of my greatest enjoyments in life you may gather the extent of my appreciation of this gentle Botticelli".[99]

This fulsome praise for Botticelli is very telling and instructive, as Botticelli had been rediscovered by the Pre-Raphaelites and admired by Ruskin. In addition Walter Pater, the apostle of Aestheticism, had dedicated an eloquent essay to him.[100] Stott would have had no difficulty in embracing Botticelli's Neo-Platonist philosophy, as interpreted by Pater, which regarded Beauty as an embodiment of the Divine. The reinstated Botticelli was to become one of the significant influences on the Symbolist movement of the late nineteenth century. In England his work was especially admired by Edward Burne-Jones and the mannered and elongated female figures in some of Stott's later work, such as *The Happy Valley, Hide and Seek* and *Idlers* (fig. 36, cat. 67, 65), certainly reveal evidence of his own admiration for the ornamental and evocative work of Botticelli.

Stott's passion for Keats is also interesting, given that this poet was again a source of inspiration for the Pre-Raphaelites. It has been said that Keats "... with his sensuous lyricism and virtuoso evocations of physical delight has been seen as a forerunner of Aestheticism".[101] Stott attached to his picture entitled *Autumn*, which was exhibited at the Royal Academy in 1898, a verse from the poem *To Autumn* by Keats. Indeed, in the manner of Rossetti, Stott attached a verse of poetry to several of his later works, for example, *The Birth of Venus* (Hesiod) and *The Awakening of the Spirit of the Rose*

(Lovelace). But the parallel with Rossetti ends there. Stott lacked Rossetti's sophistication and sense of decadence. His goddesses and nymphs are idealized for their aesthetic beauty and their harmony with their setting and contain none of the menace or mystery of Rossetti's female subjects. As a 'poet-painter' Stott found his inspiration in the beauty of nature rather than the souls of people. In the catalogue to a one-man show for Stott at the Goupil Gallery in 1896, Hall Caine says: "In these canvases, I think, the spirit of Keats is expressed as it has never been expressed before – Keats in his love of beauty and in his love of colour, Keats in his power of vision and in his delight in dream, Keats in his quality, and perhaps, in his excess, Keats in his poetic spirituality ...".[102]

The eclectic nature of Stott's later work seems to show a desperation to find the right formula to satisfy both his own intellectual needs and the popular demands of the Academy. It gave him a reputation for being unpredictable, individual and uneven in his output. His apparent lack of consistency perplexed the critics, although they, along with his fellow artists, never doubted his industry and the sincerity of his intentions. There is no doubt that William Stott was a significant figure in British art of the 1890s. Some critics thought he was ahead of his time, while others thought he had overreached himself, but one thing is certain, he was never dull. He was well liked in artistic circles and still had many friends from his Paris days. Most of the former Whistler associates remained supportive. Walter Sickert, in particular, remained loyal, always writing positively of Stott's work in his Press reviews. Indeed, Sickert in a letter to *The Sun* in February 1897 pointed out what he considered to be glaring omissions from the ranks of the Royal Academy. Dutifully he wrote, "First and foremost there is the monumental case of Whistler, one of the two greatest living painters of the world". He then goes on to mention "names that leap to the lips of every serious student of art, but which I never see mentioned in paragraphs of probabilities".[103] Whistler may well have choked on his croissant if he had read on, for Sickert, ever the fair-minded, rational observer, goes on to say: "First, it seems to me that the claims of William Stott cannot be overlooked. He has painted several masterpieces, which it does not fall to the lot of many painters to achieve in a lifetime .... His 'Wood Nymph' is a picture for the National Gallery. He gets little recognition."[104] John Lavery, perhaps remembering the happy days at Grez, was another who remained loyal to Stott, although their careers had taken very different paths. In 1899 Lavery proposed Stott for membership of the International Society of Sculptors, Painters and Gravers, of which Whistler was President. The suggestion did not meet with approval, as Whistler had still not forgiven Stott for the *Venus* affair. Lavery records in his biography how, some months later, he was walking down Cheyne Walk with Whistler, when he noticed "Death of William Stott of Oldham on board ship" on a newspaper poster and pointed it out to Whistler, whose comment was, "Umph, so he died at sea, where he always was!"[105]

4
In Memoriam

"Stott of Oldham is dead, and already he is half forgotten; those who remember him best are mainly old-time students at Gres [*sic*] .... And Frank O'Meara, who had a following at Gres, he, too, is gone, dying young, and few now know his name. For a few brief years there was intrepid courage with high ambition, with cheerfulness, with friendship; and then, all of a sudden, death came, and one more youthful reputation began to fade into the dead and crumbled past."[106]

Walter Shaw-Sparrow,
John Lavery and his Work, 1911

Like many of Whistler's aphorisms, his comment about Stott (see p. 47) contained an element of truth. It did seem to many observers that in his later years he was 'at sea' artistically. His eclecticism became a disadvantage and his defiance of convention made it difficult for him to find a 'spiritual home' in artistic terms. Nor did he have that completeness of character or clearness of vision to create a new 'school' around himself. The one theme that is universal in his obituaries is that he was a talented and significant figure, who did not, however, match up to early potential and who 'lost his way' artistically. One is again reminded of Zola's novel *L'Œuvre* and the artist who can find no satisfactory solution to the 'artistic problem'. As Zola explained, "... Claude Lantier, never satisfied, distracted, because he cannot give birth to the genius within him – a creative artist with too wide an ambition."[107] In tributes at Stott's death, and later assessments of his work, the most frequently used adjectives are "individual" and "original". The following obituary is typical of many: "Mr William Stott of Oldham, an artist of striking originality, whose work is far too little known to the general public, has died at sea in the course of a short voyage taken in the hope of recovering his health after a serious illness .... Mr Stott's later work, beautiful and imaginative as it is, is of somewhat too uncommon a kind to find acceptance with the majority of picture viewers in his own country, although it is highly esteemed in France and Germany."[108]

No doubt Stott's deep and ingrained connections in the Parisian art world did nothing to assist his acceptance at home. Many of his contemporaries at the Ecole des Beaux-Arts had returned to Britain immediately after their training and begun the process of establishing themselves in one 'school' or another. Stott, on the other hand, retained his studio in Paris, off the rue de Vaugirard, throughout the 1880s, and therefore became more deeply involved with the European *avant-garde* and the emerging Symbolist movement in France. The 'art for arts sake' aesthetic of Whistler had appealed to the romantic in Stott, as well as giving him influential connections in Paris; but he was to realise, too late, that the association with Whistler was a curse. The two men were temperamentally unsuited and Stott was too much his own man to be a 'disciple' of anyone. None of the 'followers' were to become Associates of the Royal Academy (except Walter Sickert belatedly in 1924); Stott was to spend the last ten years of his life desperately seeking recognition from the Academy, perhaps prescient of an early death owing to his constant ill-health.[109] Controversy seemed to dog Stott's whole career, from the early days, when he was told by the critics he was "less original and inventive than dexterous and intelligent",[110] to his later years, when he was criticized for being too original to be understood! One critic writing in 1896 believed that Stott was underestimated for this reason: "This painter's delicate perception of exquisite tones of colour mark him as one of our foremost artists. He is a little in advance of his time, however, and the usual lack of support accorded to an original man during his best days is exemplified to some extent in his artistic career."[111] Even in 1889 Alice Corkran had written of Stott, "By some critics he is put into a sort of pillory ... others largely recognize the artist's power, but lament his eccentricities ... and some most eminent painters admire his work passionately ...."[112]

In October 1901 a memorial exhibition of Stott's work was held in London. One might expect that, nearly two years after his death, a clear, unambiguous evaluation of his

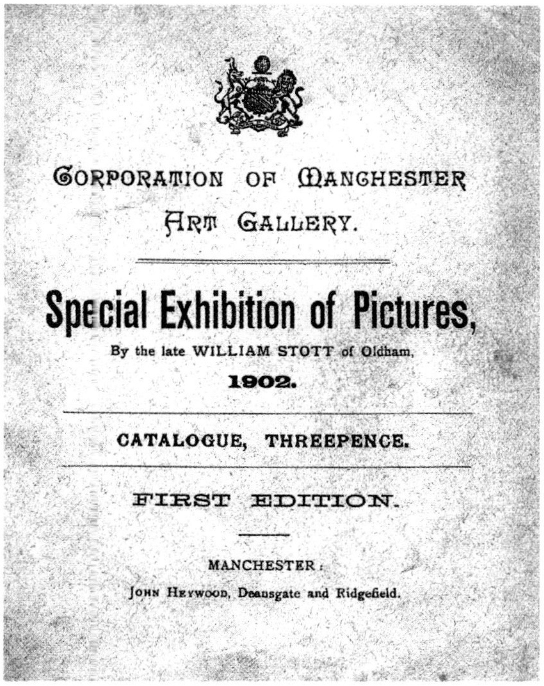
Corporation of Manchester
Art Gallery.

Special Exhibition of Pictures,
By the late WILLIAM STOTT of Oldham.
1902.

CATALOGUE, THREEPENCE.

FIRST EDITION.

MANCHESTER:
John Heywood, Deansgate and Ridgefield.

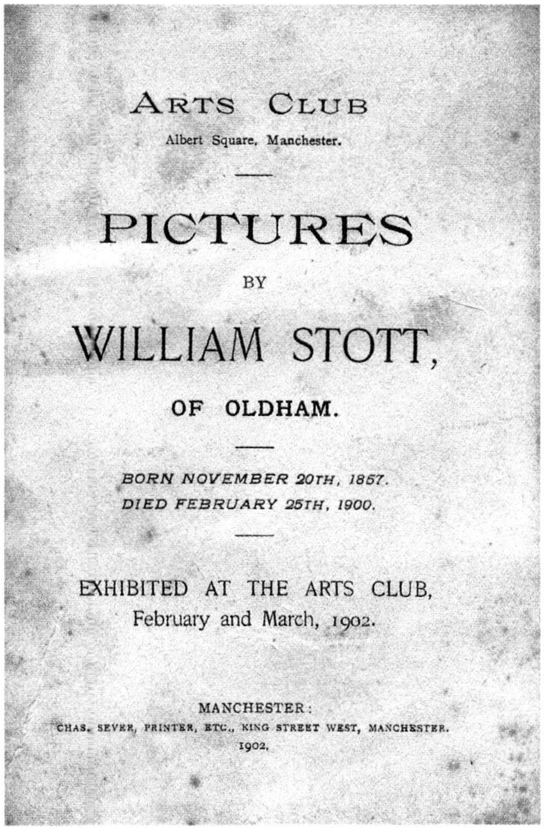
ARTS CLUB
Albert Square, Manchester.

PICTURES
BY
WILLIAM STOTT,
OF OLDHAM.

BORN NOVEMBER 20TH, 1857.
DIED FEBRUARY 25TH, 1900.

EXHIBITED AT THE ARTS CLUB,
February and March, 1902.

MANCHESTER:
CHAS. SEVER, PRINTER, ETC., KING STREET WEST, MANCHESTER.
1902.

work and achievements would be possible, but from the reviews it seems that Stott was still a controversial figure, whose disparate output continued to puzzle and confuse the critics. The anonymous reviewer in the *Magazine of Art*, after conceding that William Stott "was a charming personality, much beloved of his friends", states bluntly, "The fact is, the artist's mental qualities were beyond his powers of accomplishment .... He was delightfully but incompletely endowed. His individuality was striking – his pictures are like those of no one else."[113] Stott's later works, such as *Hide and Seek* (cat. 67) and *The Happy Valley* (fig. 36), are dismissed as "ingenious and elaborately worked out" but "curiously artifical". The most lavish praise is reserved for his Alpine scenes, which have "an elegance and a refinement not too common nowadays". *Summer's Day* (cat. 49) is singled out by the writer in *Magazine of Art* as Stott's "masterpiece", although the comment implies that Stott might have been more successful had he stuck with the realist genre of his early works. "The canvas is one which will keep Stott's name alive. And future beholders will assuredly ask themselves why a painter who could do so well could allow himself to wander into a Valley of his own, which might be Happy perhaps for him, but which tempted him from the more rugged path of artistic duty and success."[114] *The Daily Telegraph* on the other hand takes a rather more thoughtful and perceptive view of the work on display. After praising *Summer's Day* as "the finest piece of mere painting in the gallery" (it is interesting how views on this work appear to have changed in the fifteen years since it was slated at the Society of British Artists), the *Daily Telegraph* critic shows understanding of Stott's ambitions when he adds, "Still, this, though a remarkable achievement, is mere unambitious realism, and as such it is not as distinctive of Stott's art, at its truest and highest, as some of the less perfect things that have been named."[115] But these "less perfect things" are forgiven because Stott "belonged to the band of those innovators who cannot be ignored", and here we have a clue to Stott's apparent eccentricity - he was a compulsive innovator, always looking for new ways of achieving perfection in his work. The *Daily Telegraph* summing-up is helpful in giving us an insight into the reasons behind his varied fortunes and the misconceptions that surrounded so much of his career: "He is unquestionably very unequal, and when he fails in some bold attempt comes dangerously near to shipwreck on the rocks of the ridiculous. But every innovator who has his cause at heart must risk disaster and brave misunderstanding if he is to force the good cause on a step."[116]

In the introduction to the catalogue for the London exhibition Richard Whiteing, a friend from his Paris days, seems to confirm that Stott had a restless, enquiring mind, and this perhaps gives us a further clue to his eclecticism: "He had the passion for experiment of the epoch of French art in which his lot was cast, and of his own eminently scientific mind .... He was ever trying something new, as though in weariness of the thing achieved."[117] The reviewer of the exhibition in the *Magazine of Art* picks up on this suggestion, but is less than sympathetic in his comments: "Mr Whiteing tells us that it was by his love of experiment that he was led away – that he was half a man of science. That explains it all. It is an explanation, but it is not an excuse. An artist who allows his science to step in between him and poetry, not as an assistant, but as a deterrent, must accept the verdict of his selected fate."[118]

There is one sense in which William Stott was consistent. From first to last he was

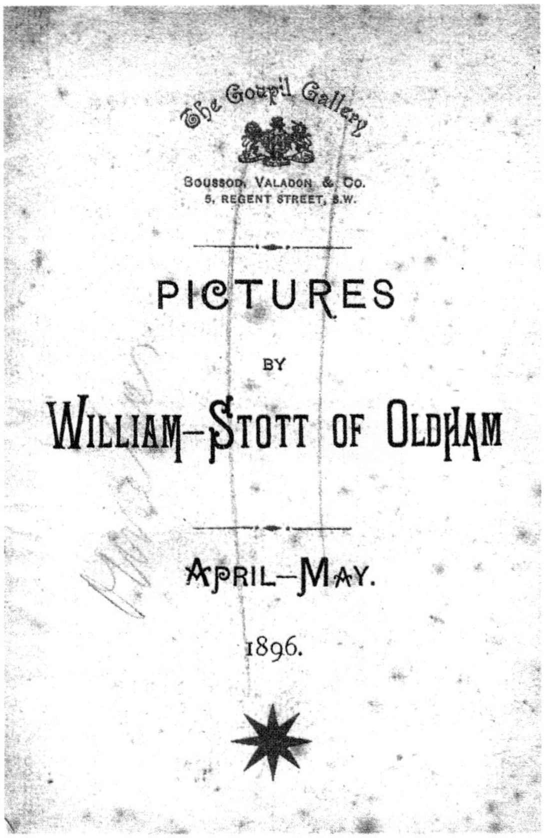
The Goupil Gallery

Boussod, Valadon & Co.
5, Regent Street, S.W.

PICTURES

BY

WILLIAM-STOTT OF OLDHAM

APRIL–MAY.

1896.

concerned with Man's relationship with, and to, nature. His strength, and also his failure, was to strive consistently and relentlessly for perfection in achieving this aim. In the beginning he was an innovator and he died an innovator. Once he had assimulated and adapted the lessons of Bastien-Lepage, Whistler, Degas, Puvis de Chavannes and a host of other influential painters with whom he came into contact, he moved on in his relentless search for his own 'solution'. Even as early as 1882 *The Manchester Guardian*, when reporting the success of a young Lancashire painter, Mr William Stott, at the Paris Salon, stated, with considerable perspicacity: "In so far as such an artist may be supposed to have a theory of his art, and as such theory may be divined from his pictures, one would suppose that he looks upon every scene in landscape as a complete harmonious whole; that is to say he will not study the figures apart from the landscape or the landscape apart from the figures where the latter are introduced."[119] The same could have been written about *Hide and Seek*, the last picture Stott sent to the Royal Academy, in 1899.

Even in 1882 the young Stott was being seen as an innovator, as *The Manchester Guardian*, in discussing *The Ferry*, commented, "It is a poetic landscape, but it is also in some degree scientific. It is distinctly modern; in fact it is new."[120] It is no wonder then that in Paris and at Grez he attracted a group of fellow artists eager to explore his innovative ideas. Indeed, throughout his career other artists, in particular, admired his work, not necessarily for its skill, but for its ideas and intention. The verdict has to be that Stott was a significant and influential figure in his time. Some of his work may have attracted ridicule at times, yet this is often the case with innovators and explorers. But his work never went unnoticed and was always intellectually challenging and instructive.

In his novel *L'Œuvre* Zola depicts the artist's continual struggle with nature, "... the perpetual battling with truth, the endless failures, the ceaseless wrestling with the Angel."[121] Stott would have identified with these words, as throughout his life he was filled with self-doubt and despair and, like Zola's Claude Lantier, he became a victim of his own ideals. The parallel between Stott and Zola's anti-hero is compelling. Stott's words to Forbes White in 1882, although penned four years before *L'Œuvre* was published, could well have been spoken by Claude Lantier: "... and fearful doubts will come sometimes about my capability and these doubts of all things are the most cruel pangs. If I can't be a painter I *won't* be anything and this idea which will come sometimes of perhaps not having the power within to become an artist is agonizing."[122]

William Stott made his mark in his time, but it was not sufficiently indelible, for it faded quickly after his death. We will never know whether his premature death saved him further frustration, heartache and disappointment or whether it robbed him of eventual recognition and a permanent place in the canon of nineteenth-century British art. In *L'Œuvre* the writer Sandoz, speaking after the suicide of his artist friend Lantier, delivers the following judgement, which, sadly, could equally apply to the life and work of William Stott of Oldham: "His trouble was this: he was not the man for his own artistic formula. By that I mean he hadn't quite the genius necessary to plant it on a firm foundation and impose it on the world in the form of some definitive work ... and now what is there to see for all he has done?"[123]

Notes

1. R.A.M. Stevenson, 'William Stott of Oldham', *The Studio*, October 1894, pp. 3–15.
2. Stott's notebook is clearly written retrospectively and may therefore contain lapses of memory or chronology, but it has proved a valuable source and reveals hitherto unknown information about his early artistic endeavours. It finishes in 1888 and is simply a record of his work and sales with no comments on style or substance. I am indebted to a member of the Stott family for the opportunity to be the first 'outsider' to study it.
3. Most biographical sketches state that Stott went to France in 1879. This error has been perpetuated by accepting Stevenson's date. Examination of the Salon records has revealed that he had two watercolours accepted at the Salon of 1878 and was listed as an "*élève de M. Gérôme*". For the full Salon record see Appendix 3.
4. Alice Corkran, 'William Stott of Oldham', *Scottish Art Review*, April 1889, pp. 319–25.
5. John Houghton Hague exhibited four times at the Royal Academy between 1875 and 1886. He taught at Oldham School of Art 1873–78. He painted also in Belgium and Sweden and was a member of the Belgian Academy of Fine Arts.
6. Houghton Hague file in Gallery Oldham. Stott records in his notebook several watercolours and an oil *pochard* [*sic*] of Heysham.
7. Leading members of the group included Weissenbruch, Bosboom, Israels, Mauve, the Maris brothers and Mesdag. See *The Hague School: Dutch Masters of the 19th Century*, exhibition catalogue, Haags Gemeentemuseum, The Hague, 1983.
8. John Ruskin, *Modern Painters*, edn New York 1883, I, p. 21.
9. For a good description of the system, see Quentin Bell, *The Schools of Design*, London 1963.
10. See Jeanne Sheehy, 'The Flight from South Kensington: British Artists at the Antwerp Academy 1877–1885', *Art History*, March 1997, pp. 124–53; also Anna Gruetzner, 'Two Reactions to French Painting in Britain', in *Post-Impressionism*, exhibition catalogue, London, 1979, pp. 178–82.
11. Research has been unable to substantiate this anecdotal evidence. If he did have an introduction to Gérôme it could have come from Houghton Hague or from one of the honorary members of the Manchester Academy of Fine Arts (where Stott attended life classes) such as Sir Edward Poynter, who studied in Paris under Gleyre, whose mantle Gérôme had taken over. But this may be stretching speculation too far!
12. Impressionist exhibitions were held in 1874, 1876, 1877, 1879, 1880, 1881, 1882 and 1886. They were a 'closed' group, where one exhibited by invitation. See John Rewald, *The History of Impressionism*, 4th edn New York 1973.
13. James Paterson, *Early Memories* (unpublished), 1921, p. 12.
14. This portrait came to light in 1997 in the gallery of a New York dealer. I am indebted to Mr Peyton Skipwith of The Fine Art Society plc for drawing my attention to it and to the Spanierman Gallery, New York, for sending me a photograph. Stott's companions on the sketching trip to the Bois de Clamart were the Americans Theodore Robinson (1852–1896) and Kenyon Cox (1856–1919), who both studied under Carolus-Duran and Gérôme, and Charles Gifford Dyer (1846–1912), who at the time was Paris-based, but had also studied in Munich.
15. John Shirley Fox, *An Art Student's Reminiscences of Paris in the Eighties*, London 1909, p. 74.
16. Kenyon Cox, *Century Magazine*, 1886, p. 635.
17. Charles Moreau-Vathier, *Gérôme, peintre et sculpteur*, Paris 1906, quoted in Gerald M. Ackerman, *The Life and Work of Jean-Léon Gérôme*, London 1986, p. 160.
18. Corkran, *op. cit.* (note 4), p. 320.
19. *Ibid.*, p. 320.
20. Albert Boime, *The Academy and French Painting in the Nineteenth Century*, London 1971, p. 17.
21. Walter Shaw Sparrow, *John Lavery and his Work*, London 1911, p. 41.
22. William H. Low, *A Chronicle of Friendships 1873–1900*, London 1908, gives a full and fascinating account of artists' lives at Barbizon and Grez. See also Michael Jacobs, *The Good and Simple Life*, Oxford 1986, for an excellent chapter on Grez.
23. Corkran, *op. cit.* (note 4), p. 320.
24. Julian Campbell, *The Irish Impressionists*, exhibition catalogue, Dublin, 1984, p. 49.
25. See Julian Campbell, *Frank O'Meara and his contemporaries*, exhibition catalogue, Dublin, 1989, for an excellent assessment of O'Meara's work and influence at Grez.
26. Quoted by Richard Ormond in *John Singer Sargent*, London 1970, p. 17.
27. Obituary in *Scottish Art Review*, I, no. 6, November 1888, pp. 156–57.
28. Stevenson, *op. cit.* (note 1), p. 9.
29. This picture is often referred to as *The Bathers*, but the correct translation is *The Bathing Place*. It was exhibited at the Royal Academy Exhibition of 1891 as *The Bathing Place*, no. 239.
30. Corkran, *op. cit.* (note 4), p. 320.
31. Gabriel P. Weisberg, 'Jean-Charles Cazin's reception in America', *Apollo*, February 1999, p. 36.
32. John Lavery, letter to Fernande Sadler, author of the pamphlet, *L'Hôtel Chevillon et les Artistes de Grez sur Loing*, Grez 1931, p. 14 (translated by Julian Campbell).
33. H. Houssaye, 'Le Salon de 1882–II', *Revue des Deux Mondes*, June 1882, p. 863.
34. Antonin Proust, 'Le Salon de 1882', *Gazette des Beaux-Arts*, July 1882, p. 148.
35. *Art Journal*, 1882, p. 218.
36. *Magazine of Art*, V, 1882, p. xli.
37. George Moore, *Confessions of a Young Man*, London 1886 (edn London 1939, p. 103).
38. Quoted in Ina Mary Harrower, *John Forbes White*, London 1918, p. 73.
39. Corkran, *op. cit.* (note 4), p. 320.
40. *Art Journal*, 1886, p. 223.
41. The Salon des Refusés was an exhibition put on in Paris in 1863 to show works rejected that year from the official Salon. It included works by Manet, Boudin, Fantin-Latour, Pissarro, Whistler and others, who were seen at the time as *avant-garde* but who by the end of the century were revered figures in the art world.
42. Paul Mantz, 'Exposition de la Société Internationale', *Le Temps*, December 1882, p. 3.
43. Mortimer Menpes, *Whistler as I Knew Him*, London 1904, pp. 23–24.
44. The Neo-Platonists regarded Beauty as the visible token of the Divine.
45. Stevenson, *op. cit.* (note 1), p. 9.
46. Whistler's 'Ten O'Clock Lecture' was delivered in 1885 and published by him in *The Gentle Art of Making Enemies*, London 1890, pp. 131ff.
47. *Portrait of Lady Meux* and three Venice etchings.
48. Bruce Laughton, 'The British and American contribution to Les XX, 1884–93', *Apollo*, November 1967, p. 373.
49. Letter from Stott to John Forbes White, August 1883 (Ravenglass).
50. We know from Stott's notebook that the two were acquainted as he records in 1884 working on an etched portrait of Degas. See also Whistler's letter to Degas (note 84).
51. From 1860 onwards it has been estimated that Degas produced over seven hundred works in pastel, more than in any other medium, and it has been said that he "... pushed the medium of pastel to an expressive range that has never before or since been challenged": see Jean Sutherland Boggs and Anne Maheux, *Degas Pastels*, London 1992, p. 7.
52. Letter from Stott to John Forbes White, August 1883 (Paris): "Whistler's portrait of his mother, which I thought the finest portrait, except one by Puvis de Chavannes ..." (this was *Portrait de Mme M.C.* (Marie Cantacuzene)).
53. Quoted in Corkran (p. 322) but unattributed.

54. Corkran, *op. cit.* (note 4), p. 320.
55. Quoted in Corkran (p. 322) but unattributed.
56. Corkran, *op. cit.* (note 4), p. 322.
57. Elizabeth and Joseph Pennell, *The Life of James McNeill Whistler,* London 1909, I, p. 61.
58. *Court and Society Review*, 29 July 1886, p. 678.
59. Glasgow University Library (henceforward GUL), Whistler Collection, W703: letter to Nellie, his sister-in-law, dated 3 September 1886.
60. GUL Whistler Collection, PC, vol. VII, *Pall Mall Gazette*, 30 November 1886.
61. Letter from Stott to John Forbes White, April 1883 (Paris): "Sargent likes Alice the most of anything he has seen of mine – Helleu & L'Hermitte – the latter especially – were very pleased – L'Hermitte especially admired it in movement & standing & the delicate effect of 'indoors'."
62. GUL Whistler Collection, PC, vol. VII, *The Standard*, 30 November 1886.
63. GUL Whistler Collection, PC, vol. VII (unidentified press-cutting).
64. Stevenson, *op. cit.* (note 1), p. 13.
65. The picture also seems to make reference to Degas's *Young Spartans* (National Gallery, London) with the careful positioning of the figures like statues frozen in movement. Degas kept *Young Spartans* visible in his studio for young artists to study and Stott may have seen it there.
66. Stevenson, *op. cit.* (note 1), p. 13.
67. George Du Maurier, *Trilby*, London, 1895, p. 95.
68. Stevenson, *op. cit.* (note 1), p. 14.
69. In 1886, in an article in *Le Figaro*, Jean Moréas gave the name "*Le Symbolisme*" to the French school of poets led by Stéphane Mallarmé, who were also closely associated with the Aesthetic Movement in art. The Symbolists rejected objectivity in favour of the subjective as a reaction to the the principles of Realism as expounded by Courbet, who said that painting should only deal with "real and existing things". They concerned themselves with the metaphysical and the mystical and sought to express ideas and emotions by the use of symbolic language and images. See Edward Lucie-Smith, *Symbolist Art*, London 1972.
70. Pictures for the British Section were chosen by Sir Frederick Leighton, President of the Royal Academy.
71. Stevenson, *op. cit.* (note 1), p. 14.
72. Cited in Stanley Weintraub, *Whistler: A Biography*, London 1974, p. 325.
73. Emile Zola (1840–1902), the novelist and art critic, was the leading practitioner of literary naturalism with a series of novels concerned with everyday life and the belief that people's fates were determined by environmental and social forces beyond their control. As an art critic he supported the naturalist movement in art, particularly the career of Jules Bastien-Lepage, and was also acquainted with the Impressionist circle.
74. Corkran, *op. cit.* (note 4), p. 325. Corkran quotes from notes by Stott about *Venus*, but adds her own comment: "What disappoints us is the Venus herself".
75. See note 58.
76. *Manchester Examiner*, 2 December 1887.
77. Weintraub, *op. cit.* (note 72), p. 326.
78. *Ibid.*, p. 325.
79. Corkran, *op. cit.* (note 4), p. 325.
80. Stevenson, *op. cit.* (note 1), p. 15.
81. GUL Whistler Collection, H241, H247, H251: letters about the Hogarth Club affair.
82. *The Evening Post*, 11 January 1889.
83. GUL Whistler Collection, S223.
84. GUL Whistler Collection, D22.
85. GUL Whistler Collection, S84.
86. The only picture Stott ever exhibited at the NEAC was *Amethyst Cloud, Jungfrau*, in November 1890.
87. Corkran, *op. cit.* (note 4), p. 325.
88. The previous year a Mr James McNeill Whistler was on the Hanging Committee. Stott's exhibit *The Alps by Night* was purchased by Liverpool City Council but there was considerable opposition to the purchase.
89. Corkran, *op. cit.* (note 4), p. 325.
90. *Ibid.*, p. 325.
91. Richard Whiteing, 'William Stott and his Work', in the exhibition catalogue for *Pictures by William Stott of Oldham*, a memorial exhibition held at the Royal Watercolour Society Galleries, London, 1901, p. 5.
92. Cited in Chistopher Wood, *The Pre-Raphaelites*, London 1981, p. 10.
93. *Ibid.*, p. 12.
94. His exhibit was *The Eiger.* It was the only time he exhibited with the Guild at the New Gallery.
95. *Oldham Standard*, 21 February 1893.
96. *Ibid.*
97. *Ibid.*
98. *Manchester Guardian*, 23 February 1889.
99. *Ibid.*
100. Walter Pater, *Studies in the History of the Renaissance*, London 1873.
101. Andrew Wilton, 'Symbolism in Britain', in *The Age of Rossetti, Burne-Jones and Watts,* exhibition catalogue, London, 1997, p. 20.
102. Hall Caine, 'L'Envoi', in catalogue to *Pictures by William Stott of Oldham* at the Goupil Gallery, London, April 1896.
103. *The Sun*, 10 February 1897.
104. *Ibid.*
105. John Lavery, *The Life of a Painter,* London 1911, p. 116.
106. Shaw Sparrow, *op. cit.* (note 21), p. 44.
107. Quoted in the introduction to Zola's *L'Œuvre* (The Masterpiece), translated by Thomas Walton, University of Michigan 1968, p. 8.
108. *The Echo*, 28 February 1900 (Tate Gallery Archive).
109. The records of the Royal Academy show that Stott was nominated in November 1895 by E. Onslow Ford and (Sir) George Frampton, both sculptors who at the time were members of the progressive New Sculpture Movement. However, Stott's name was never placed on the list of candidates put to the vote and the entry is crossed out in pencil with the note "deceased". I am grateful to Mark Pomeroy, Archivist at the Royal Academy, for this information.
110. *Magazine of Art*, V, 1882, p. xli.
111. *Art Journal,* June 1896: review of one-man show at Goupil Gallery, London.
112. Corkran, *op. cit.* (note 4), p. 319.
113. *Magazine of Art*, December 1901, p. 82. The review is just signed 'S'.
114. *Ibid.*, p. 82.
115. *The Daily Telegraph*, 15 October 1901.
116. *Ibid.*
117. Whiteing, *op. cit.* (note 91), p. 4.
118. *Magazine of Art*, *op. cit.* (note 113), p. 82.
119. *Manchester Guardian*, 9 June 1882.
120. *Ibid.*
121. Zola, *op. cit.* (note 107), p. 8.
122. Letter from Stott to John Forbes White, 17 November 1882 (Ravenglass).
123. Zola, *op. cit.* (note 107), p. 363.

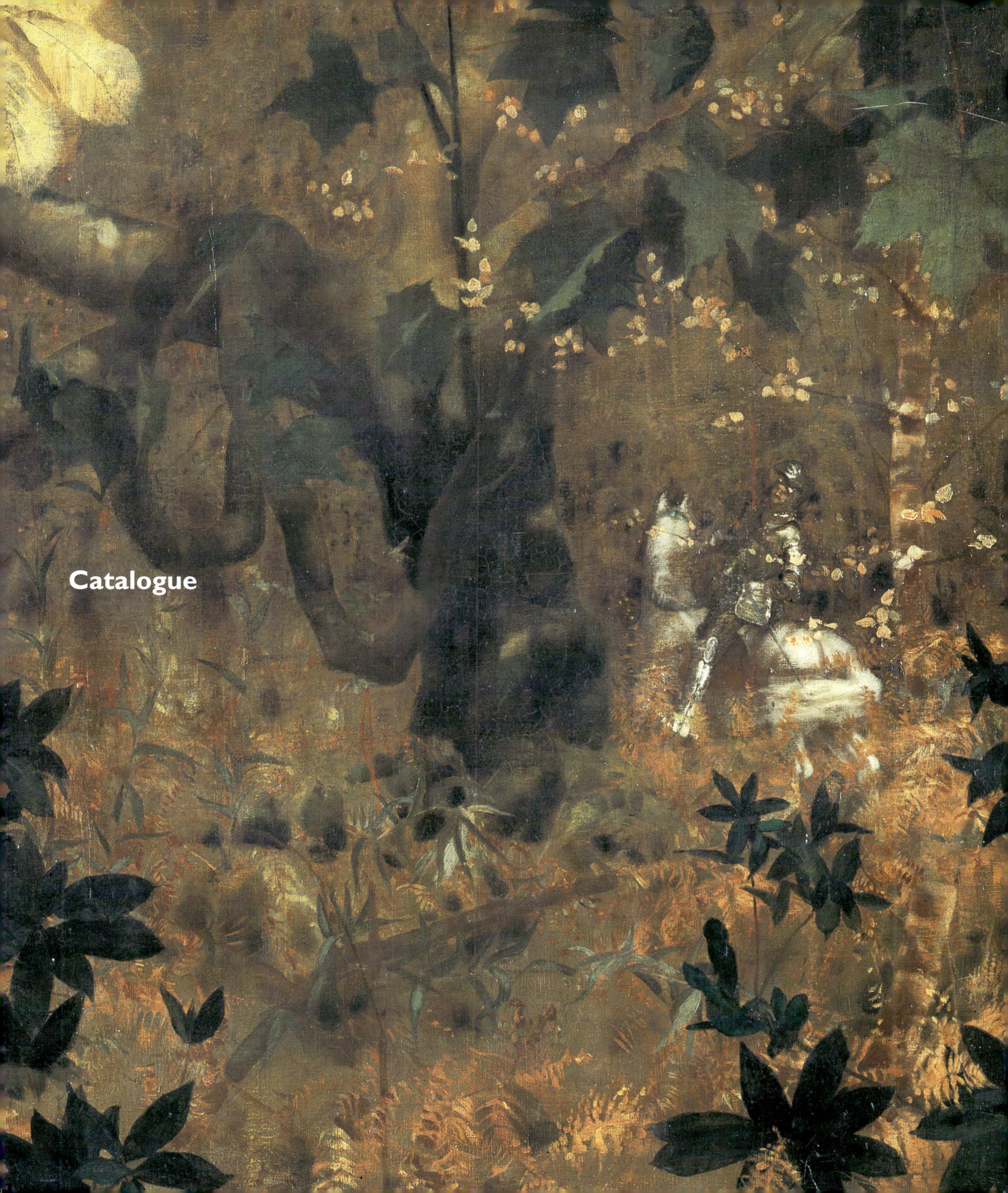

Catalogue

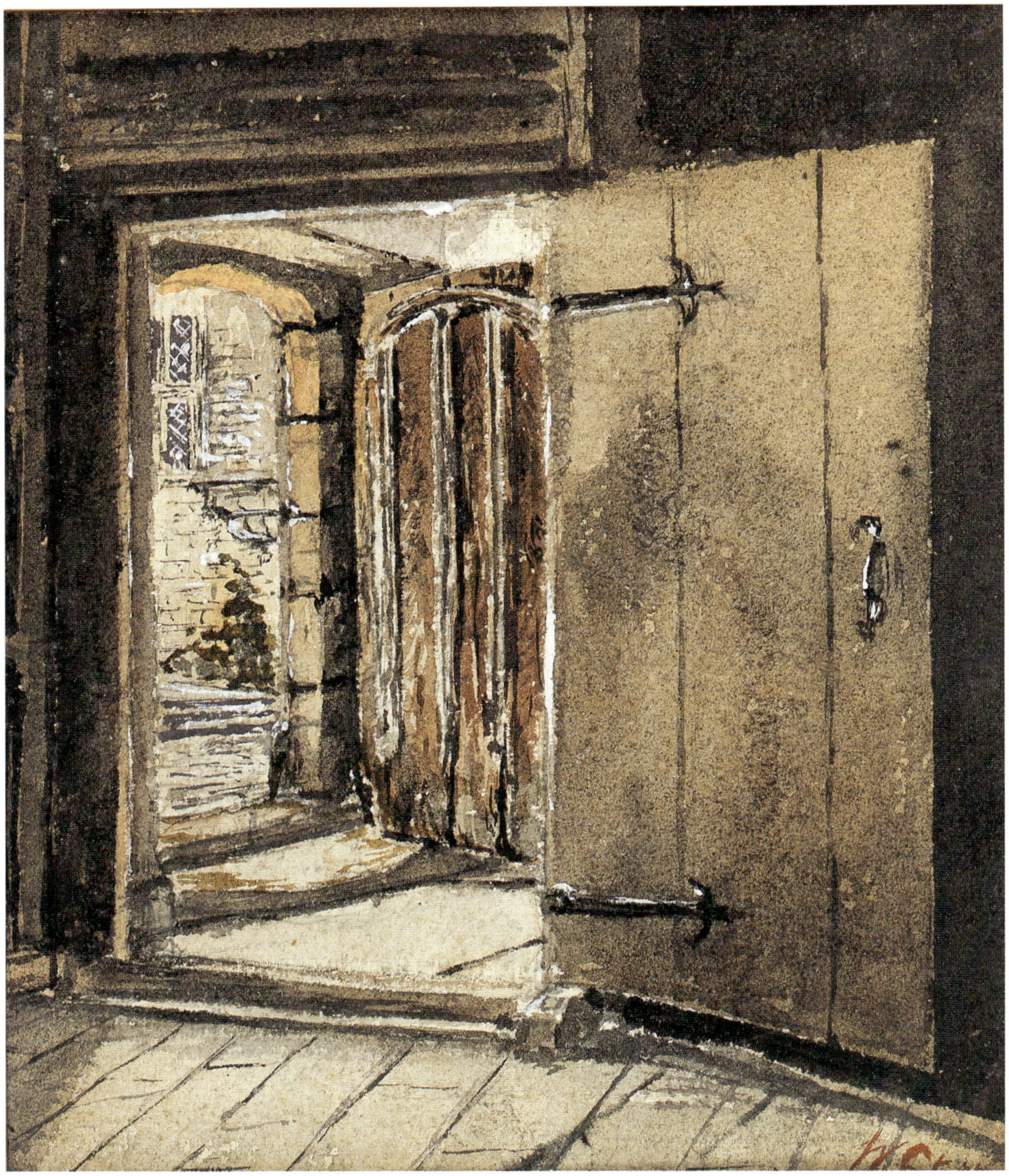

Early Days

1 Chaplain's Porch, Haddon Hall

1876

Signed *W. Stott*

Ink and watercolour, 24.1 x 19 cm ($9^1/_2$" x $7^1/_2$")

Private collection

This is the earliest known work by William Stott. It was painted *in situ* on a visit to Haddon Hall, Derbyshire, in 1876, while he was still a student at Oldham Art School.

It reflects a knowledge of the Dutch genre painters, such as Pieter van Hooch and Jan Vermeer, and, for an eighteen-year-old student, a good understanding of perspective and the use of light and shade.

2 River in Flood

1877
Signed *W. Stott* and dated *1877*
Watercolour, 33 × 48.3 cm (13" × 19")
Gallery Oldham

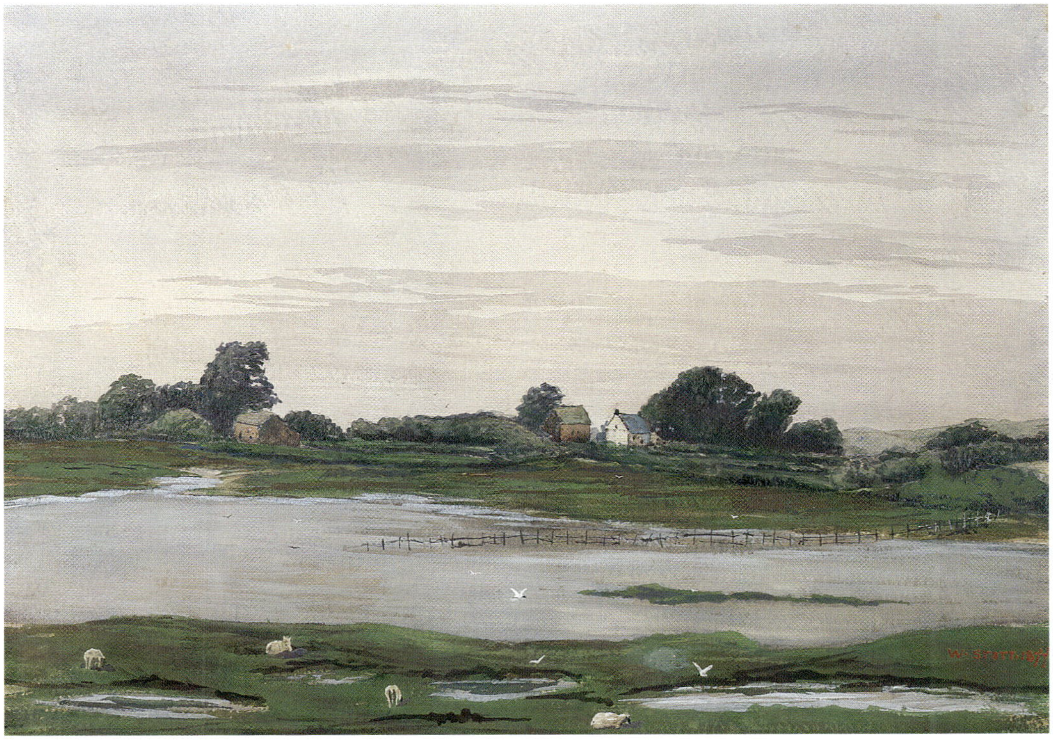

3 Boat at Low Tide

1877
Signed *W. Stott* and dated *1877*
Watercolour, 33 × 48.3 cm (13" × 19")
Private collection

Both these student works are suggestive of the Hague School, a group of Dutch realist painters whose work became popular with collectors in Britain from 1870 onwards. Their work was characterized by a sensitivity to the effects of light and atmosphere – qualities which the young Stott strives for here. Both pictures were painted at Ravenglass, on the Cumbrian coast, where the Stott family rented a house which was later to become a home and studio for William and his wife. In *Boat at Low Tide* the village of Ravenglass can be seen across the estuary of the River Mite.

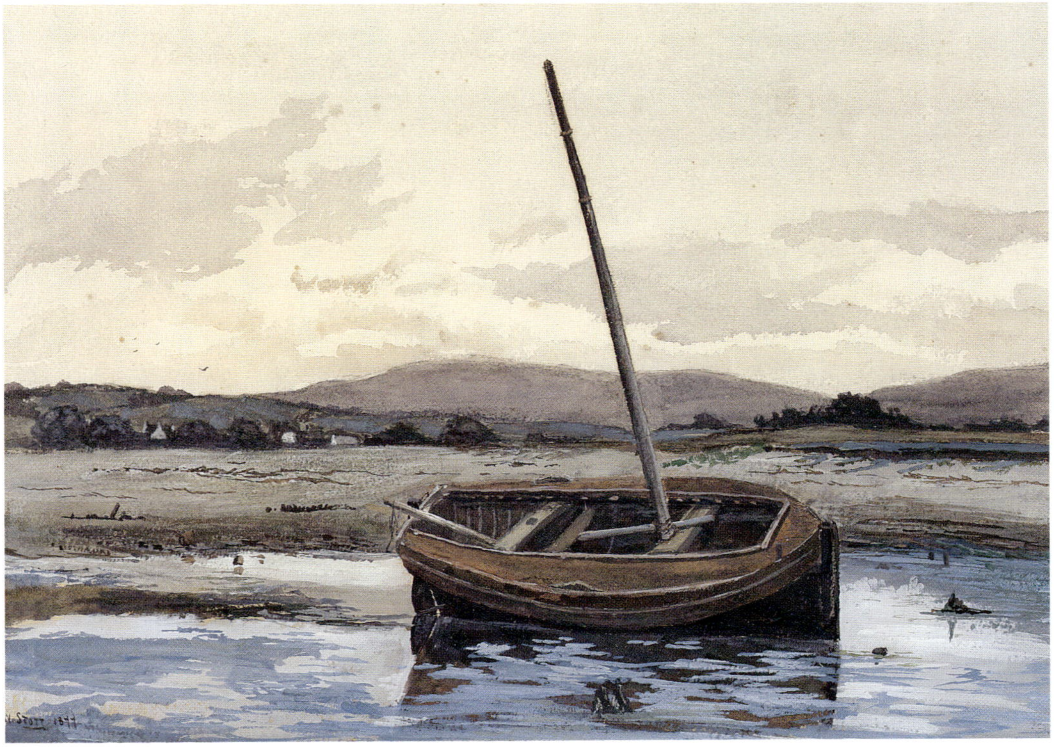

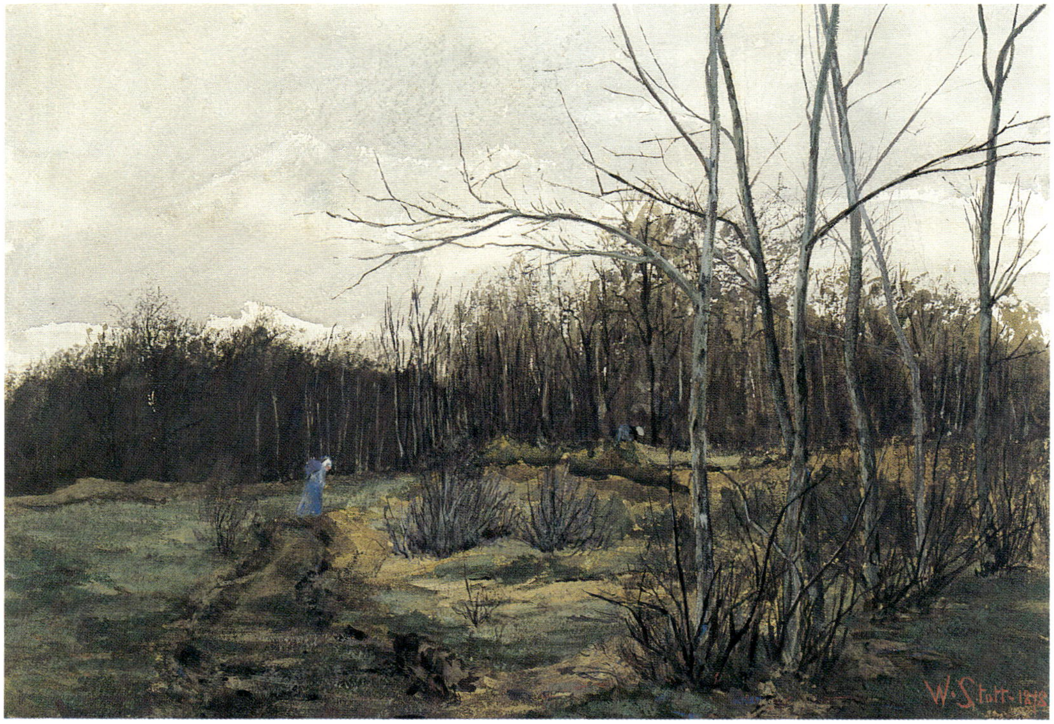

4 Woodgathering

1878
Signed *W. Stott* and dated *1878*
Watercolour, 22.8 × 24.3 cm (9" × 13½")
Gallery Oldham

Early in 1878 Stott went to France for the first time, and stayed at Meudon, on the Seine, close to Paris. This late-winter scene was painted in the Bois de Clamart and reflects the work of the Barbizon School, with its earthy colours and subdued tones. It was the first painting by Stott accepted for the Paris Salon, where it was exhibited that same year as *Un temps gris* (no. 3860).

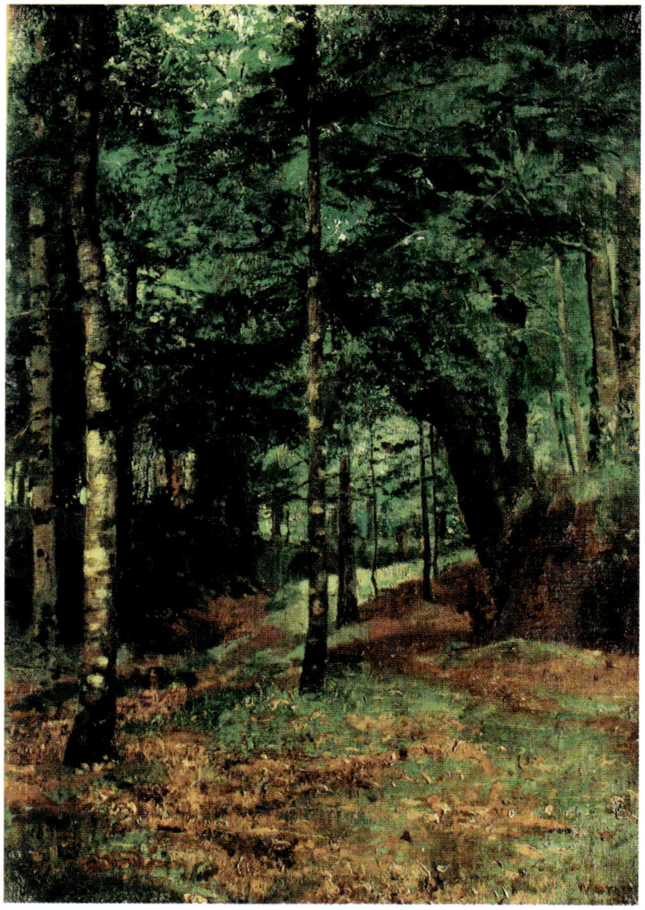

5 Study of sun shining through trees – Concarneau

1879
Signed *W. Stott* and dated *1879*
Oil on canvas, 45.4 × 32.4 cm (18" × 12¾")
Private collection

During the summer of 1879 Stott spent some time at Concarneau in Brittany, where there was a thriving colony of artists, predominantly American. It is may be that this is when he first came into contact with two expatriate Americans, Alexander Harrison, who had also studied under Jean-Léon Gérôme, and John Singer Sargent.

This study, the earliest existing oil-painting by Stott, is typical of the *sous-bois* subject popular with painters of the Barbizon School. With its confident brushwork and mastery of perspective and *chiaroscuro* it illustrates the progress the young Stott had made during his first year studying in Paris.

6 Italian Woman and Man Reading

1877
Unsigned
Watercolour and bodycolour, both 34.3 x 21 cm
(13½" x 8¼")
Gallery Oldham

These two student studies were perhaps examination pieces for the Oldham Art School.

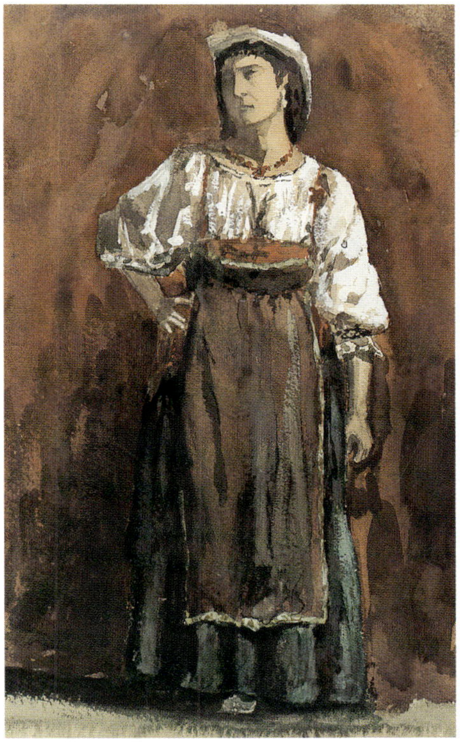

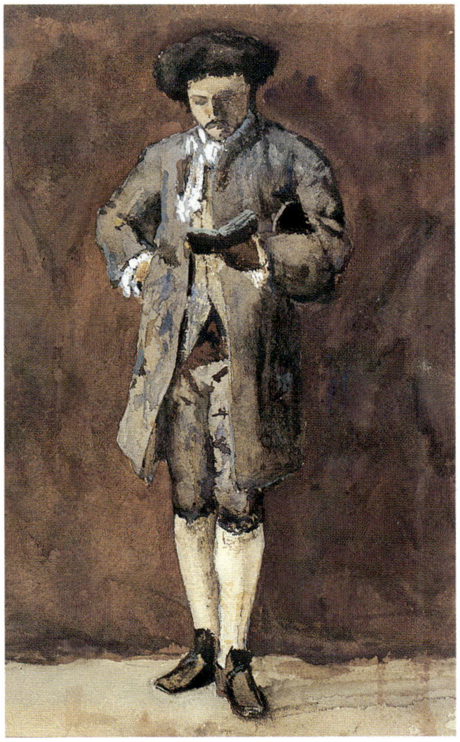

7 Study of a Head

ca. 1879
Unsigned
Watercolour, 25.4 x 19 cm (10" x 7½")
Private collection

This early student study is possibly the only work surviving from Stott's time at the Ecole des Beaux-Arts in Paris.

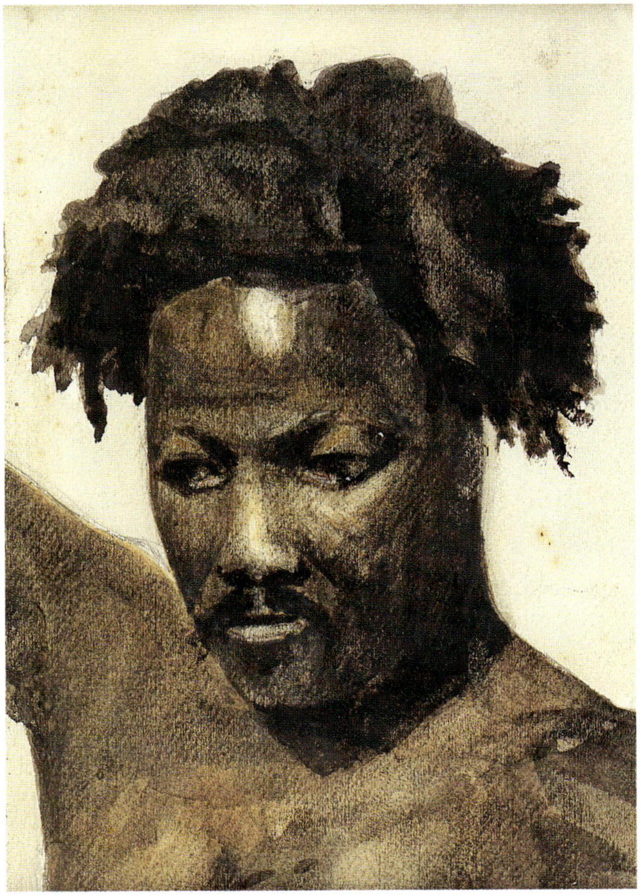

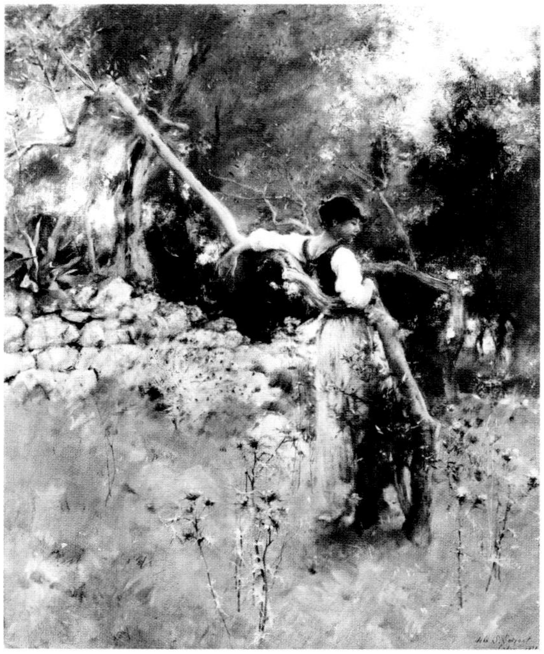

Fig. 37 John Singer Sargent (1856–1925)
A Capriote, 1878
Oil on canvas, 76.8 x 63.2 cm
Museum of Fine Arts, Boston

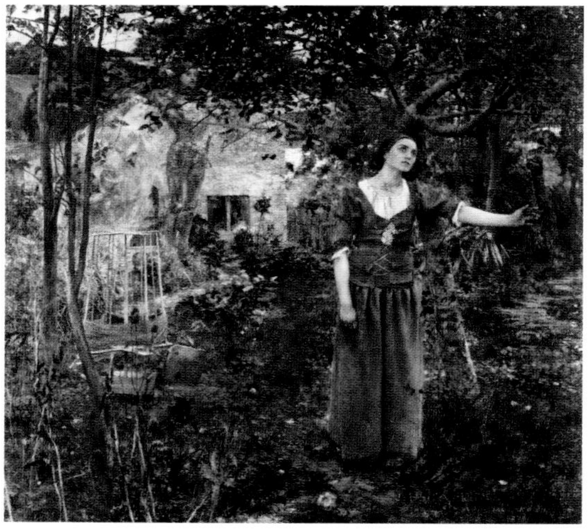

Fig. 38 Jules Bastien-Lepage (1848–1884)
Joan of Arc listening to the Voices, 1879
Oil on canvas, 254 x 278.7 cm
The Metropolitan Museum of Art, New York

8 Prince or Shepherd?

[Prince ou Berger?]
(subsequently known as *A Girl in a Meadow*)
1880
Signed *W. Stott* and dated *1880*
Oil on canvas, 71.7 x 57.8 cm (28¼" x 22¾")
Tate, London

In the summer of 1880 Stott paid his first visit to Grez-sur-Loing, a peaceful, picturesque village on the edge of the Forest of Fontainebleau. It had been 'discovered' by a group of American artists, together with the Scottish art critic R.A.M. Stevenson and his cousin the writer R.L. Stevenson, on a day trip from Barbizon in August 1875. Over the next twenty years it became home to an international colony of mainly British, American and Scandinavian artists, and "a crucible of the *plein-air* movement that spread across Europe". Robert Louis Stevenson, writing home to his mother, described Grez as "a pretty and very melancholy village on the plain. A low bridge of many arches choked with sedge; great fields of white and yellow water-lillies ... and about it all such an atmosphere of sadness and slackness ...".

The great advantage of Grez over Barbizon was the river with its numerous motifs, including an ancient stone bridge, which was to appear in countless paintings by artists of many nationalities. The river also provided recreation – boating, fishing and swimming – when they were relaxing or waiting for the weather to change. In addition, the village boasted two riverside inns which were tolerant of the whimsical demands of the artists.

William Stott was clearly immediately inspired by the milieu and the mood of the little community to paint three *plein-air* oils on a scale larger than anything he had attempted before. All three works, *Girl Knitting* (*La Tricoteuse*), *Daydream* (*Rêve de Midi*) and *Prince or Shepherd?* (*Prince ou Berger?*), were clearly influenced by the work of Jules Bastien-Lepage and contain a single figure in a naturalist landscape.

Girl Knitting and *Daydream* were exhibited at the Paris Salon in 1881 and both were bought by the collector Ramon Subercaseaux, the Chilian ambassador in Paris. Their whereabouts today is unknown. *Prince or Shepherd?* was bought by a French collector from an exhibition at the Grosvenor Gallery in London in 1881, and, like its two companions, disappeared from public view. Fortuitously it reappeared in 1928, when it was bought by an English buyer at an auction in Vichy, France, who bequeathed it to the Tate Gallery in 1939. The title *Girl in a Meadow* was given to it after 1928 and was 'adopted' by the Tate Gallery, but *Prince or Shepherd?* (*Prince ou Berger?*) was William Stott's title for the picture.

The prominent central figure, the handling of the oversized weeds in the foreground and the high horizon all indicate a rather formulaic response to Bastien-Lepage. However, there are signs that Stott's work is less raw and confrontational than that of Lepage, and it displays a more poetic and enigmatic approach even at this early stage in his development. Stott's title, *Prince or Shepherd?*, presumably alludes to the daydream of the young girl. Such meditative subjects were popular with Grez artists, and almost all the works of the Irish artist Frank O'Meara, a long-standing resident of Grez, show a single contemplative figure. In the 1879 Salon O'Meara showed a work entitled *Rêverie* (fig. 41, p. 62) and in 1882 the American Alexander Harrison, a companion of Stott's both in Gérôme's studio and at Grez, showed *Castles in the Air*, depicting a young boy daydreaming.

Many commentators have suggested that *Prince or Shepherd?* was inspired by Bastien's *Joan of Arc listening to the Voices* (fig. 38), exhibited at the 1880 Salon, but in fact it shows a much stronger similarity in mood and composition to John Singer Sargent's *A Capriote* (fig. 37), shown at the Salon the previous year, where a peasant girl in an overgrown olive-grove leans in similar pose against the gnarled branch of a tree. Sargent's picture also owes a debt to Bastien-Lepage, but instead of his brash and sombre reality the mood is more lyrical and enigmatic, which would have appealed to the young romantic William Stott.

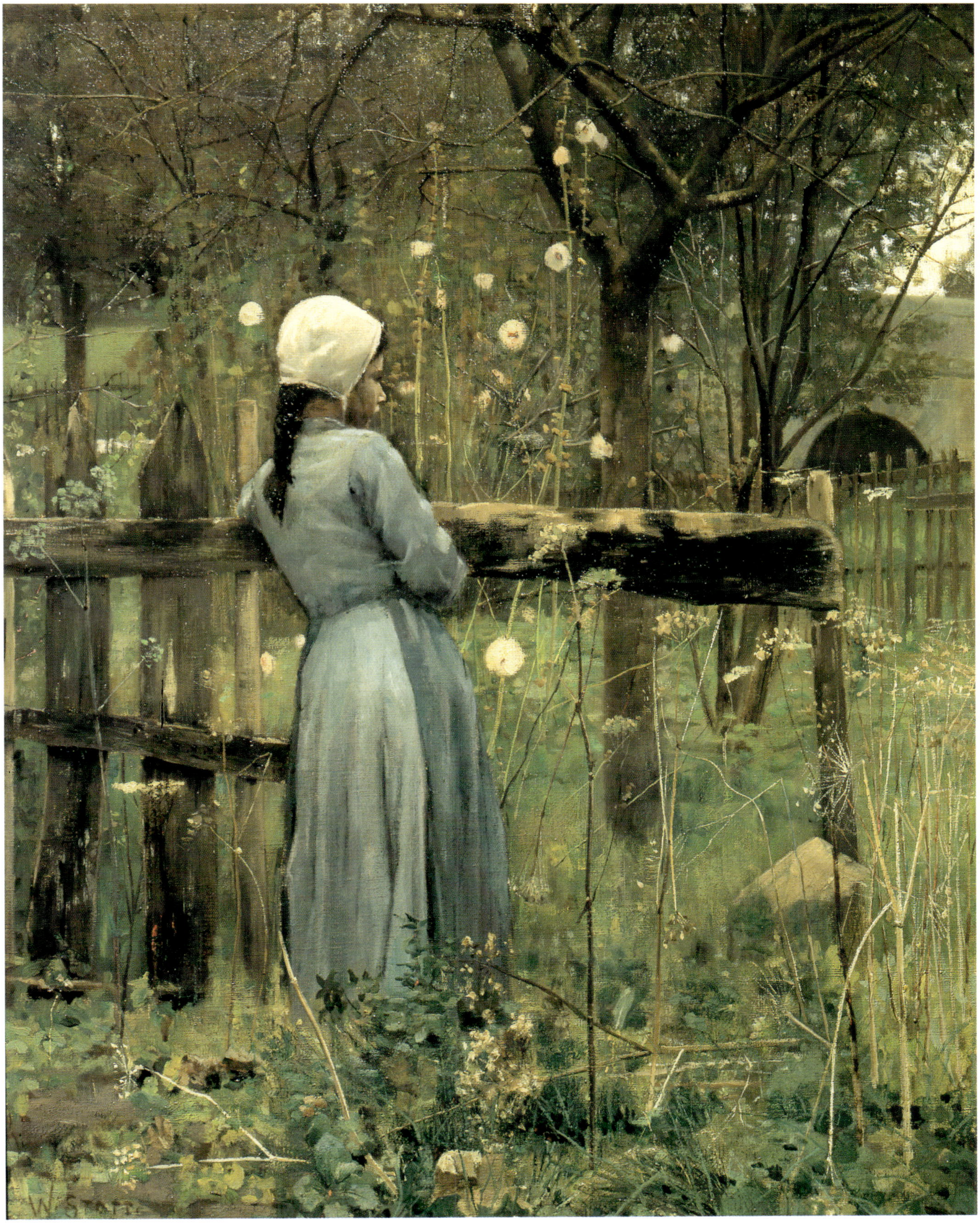

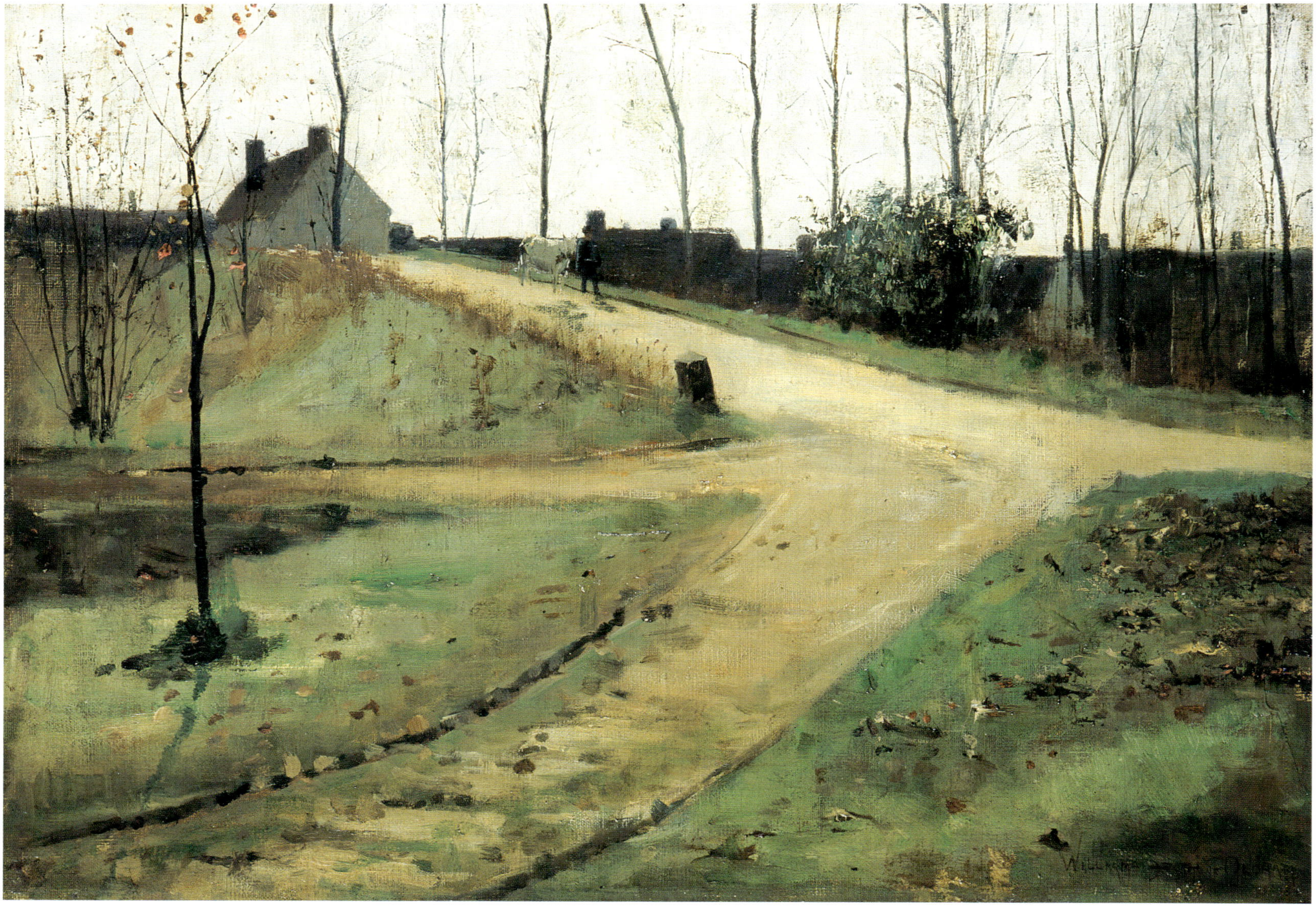

9 October Morning

1880
Signed *William Stott of Oldham*
Oil on canvas, 36.8 x 53.3 cm (14½" x 21")
The Hugh Lane Municipal Art Gallery, Dublin

In 1880 William Stott, as a sensitive and susceptible young man of twenty-three, was still absorbing the many influences he was exposed to both in Paris and at the artists' colony at Grez-sur-Loing. At that time Impressionism was gaining much critical attention and many of the British and American expatriate artists were attracted to this new and exciting manifestation of realist art.

October Morning is perhaps the nearest Stott came to adopting Impressionist techniques. The loose brushstrokes, the wide perspective and the spontaneity of the scene, with its keen observation of the light and atmosphere, all suggest a conscious shift away from the more mannered work of Bastien-Lepage, if not a complete conversion to Impressionist ideals. Stott refers to this work in his notebook as a "sketch", which may explain the painterly manner – or perhaps Stott intended it to be his token gesture to Impressionism.

A solitary figure leads a cow back to its pasture. It is a dank, grey autumn morning, but with a hint of brightness in the sky beyond the trees and buildings. The work is very suggestive of works painted by Camille Pissarro around Louveciennes – with a solitary figure on a road that stretches into the distance under a leaden winter sky (fig. 39). Most writers have assumed that *October Morning* represents the entrance to the village of Grez-sur-Loing, but we now know from Stott's notebook that it was painted at the "cross roads, Montcour", a small village on the Loing canal about two kilometres from Grez.

The picture was exhibited at the Fine Art Society in 1884 and bought by the distinguished collector and connoisseur James Staats Forbes, who collected mostly Barbizon and nineteenth-century Dutch paintings, but who also owned several works by Whistler.

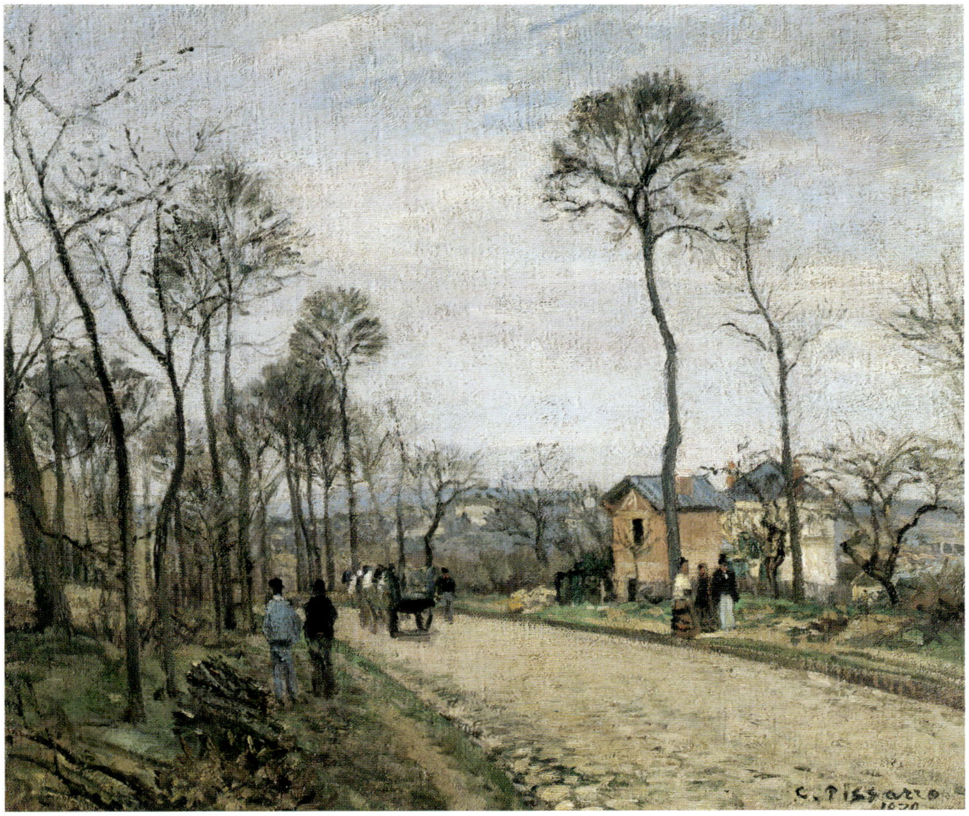

Fig. 39 Camille Pissarro (1831–1903)
The Road from Louveciennes, 1870
Oil on canvas, 46.5 x 55 cm
Musée d'Orsay, Paris

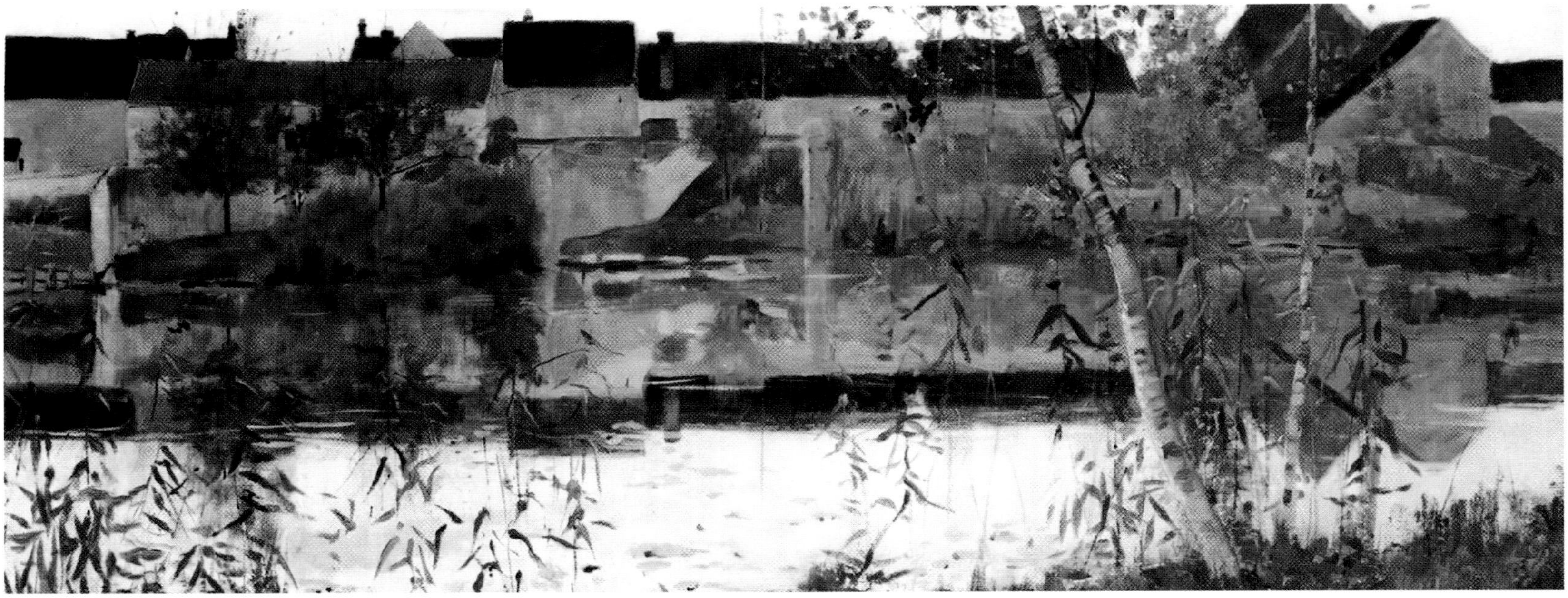

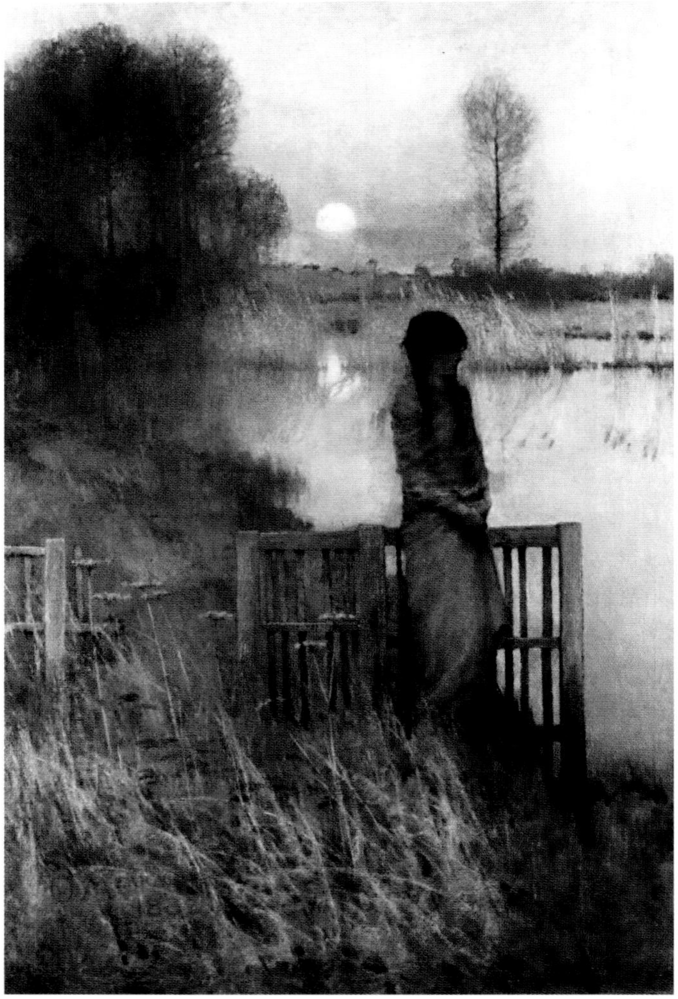

Fig. 40 (above)
William Stott of Oldham
Study for *The Ferry*
Oil on canvas,
39.1 x 110 cm
Private collection
(courtesy of The Fine Art Society plc)

Fig. 41 (left)
Frank O'Meara
(1853–1888)
Rêverie, 1882
Oil on canvas,
180 x 129.5 cm
Private collection
(courtesy of Pym's Gallery, London)

10 The Ferry

[*Le Passeur*]
1881
Signed *William Stott of Oldham*
Oil on canvas, 109 x 213.9 cm (43" x 84 1/4")
Private collection

This is perhaps Stott's best-known painting. It was painted in 1881 at Grez-sur-Loing in France, a picturesque, rather melancholy village which was home to an international colony of artists from 1875 to the turn of the century. With its companion work *The Bathing Place* (*La Baignade*; fig. 17, p. 21) it received much acclaim at the Paris Salon of 1882 and marked William Stott out as one of the more talented and progressive English painters.

The Ferry became a seminal picture in the development of British *plein-airism* and with its horizontal format and subdued tonalities cast an influence over painters such as John Lavery, the 'Glasgow Boys' James Guthrie, Arthur Melville, William Kennedy and Alexander Roche, and the Americans Alexander Harrison and Daniel Ridgeway Knight. Although showing a strong affinity with the work of Bastien-Lepage, Stott is moving towards a more decorative and poetic form of naturalism, which in turn reflects his

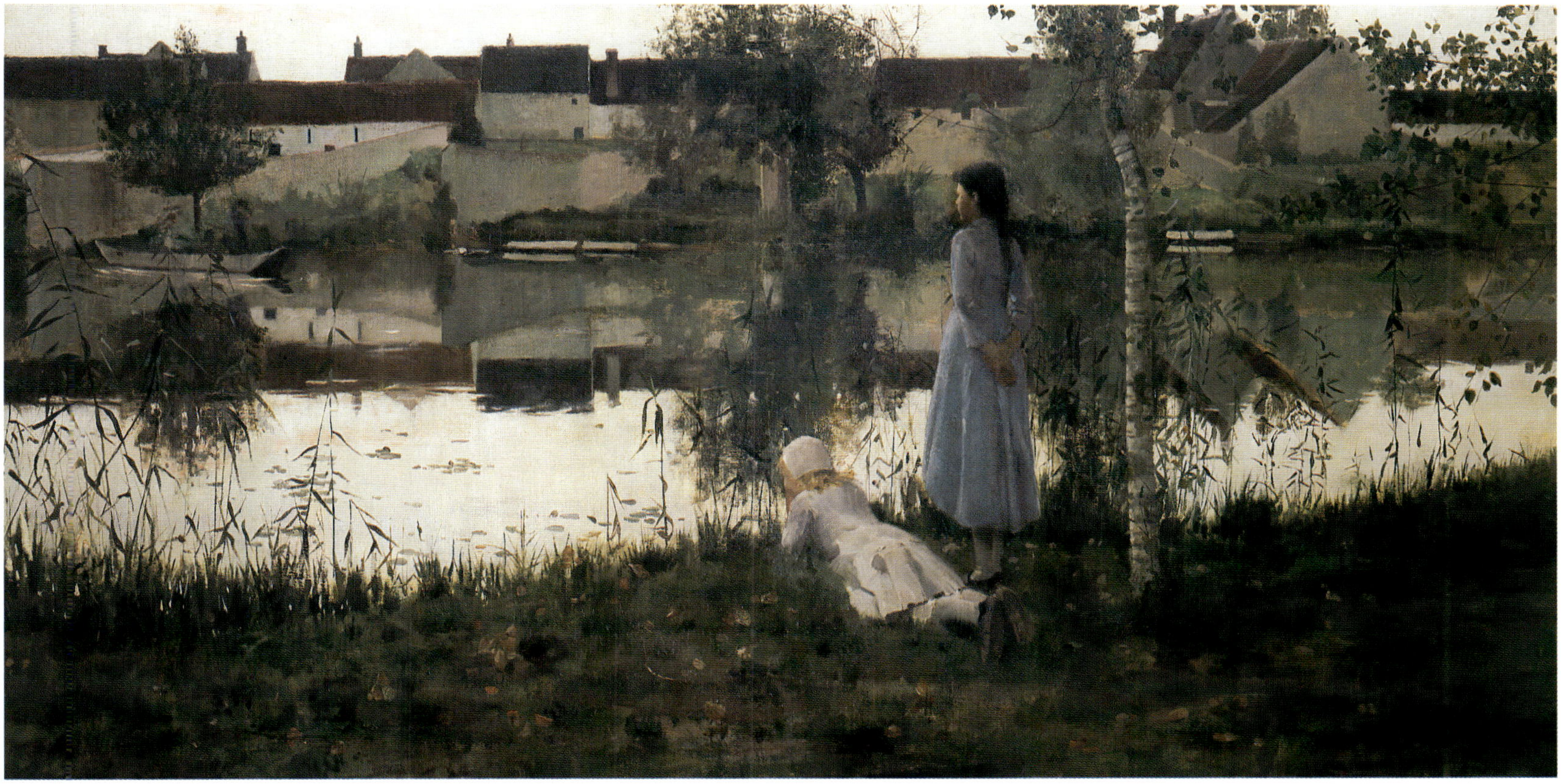

contact with the Irish artist Frank O'Meara, who specialized in thoughtful, crepuscular works with a strong underlying theme on the brevity of life and the passing of time (see fig. 41).

In *The Ferry* Stott seems to be introducing a covert symbolism into what appears to be a straightforward naturalist picture. Two little country girls wait patiently in the evening stillness for the ferry-boat which is setting off from the far shore. The river, a favoured Victorian metaphor for the passage of life, flows placidly, inexorably, past. Stott's original title for the picture was *Le Passeur*, which strictly translated means 'the ferryman'. Could he have intended this charming picture, which Alice Corkran (*Scottish Arts Review*, April 1889, p. 320) described as possessing "witching harmony and restfulness, unbroken by any intrusive emotion brought into it by the human world" to have been an allegory on the story of Charon, the old man who ferried the spirits of the dead over the rivers Styx and Acheron to Elysium?

The apparent innocence and poetic charm of *The Ferry* and its companion *The Bathing Place* brought lavish praise from most of the French critics. One wrote, "It is an Englishman, Mr William Stott, to whom go the plaudits of the connoisseurs, surprised, charmed and overcome by the sincerity, absolute originality and the captivating rare delicacy of his works" (Victor Champier, *Le Paysage et la mer*, in Goupil & Cie, *L'Exposition des Beaux-Arts (Salon 1882)*, Paris 1882, p. 222).

The London commentators, conscious of the picture's French provenance, were more grudging in their comments. The critic in the *Art Journal* conceded that "the desired impression, repose, has been admirably caught" but went on to say it was achieved "with the sacrifice … of many details which would vex the soul of the majority of English landscape painters" (*Art Journal*, 1882, p. 218). The *Magazine of Art* was equally ambiguous in praising "the workmanship and treatment of nature" but commented that "Mr Stott (who is a pupil of Gérôme) has been taken, however, with the manner of Bastien-Lepage …' (*Magazine of Art*, V, 1882, p. XLI). It was left to *The Manchester Guardian* to declare its local hero to be "profoundly original" (9 June 1882).

The first owner of *The Ferry* was the Aberdeen merchant and art connoisseur John Forbes White, with whom William Stott and his wife stayed following their marriage in 1882.

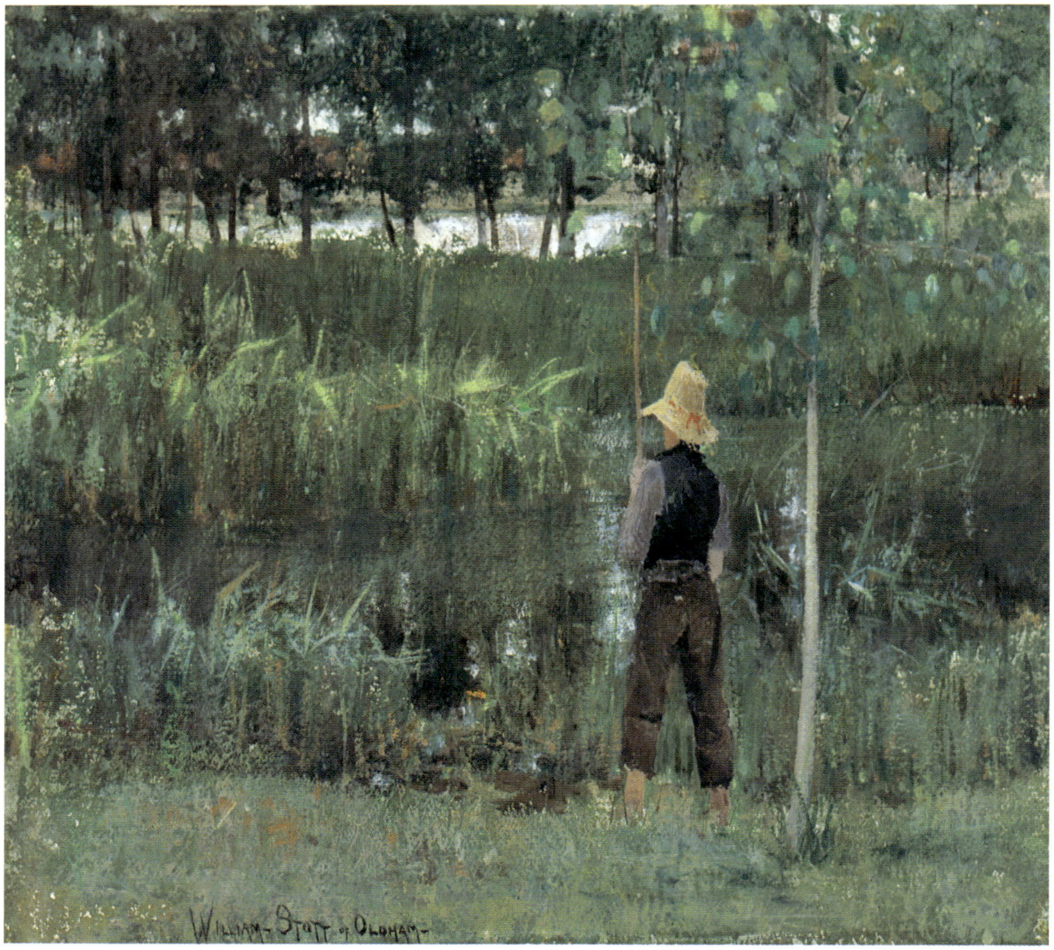

11 Boy Fishing at Grez

1881
Signed *William Stott of Oldham*
Watercolour, 25.4 x 34.3 cm (10" x 13½")
Private collection

This is the only small *plein-air* watercolour study we have from Stott's days at Grez-sur-Loing. At this stage he was still using watercolour for preliminary sketches, although he later moved almost exclusively to pastel. The young angler appears to be the same boy that appears in *Return from Fishing* (untraced; fig. 00), which was shown at the Royal Academy in 1882. It is possible that this is a study Stott intended working up into an exhibition picture at a later date.

12 Wild Flower

[Fleur Sauvage]
1881
Signed *W. Stott* and dated *1881*
Oil in canvas, 81.9 x 48.3 cm (32¼" x 19")
Gallery Oldham

Just why Stott was prompted to break off from a series of *plein-air* landscapes with figures to produce this enigmatic studio composition is a mystery. *Wild Flower* was painted in Paris during the winter of 1880–81, between two summers spent at Grez-sur-Loing. The previous year at Grez he had produced *Girl in a Meadow* (cat. 8) and *October Morning* (cat. 9) and later in 1881 he would paint *The Ferry* (cat. 00) and *The Bathing Place* (fig. 00), his two outstanding works in the realist mode that caused a stir at the 1882 Paris Salon. There is no evidence from his notebook of any other life studies at this time and indeed the next nude studies recorded by Stott are in 1885: "Pastel of Nymph with roses" and "Pastel first draught of Venus rising from the sea foam – destroyed".

Stott's notebook entry for *Wild Flower* ("*Jeune fille en blanc/ Fleur Sauvage*") seems to allude to Whistler's *The White Girl*, which caused a sensation at the Salon des Refusés in 1863, but the timing is puzzling. William Stott arrived in Paris in 1878, the year of the Whistler *v.* Ruskin libel trial, so there may well have already been a latent sympathy with Whistler's 'art for art's sake' aesthetic stirring in his breast as early as 1881. Certainly Stott later became a 'follower' of Whistler, until their estrangement over *Venus* (cat. 00) in 1887, and we know that a correspondent to *L'Art moderne* in 1883 referred to Stott as "… an Englishman who only dreams of Whistler". But Whistler was in London during the winter of 1880–81 and did not start exhibiting at the Salon again until 1882, and *The White Girl* had been in America for sometime.

However, the arcane title, the lack of narrative, the flowers with their petals falling, the rug and the model's dishevelled hair all point to a conscious plagiarism on Stott's part. Another pointer is that, almost uniquely, Stott signed *Wild Flower* at the top, and Whistler signed and dated *The White Girl* at the top right of his picture. *Wild Flower* also creates in the viewer a feeling of unease like that induced by *The White Girl*, with an uncomfortable and conflicting symbolism of chastity and corruption, which leaves an impression of gratuitous decadence.

Alison Smith, the author of *The Victorian Nude*, has said of *Wild Flower*, "… the theme of tainted innocence subtly implied in *The White Girl* is treated with much greater daring in Stott's image …. Although it was customary for children and adolescents to pose as models, the absence of any allegorical or mythological message in his painting enhances the viewer's sense of tense psychological intensity" (*Exposed: The Victorian Nude*, Tate Britain, 2001, p. 251). But it has been suggested that Stott used a lay figure, a jointed wooden manikin, for the painting rather than a live model. This could explain the rather 'wooden' appearance of the torso and arms, while the face and legs seem more natural.

Probably because of the sensitive nature of the painting, *Wild Flower* was exhibited only once during Stott's lifetime, in 1882 at the Cercle des Arts Liberaux, an *avant-garde* exhibition venue in Paris. At his death in 1900 it was listed for probate purposes as being in the drawing room of his London home. It was sold by his son at Christie's in 1913 and reappeared at the Oldham Art Gallery Spring Exhibition in 1921 (no. 25) with the caption *Presented by F. Hindley Smith, Esq.*

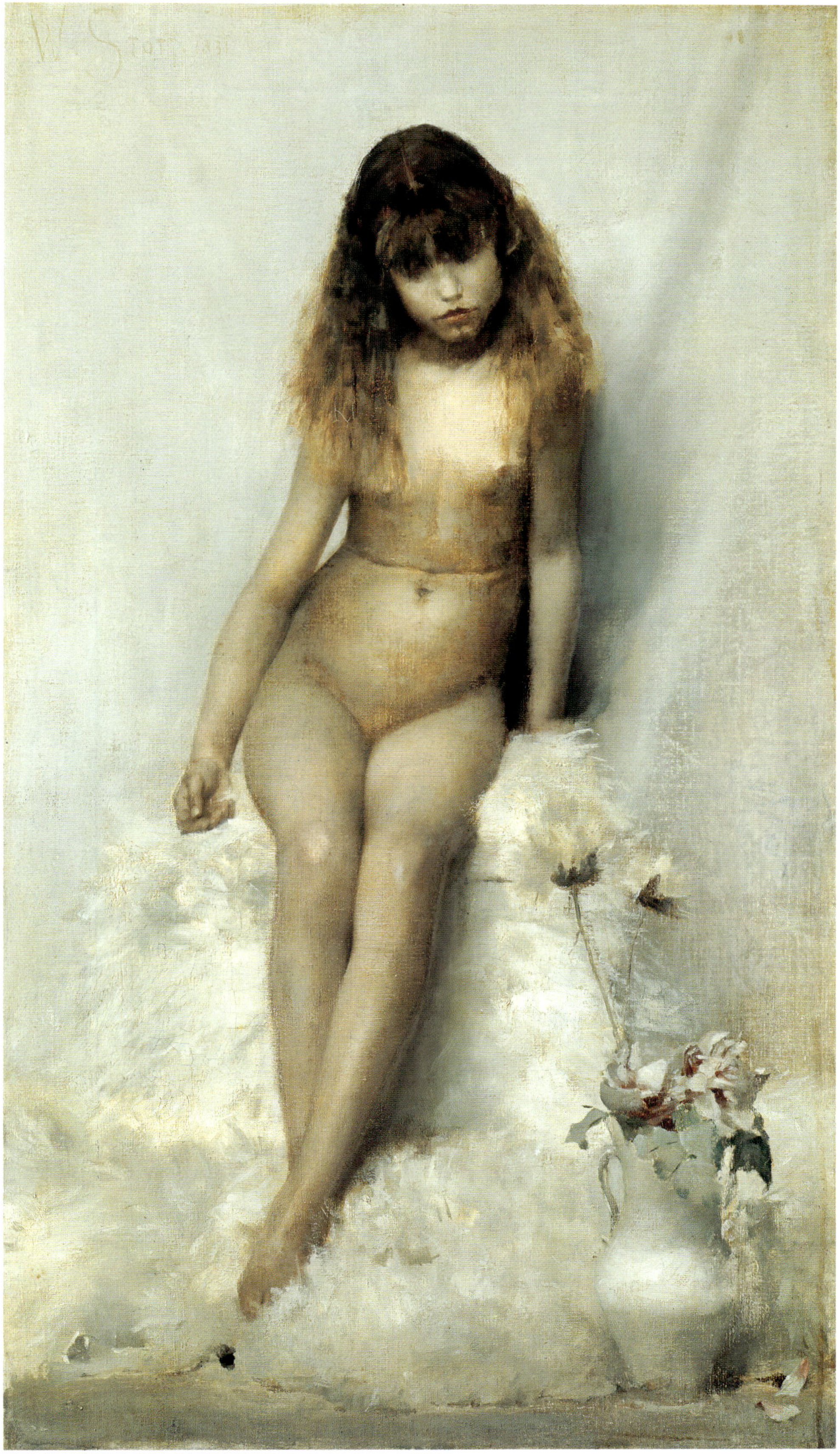

13 Tom Millie Dow

1882
Signed *W. Stott* and dated *1882*
Inscribed *To my friend Tom Dow*
Oil on canvas, 104.1 x 81.3 cm (41" x 32")
National Gallery of Scotland, Edinburgh

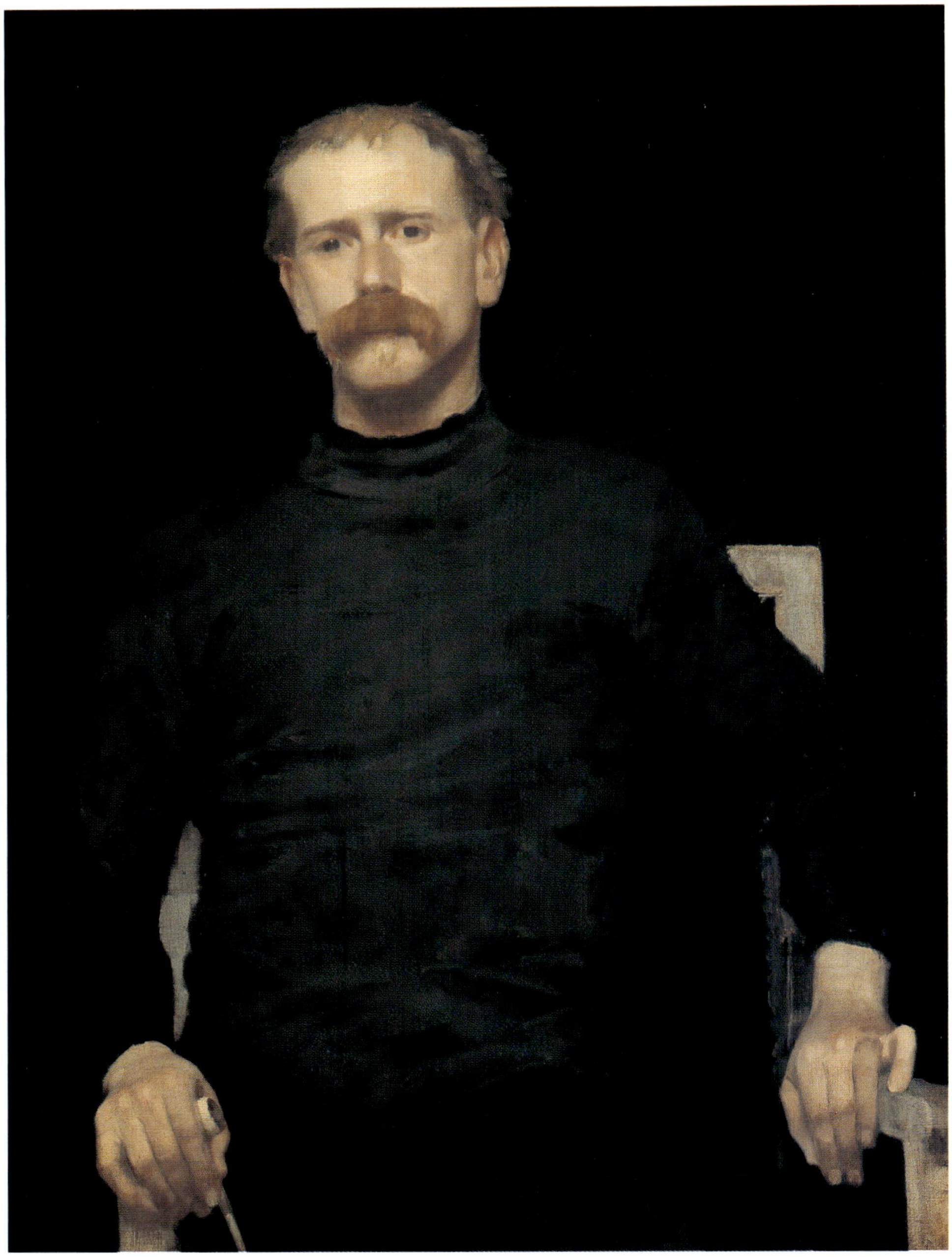

Thomas Millie Dow was born in Dysart in Fife in 1848 and trained as a lawyer in Edinburgh. However, in 1877 he gave up the law and went to Paris to study art, enrolling for classes at the Ecole des Beaux-Arts under Jean-Leon Gérôme. Here he met William Stott, who arrived in Paris a year later to study in Gérôme's *atelier*. The two men immediately struck up a close friendship which was to last throughou´t their lives. Stott christened his son, born in 1883, Millie Dow Stott (see cat. 19), and Dow was an executor for Stott's estate and remained in touch with his widow.

Their friendship was firmly established during the three summers they spent together at Grez-sur-Loing, where they also made many mutual friends in the artistic community. Later they painted together in Scotland, and Dow accompanied Stott on his trip to the Swiss Alps in 1888. On his return from Paris Dow took a studio in Glasgow and became a member of the loose association of artists known as the 'Glasgow Boys'. Most of this group, which included John Lavery, Alexander Roche, James Paterson and Alexander Mann, had trained in Paris, and now came to represent the progressive and anti-establishment scion of Scottish art.

Although he was nearly ten years older, it seems that Dow looked up to Stott artistically and was influenced by his companion's success. Roger Billcliffe has said that William Stott "was to become something of an idol for many of the Glasgow Boys – a home-grown Bastien-Lepage who formed a link for them with Whistler and other *avant-garde* painters working in London" (*The Glasgow Boys*, 1985, p. 24). Like Stott, in the 1890s Dow moved away from his early Realism and started painting allegorical works with titles such as *Spring* and *The Herald of Winter*. In 1895 he moved to St Ives and became an active member of the St Ives Arts Club, serving as President in 1898. He died in 1919 and is buried at Zennor, near St Ives.

In this portrait, William Stott achieves a spontaneity and directness which is reminiscent of the portrait masters Rembrandt and Frans Hals but also shows a sophisticated understanding of Whistler and Degas.

14 The Two Sisters

[*Les Deux Sœurs*]
Signed and dated *William Stott of Oldham 1882*
Oil on canvas, 142.2. x 215.9 (56" x 85")
Rochdale Art Gallery

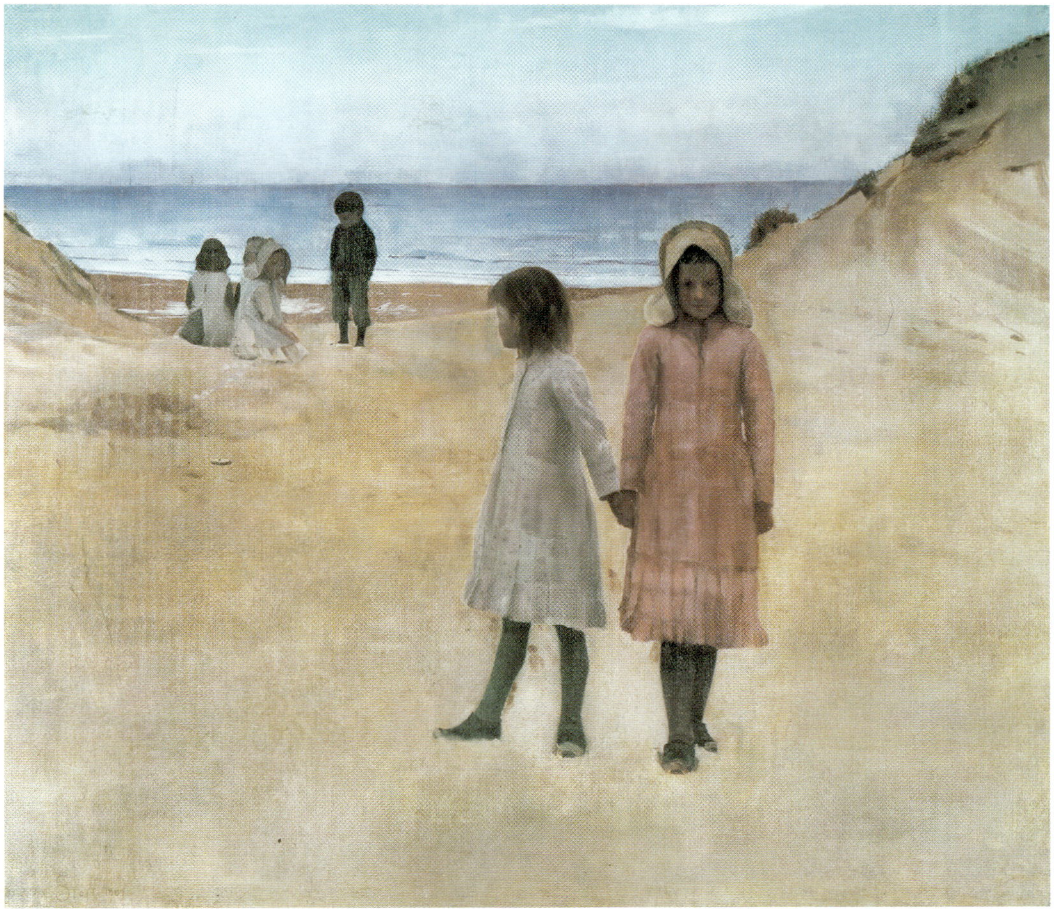

In the autumn and winter of 1882 Stott was at Ravenglass working on two monumental canvases which were to mark a further shift in his stylistic development. Both *The Two Sisters* (*Les Deux Sœurs*) and *The Kissing Ring* (*Ronde d'Enfants*; fig. 24, p. 26) have the sombre, haunting mood of a Cumbrian twilight. Stott's adherence to *plein-air* principles is illustrated in a letter he wrote in November 1882 to the collector and art critic John Forbes White: "Lately I have worked outside in this bitter weather .... I cannot bear the cold much longer .... I have worked often until my fingers were so numb that no feeling was left in them. On a hill with mist and a cold wind piercing you is not a situation desirable."

The subdued, pale colours and flatness of the picture surface in *The Two Sisters* shows an influence from the Irish artist Frank O'Meara, a companion at Grez, who also applied his paint thinly and sparingly. O'Meara was in turn influenced by the work of the much revered French mural painter Puvis de Chavannes. In the 1882 Paris Salon Stott would have seen Puvis's *The Poor Fisherman* (fig. 16, p. 20), and *The Two Sisters* seems to be a direct response to its simplified forms, large flat areas of colour and disturbing mood.

In *The Two Sisters* Stott is developing a stage further the intention, expressed tentatively in *The Ferry* (cat. 10) and *The Bathing Place* (fig. 17, p. 21), of creating atmospheric and tonal harmony in a picture. From now on, for the rest of his erratic artistic life, the one thread running through all his work was this desire to represent human beings only in relation to the general harmony of their setting. As Alice Corkran wrote in 1889, "... the figures, as figures, in Mr Stott's work are, to our thinking, debateable. As effects of nature of the same order as the skies, the streams and flowers, they are equally marvellous with these in his rendering of them" (*Scottish Arts Review*, April 1889, p. 325). Certainly the children in *The Two Sisters* and *The Kissing Ring* appear to match, and be at one with, the sombre, melancholy mood of their natural surrounding.

The Two Sisters shows that Stott was working hard to absorb new lessons and maintain his position as a progressive young artist. He sent the picture for its first public show to the inaugural exhibition of the Société internationale de peintres et sculpteurs in Paris in December 1882 at the Galerie George Petit, a new exhibition space recently set up to show 'modern art'.

The original signature of *W. Stott* can still be seen, but it has been over-signed *William Stott of Oldham* at a later date, probably when it was sent to the Paris Salon in 1884.

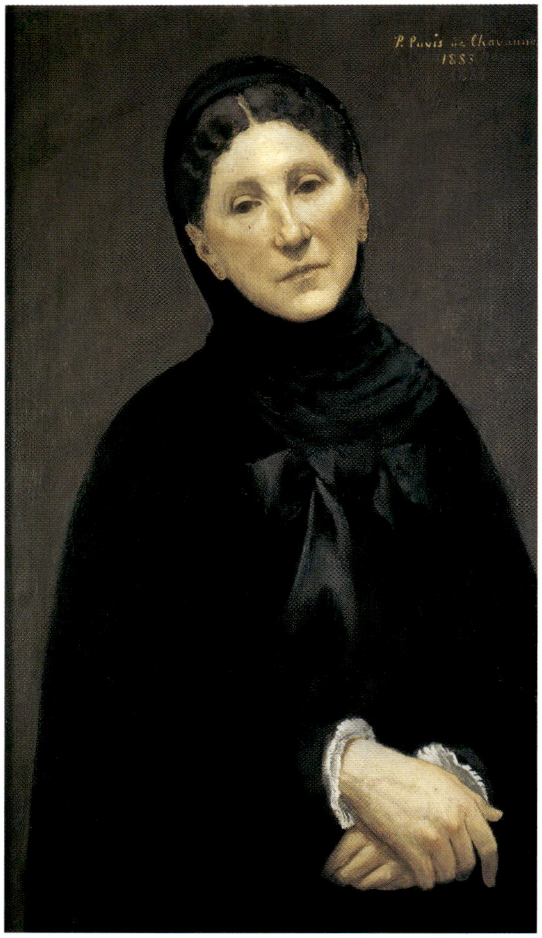

Fig. 42 Puvis de Chavannes (1824–1898)
Portrait of Mme M.C., 1883
Oil on canvas, 78 × 45.7 cm
Musée des Beaux-Arts, Lyons

Family Portraits

15 The Artist's Wife

[*CMS in black dress in easy chair*]
1884
Signed *William Stott of Oldham*
Pastel, 57 × 43.2 cm (22½" × 17")
Manchester Art Gallery

In the winter of 1883–84, while staying with his parents at Windsor Road, Oldham, Stott worked on a number of pastels of his wife Christina Mary in domestic settings. They are some of the first works he produced in pastel, but these pictures demonstrate a rapid mastery of the technique. His decision to work in pastel was almost certainly prompted by recent contact in Paris with Edgar Degas, for whom pastel was a preferred medium.

It was in 1883 that Stott became an associate of James McNeill Whistler, a close friend of Degas, and having been inspired by Whistler's *Portrait of the Painter's Mother* (fig. 25, p. 30) at the Paris Salon that year returned home to Oldham to start working on his *Portrait of My Father and Mother* (cat. 17). These domestic pastels, which were executed at the same time, as well as conveying an intimacy and sincerity reminiscent of Degas, also reveal a growing understanding of Whistler's aesthetic, with their subtle tones and careful composition. Certainly *CMS* [Christina Mary Stott] *at the piano* (cat. 18), with its view of the sitter in profile, the prominent dado and the restricted pictorial space, is redolent of Whistler's *At the Piano* (fig. 44, p. 68), which portrays his sister Deborah playing the piano to her daughter Annie in the music room of her London home. The only jarring note in Stott's picture is the rather ghostly gap in the curtains which draws attention away from the sitter.

In August 1883, when writing to John Forbes White about the highlights of that year's Paris Salon, William Stott mentioned "Whistler's portrait of his mother, which I thought the finest portrait, except one by Puvis de Chavannes ...". The portrait by the French Symbolist painter which so impressed Stott was *Portrait of Mme M.C.* (fig. 42). It clearly made a lasting impact, because his pastel drawing *The Artist's Wife*, completed six months later, has obvious parallels, in the direct gaze of the sitter, the tilt of the head and the hands resting on the lap. With these sombre realistic scenes from domestic life Stott is reinforcing his newly found enthusiasm for Whistler's aesthetic principles.

Whether intentionally or not, with these small domestic pastels and his monumental oil painting *Portrait of My Father and Mother* Stott creates a prevailing sense of *ennui* and sadness. Alice Corkran, in her article in the *Scottish Arts Review* of 1889, deplores this and says of these pictures, "Mr Stott has carried out various skilful schemes of colour and chiaroscuro with a fine realism .... Such portraits are interesting as a page out of a work on manners, but they seem to us to lack the quality of spiritual insight." She goes on to say that in his determination to represent human beings, including his wife and parents, in relation to and as part of their surroundings, "their individualities are merged into the general impression" and that he leaves us with the idea of "a well-to-do idealless *bourgeoise*" (*Scottish Arts Review*, April 1889, p. 322).

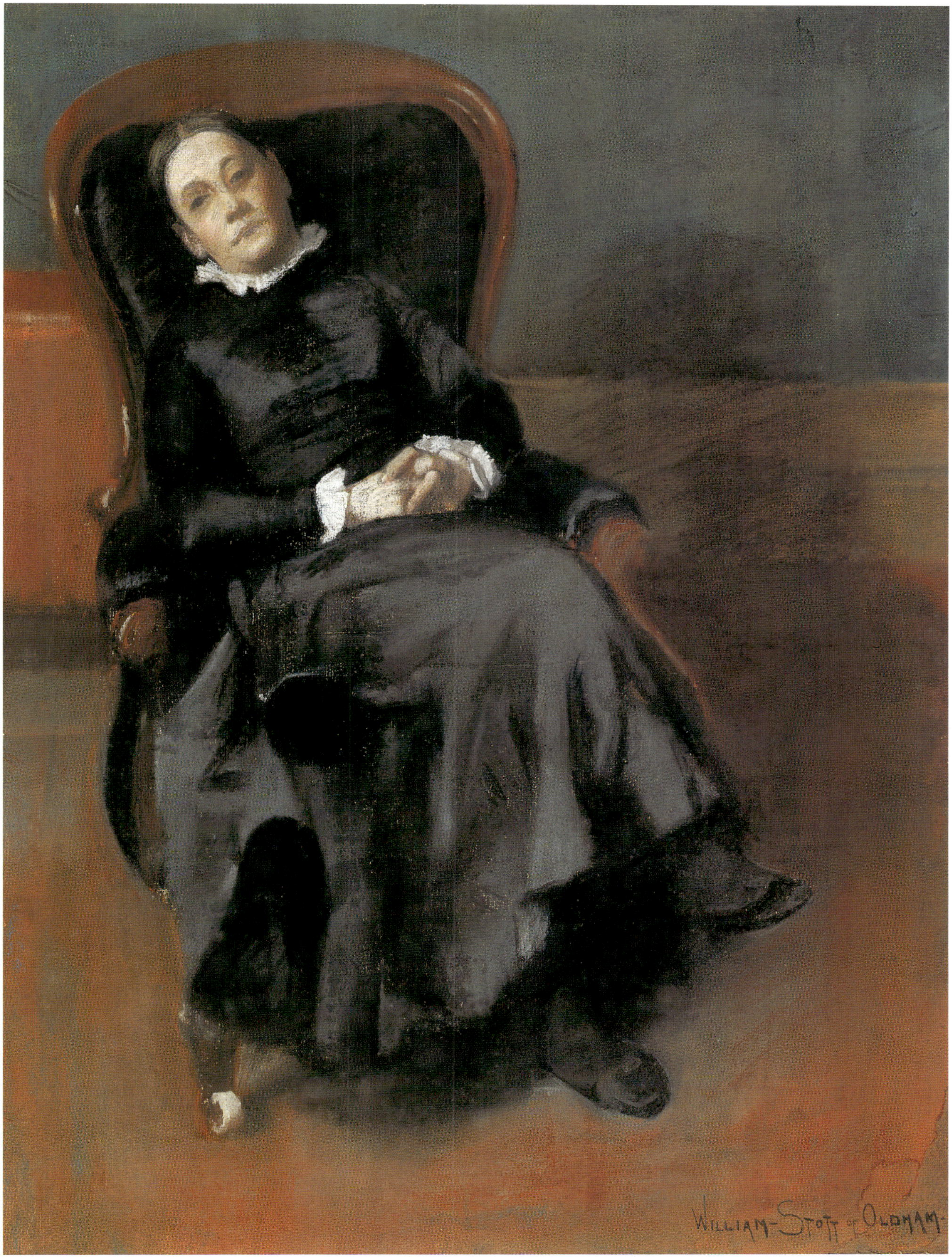
WILLIAM-STOTT OF OLDHAM-

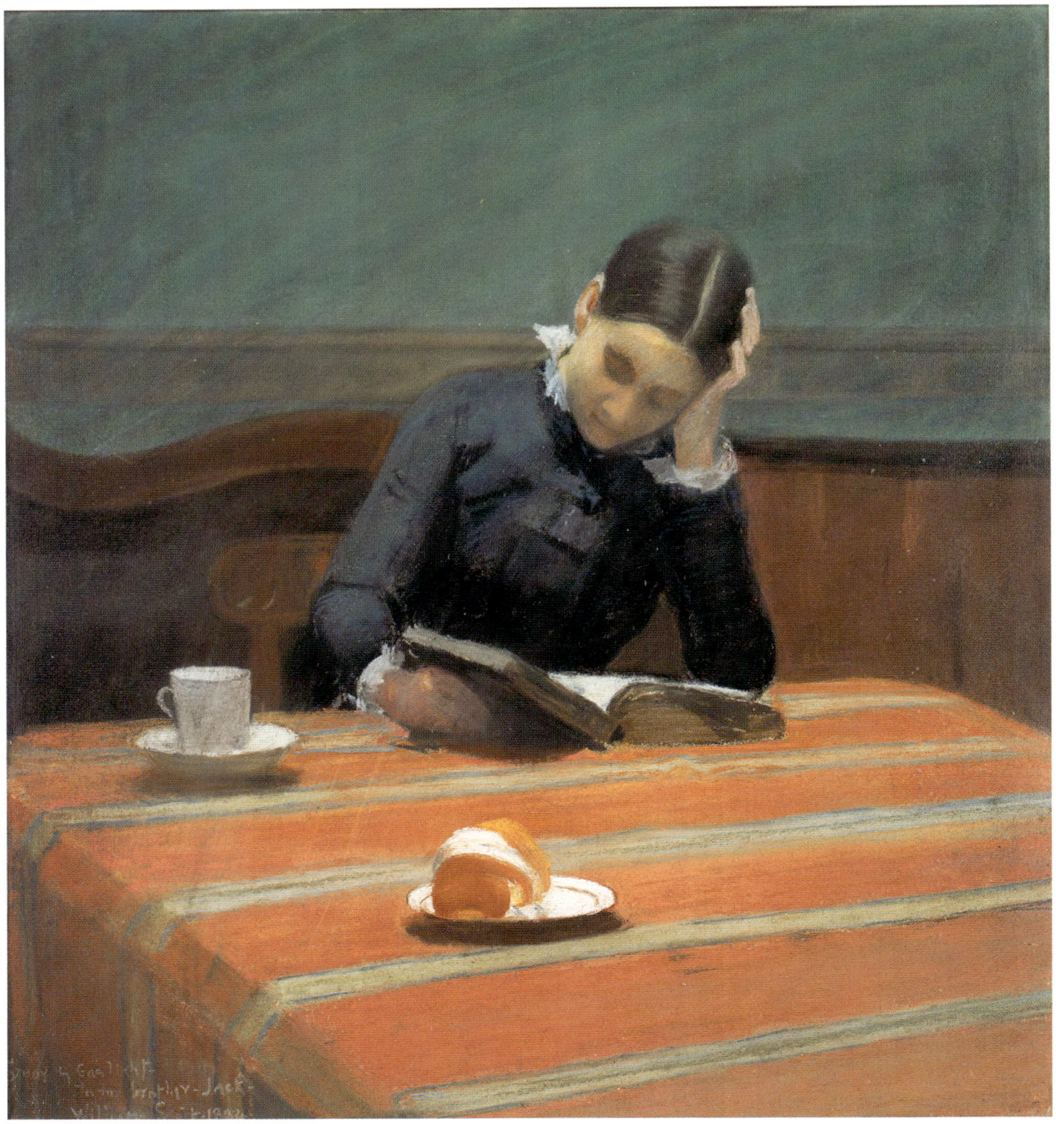

16 CMS reading by Gaslight

1884
Signed and inscribed *Study by gaslight. To my brother Jack. William Stott 1884.*
Pastel, 48.3 x 45.7 (19" x 18")
Private collection

17 Portrait of My Father and Mother

1884
Inscribed *To my Father and Mother. William Stott. 1884*
Oil on canvas, 100.3 x 153 cm (39$^{1}/_{2}$" x 60$^{1}/_{4}$")
Gallery Oldham

Inspired by Whistler's *Arrangement in Grey and Black: Portrait of the Painter's Mother* (fig. 25, p. 30), exhibited at the 1883 Paris Salon, Stott returned with his wife to his parents' home in Oldham later that year and immediately started work on *Portrait of My Father and Mother.* The careful arrangement of the composition and the precise pose of the figures, so as to create a harmonious structure to the scene, all point towards Whistler.

The influence of Whistler's *Mother* is evident in Stott's use of the strong image in profile for his father, which also has echoes of Whistler's portrait of Thomas Carlyle (Glasgow Museum and Art Gallery). Mrs Stott, with her fixed gaze and hands clasped on her lap, can be seen as representing how Mrs Whistler might look if we were sitting confronting her. But, whereas Whistler's portrait has a very concentrated spatial focus, Stott has attempted a wide-angle view of the room – with qualified success in the eyes of some critics. Walter Sickert, reviewing anonymously an exhibition at the Grafton Gallery in 1896, spotted the "Whistlerian key" in the canvas and praised the "beauty and subtlety" of its handling, suggesting it was a "great painting" that should be destined for the National Gallery. However, he goes on to comment, "This is not to say that it is faultless. The inclusion of such a large angle of sight from side to side is inartistic, and the inclusion of the fire itself sins against that canon which would wisely rule that the effect of light should be painted but never the source" ('St. P. ', review of the exhibition of *Portrait Painters* at the Grafton Gallery, *The Speaker*, 12 December 1896, p. 639).

Whistler, when asked why he called his portrait of his mother *Arrangement in Grey and Black*, replied: "To me it is interesting as a picture of my mother, but what can or ought the public care about the identity of the portrait. It must stand or fall on its merits as

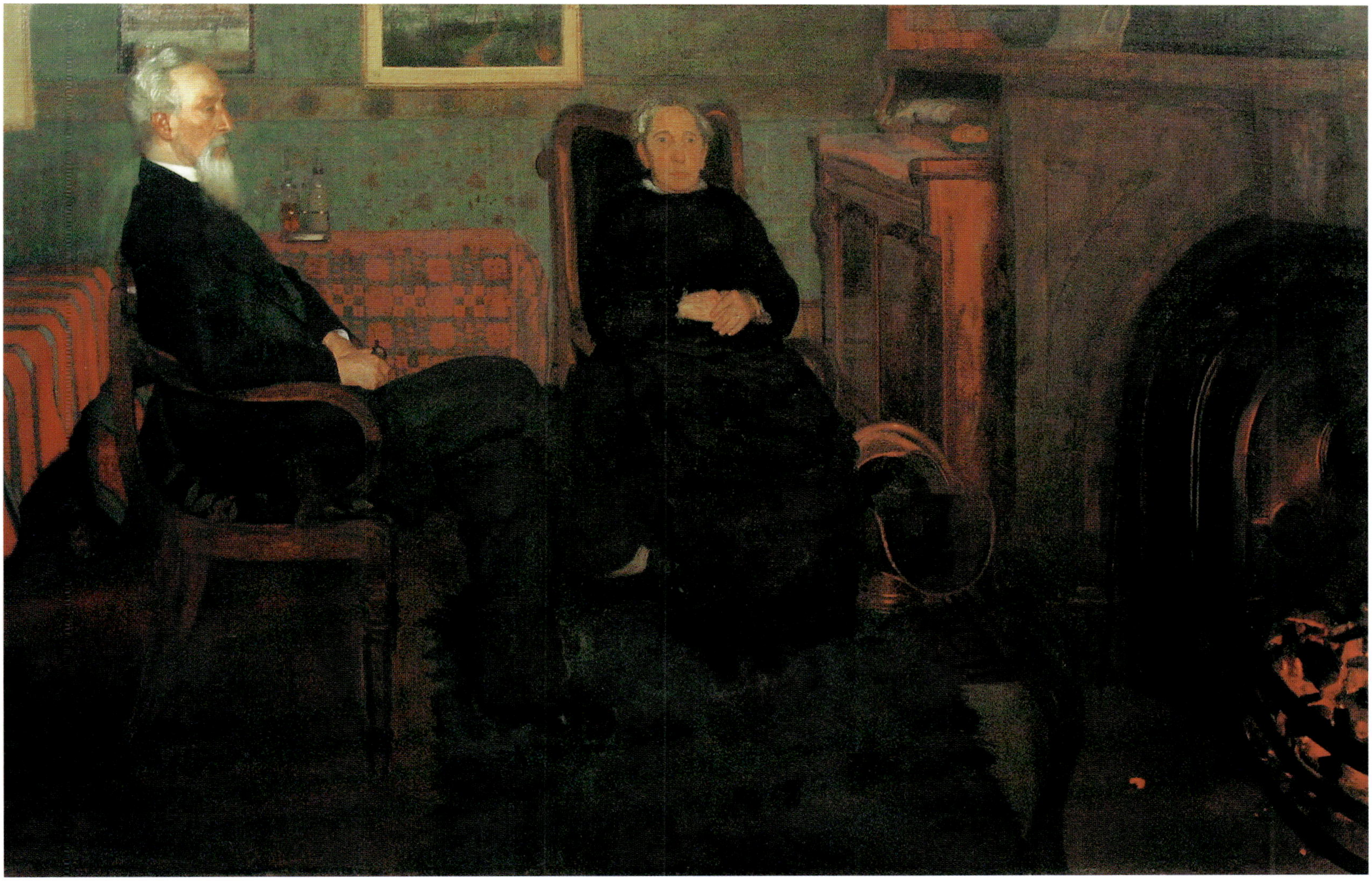

an 'arrangement'" (James McNeill Whistler, *The Gentle Art of Making Enemies*, London 1890, p. 128). In the catalogue to the Whistler exhibition at the Tate Gallery in 1994 Richard Dorment wrote, "... through his art [Whistler] can transform even the most eminent personality into a study of shape and texture and colour" (*James McNeill Whistler*, 1994, p. 144). Although Stott drew the line at calling his painting an 'arrangement', this is exactly what he attempted with *My Father and Mother*, although he lacks Whistler's sophistication, panache and psychological insight.

Alice Corkran, in her 1889 review of Stott's work, seems to imply that in this picture aesthetic values have taken over and leave a cold, austere, almost disloyal image of his devoted parents. She praises the work as "a perfect *tour de force* of technique" but goes on to say "... he has forgotten his parents, as human beings, in his ecstatic sense of their pictorial relationship to a world of colour and form. The work is not exactly a tribute of filial piety: it is only a masterpiece of art" (*Scottish Arts Review*, April 1889, p. 322).

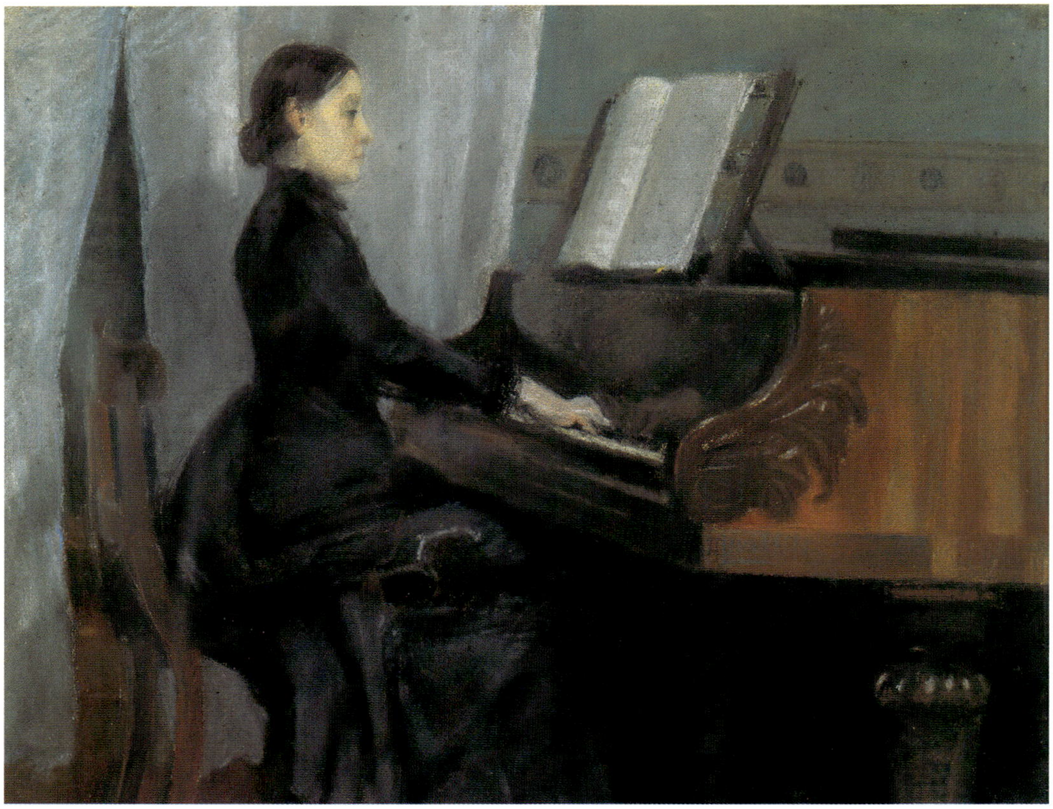

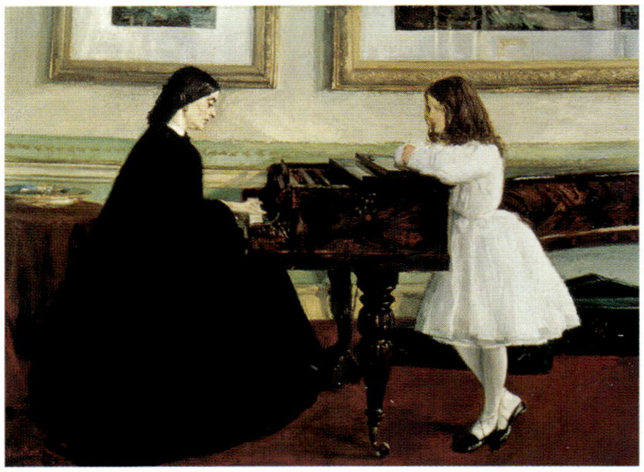

Fig. 44 James McNeill Whistler (1834–1903)
At the Piano, 1858–59
Oil on canvas, 67 x 91.6 cm
The Taft Museum, Cincinnati

18 CMS at the Piano

1884
Signed *William Stott of Oldham*
Pastel, 24.1 x 31.7 cm ($9\frac{1}{2}$" x $12\frac{1}{2}$")
Private collection

19 Millie Dow Stott

1890
Unsigned
Inscribed *Millie Dow Stott Sept 11th 1890 – aged 7*
Charcoal, 62.2 x 22.2 cm ($24\frac{1}{2}$ x $8\frac{3}{4}$")
Manchester Art Gallery

Millie Dow, the only child of William and Christina Mary Stott, was born in Paris in 1883. He died *ca.* 1956, having no children of his own. He became a chartered patent agent. This is a sketch for a large pastel that remains untraced (fig. 43).

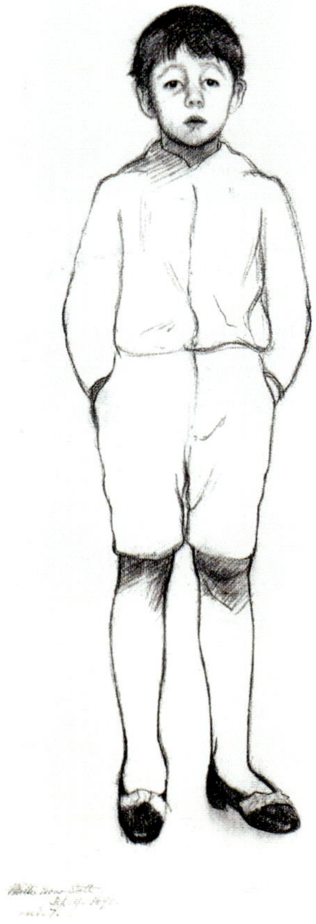

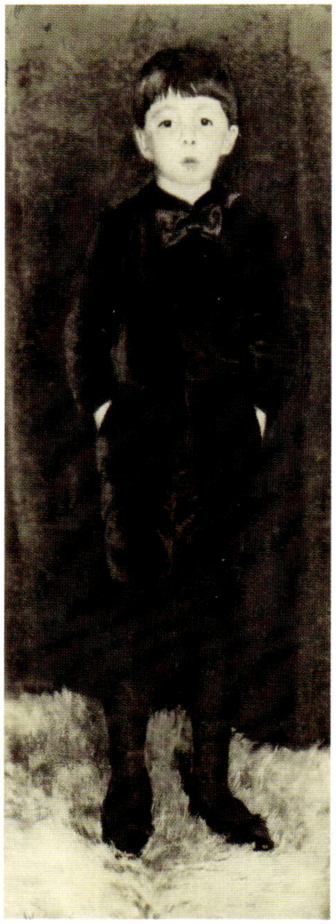

Fig. 43 William Stott of Oldham
Portrait of a Child, ca. 1890
Pastel, untraced

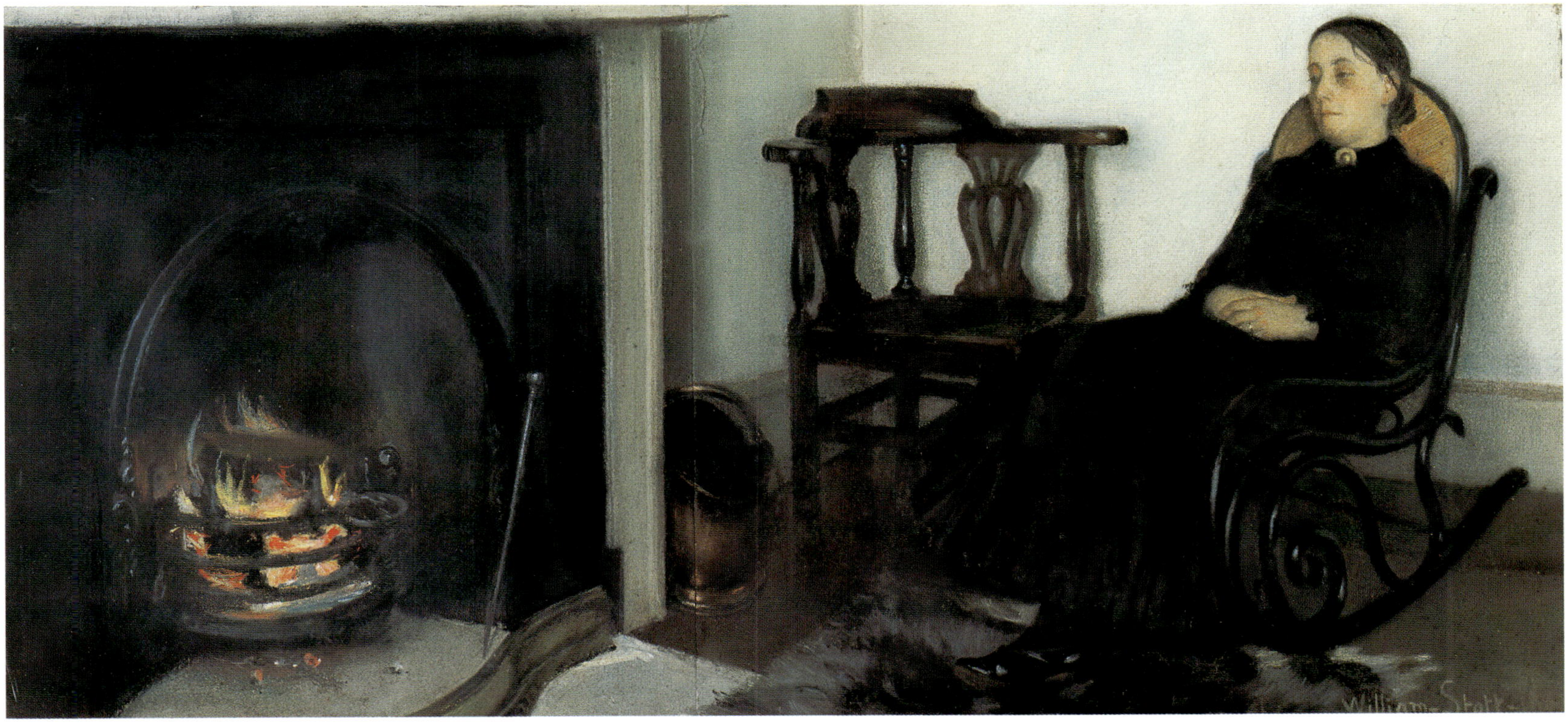

20 By the Fireside

[*Auprès du foyer*]
1884
Signed *William Stott*
Pastel, 24.4 × 54.6 cm (9¾" × 21½")
Private collection

By the Fireside is a picture of which William Stott was very proud. He gave it to his mother-in-law, Maria Bradbury, but on the understanding that it would be available for exhibitions, and, indeed, it was exhibited very widely in his lifetime. The domestic scenes he produced while he and his wife were staying with his parents in Oldham in the early part of 1884 were largely experimental, but in *By the Fireside* Stott displays with consummate skill the lessons he had learnt and produces a pastel of the very highest quality. It was completed in November 1884 and shows his wife, Christina Mary, sitting at the fireside of their house at Ravenglass in Cumberland.

The spell of Whistler is all over this picture, with its economy of expression, lack of narrative, and subtle harmonies of blacks, greys and browns. One is reminded of Whistler's statement, "Art should be independent of all claptrap – should stand alone and appeal to the artistic sense of eye or ear, without confounding this with emotions entirely foreign to it ..." (*The Gentle Art of Making Enemies,* 1890, p. 131). To aesthetes like Whistler atmosphere was everything, and in *By the Fireside* Mrs Stott, with her black dress and sombre demeanour, is in perfect tune with her setting.

Stott sent *By the Fireside* to the Paris Salon in 1885 and later that year it was shown at the Society of British Artists in London. In 1889, when he was invited for the last time to exhibit with the Belgium *avant-garde* group Les XX, *By the Fireside* was one of five works he sent to be displayed alongside paintings by Gauguin, Monet, Pissarro, Seurat and other leading artists from the progressive strand of European art. When *By the Fireside* appeared at the Third International Exhibition of Fine Arts in Vienna in 1894 it was singled out by one reviewer for comment: "... we should mention a score of portraits, all of them very distinguished: one is pastel, in slate and iron-grey colours, comfortable and cold, quite Anglican, which Mr Stott of Oldham titles *In Front of the Hearth.* With the simplest, even the most bourgeois elements of real life, the English excel in attaining style ... in order to express the mystery and indefinable qualities which are sometimes present in the simplest interiors and objects" (William Ritter, *Gazette des Beaux-Arts,* June 1894, pp. 512–20).

21 Alice White playing the Violin

1882
Signed and inscribed
Oil on canvas, 173 x 67 cm (68³/₄" x 26¹/₄")
Private collection

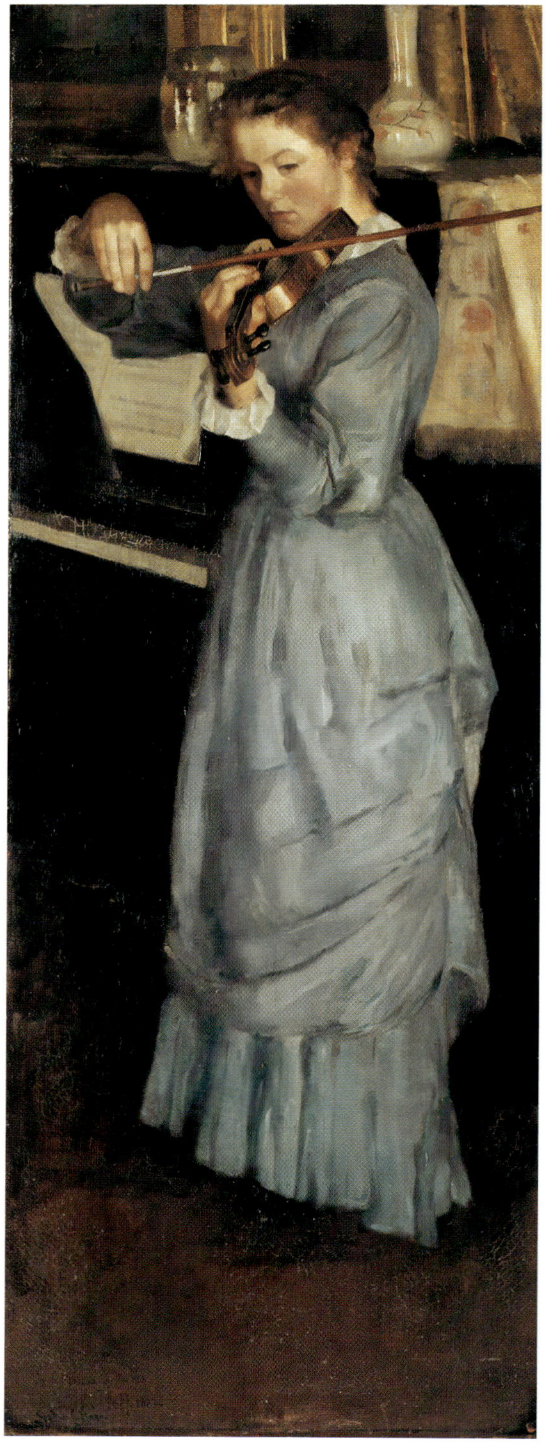

This portrait meant a great deal to William Stott, as it reminded him of a happy time spent on his honeymoon in 1882 at Seaton Cottage, the summer home of his friend and mentor John Forbes White. Following his success at the Paris Salon that year and his marriage in Oldham in June, Stott and his wife travelled to Scotland. They stayed first at Dysart at the family home of Tom Millie Dow (see cat. 13). In July they moved on to join the White family at Seaton Cottage, on the Balgownie estate just north of Aberdeen.

John Forbes White (1831–1904) was a prosperous flour-miller, a considerable scholar and a leader in the civic and cultural life of Aberdeen. A life-long Hellenist, he gave lectures on Greek language and culture. As a connoisseur and collector his knowledge of fine art was such that he was invited to contribute articles on Rembrandt and Velázquez to the *Encyclopaedia Britannica*. In addition he was one of the pioneers of photography in Scotland.

This interest in photography may have been reflected in his love of realist art. As a collector he particularly favoured the modern Dutch painters of the Hague School and invited members of the group to stay with him in Scotland. In 1873 he purchased *Souvenir d'Italie*, the first Corot to be seen in Scotland (now in the Kelvingrove Art Gallery, Glasgow). He also supported contemporary Scottish and English painters.

Forbes White was the first owner of *The Ferry* (cat. 10). On the strength of this picture he commissioned the twenty-four-year-old Stott to paint a portrait of his eldest daughter, Alice. This work, with its harmonious, low-key colours and an apparent awareness of the vogue for Japanese art, seems to point to an early admiration for the work of Whistler. The naturalistic portrait may also reflect Stott's close relationship at the time with John Singer Sargent, whose recent Salon portraits of *Mme Edouard Pailleron* (1880) and *Mme Ramon Subercaseaux* (1881), set in the natural surroundings of their home and garden, were seen by contemporary reviewers as bold and modern.

Stott's pride and pleasure in this portrait is reflected in his comments in subsequent letters to John Forbes White. He took the picture back to Paris with him and in February 1883 wrote to reassure White that he would not show it in England first: "Understand the thought of sending to England has never crossed my head. Life is too short to send pictures where people care little for them and even if they did – when they will *not hang* on just principles. I couldn't bear to send 'our Alice' to be seen by a lot of people who are simply incapable of discerning its intention, not to say – judge it." In another letter he reports excitedly that "Sargent likes Alice the most of anything he has seen of mine – Helleu and Lhermitte – the latter especially were very pleased …". Stott is clearly still 'tinkering' with Alice as he writes, "I have taken a liberty with 'Alice's' frame and gilt the interior – I think it is better and hope you will like it …. Some day if I ever find myself in Scotland and 'Alice' – I think perhaps two hours would do all I should like …."

Stott had saved *Alice* for the Salon Triennial of 1883, but it was refused. Eventually it was shown at the Salon in 1886 and was "hung well". But Stott's fears about the reaction of the English critics were to be confirmed when it was shown in London at the Society of British Artists' winter exhibition the same year. Stott must have been mortified by the comment in the *Pall Mall Gazette* about the picture which had so much personal meaning for him and in which he had invested so much. His *Portrait of Miss White* was dismissed as "a clever, but unpleasing, whole length" (30 November 1886).

The portrait of Alice has remained in the family and is currently in the possession of her granddaughter.

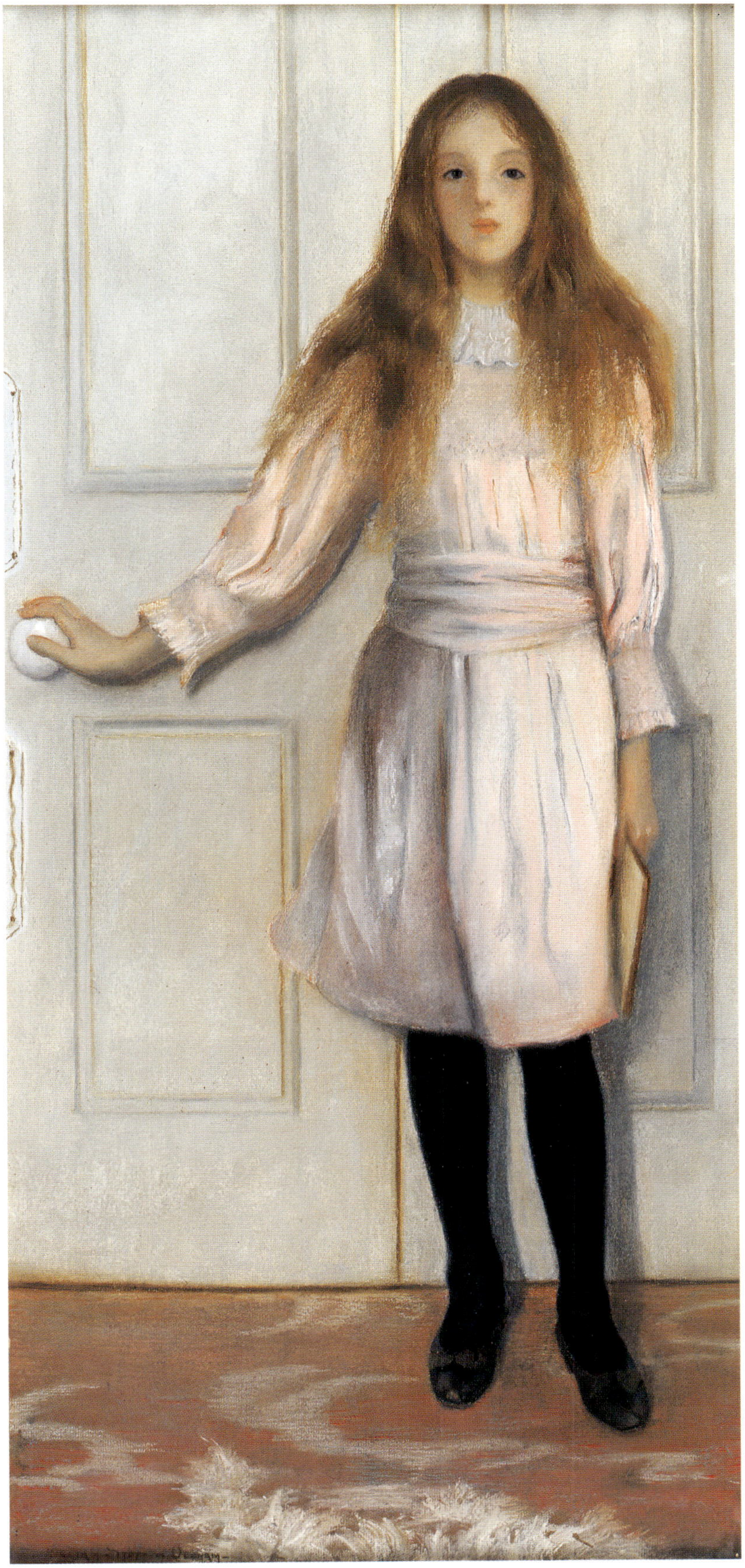

22 Beatrice

ca. 1885
Signed *William Stott of Oldham*
Pastel, 81.3 × 38.1 cm (32" × 15")
Private collection

Placing the figure in a a full-frontal pose and framing her in a cut-off doorway, Stott creates the effect a professional photographer might require. The young girl seems to stand transfixed as if waiting for the camera to click. The muted, harmonious tone and the carefully constructed composition demonstrate, as one would expect, affinity with Whistler's work. In fact, however, the picture shows that Stott was also aware of the work of the Belgian artist Fernand Khnopff, who was himself an admirer of Whistler, but who was later to become a leading member of the European Symbolist movement. Khnopff was well known in Parisian and London art circles and counted George Frederic Watts, Dante Gabriel Rossetti and Sir Edward Burne-Jones among his friends. In addition, he was a founding member of the Brussels-based *avant-garde* artists' society known as Les XX (Les Vingt, or the Twenty). Stott would have almost certainly met Khnopff when he was invited in 1884, with Whistler, to exhibit in Brussels with this group. At the 1885 exhibition of Les XX Khnopff's *Portrait of Jeanne Kéfer*, which shows interesting resemblances to this picture, was shown and it is possible Stott would have seen it there. Thus with *Beatrice* Stott is experimenting with a more radical and modern approach to portraiture than even Whistler would have felt comfortable with.

Beatrice was a second cousin of William Stott's and later became an accomplished amateur artist who exhibited at the Oldham Spring Exhibition.

Seascapes

23 Sand, Sea and Sky

Signed *William Stott of Oldham*
Oil on canvas, 61 x 91.4 cm (24" x 36")
Private collection

Marine art was extremely popular with the Victorians. Above all Britain was a mercantile power; its economy rested on sea-borne trade through its many prosperous ports and its Navy was no less important to protect and maintain this '*status quo*'.

Most marine painting in the nineteenth century, from Turner's *Fighting Temeraire* to Stanhope Forbes's *Fish Sale on a Cornish Beach*, was full of historical nostalgia, narrative incident or topographical interest. Very few Victorian artists painted pure sea-pieces, and when they did they were usually highly finished and depicted the drama of a breaking wave or storm-filled sky. Henry Moore (1831–1895) was one of the few to devote himself to pure sea subjects, recording the changing moods and colours of the sky and sea. Stott's friend and rival from his time at Grez, Alexander Harrison, after the success of his painting *The Wave* at the Salon in 1885, spent much of his time painting luminous moonlit seascapes.

William Stott's inspiration for his numerous seashore landscapes and seascapes came from two artistic mentors, Edgar Degas and James McNeill Whistler. In the 1860s both Degas and Whistler had spent time on the Normandy coast sketching the changing moods and colours of the coastline. Whistler stayed at the fashionable resort of Trouville in October 1865 with Gustave Courbet. Here he produced several oil-sketches of the empty stretches of sand and sea. At this time, under the influence of Japanese art, Whistler was lightening his palette and applying the paint more thinly to enable freer handling, so that he could work more quickly to capture the changing effects of light and movement. In *Harmony in Blue and Silver: Trouville* (fig. 46) he later superimposed the figure of Courbet in the foreground as a souvenir of their time spent together.

In 1869 Degas stayed on the Normandy coast and produced over thirty pastels – 'subject-less' vistas of empty sand, sea and sky,

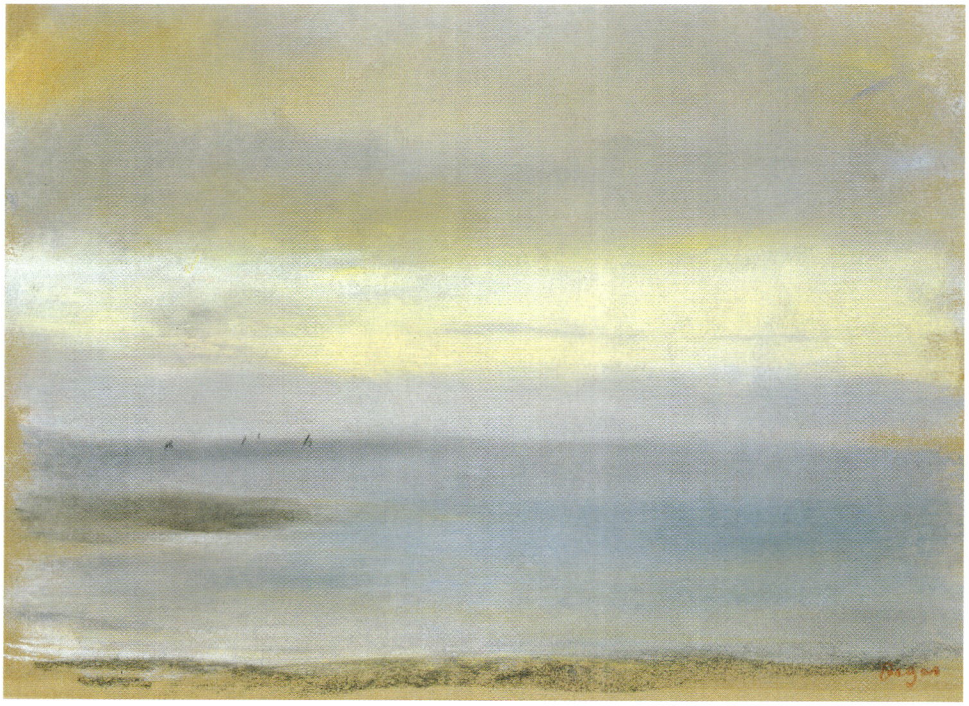

Fig. 45 Edgar Degas (1834–1917), *Marine Sunset, ca.* 1869
Pastel on paper, 21.5 x 30 cm, private collection

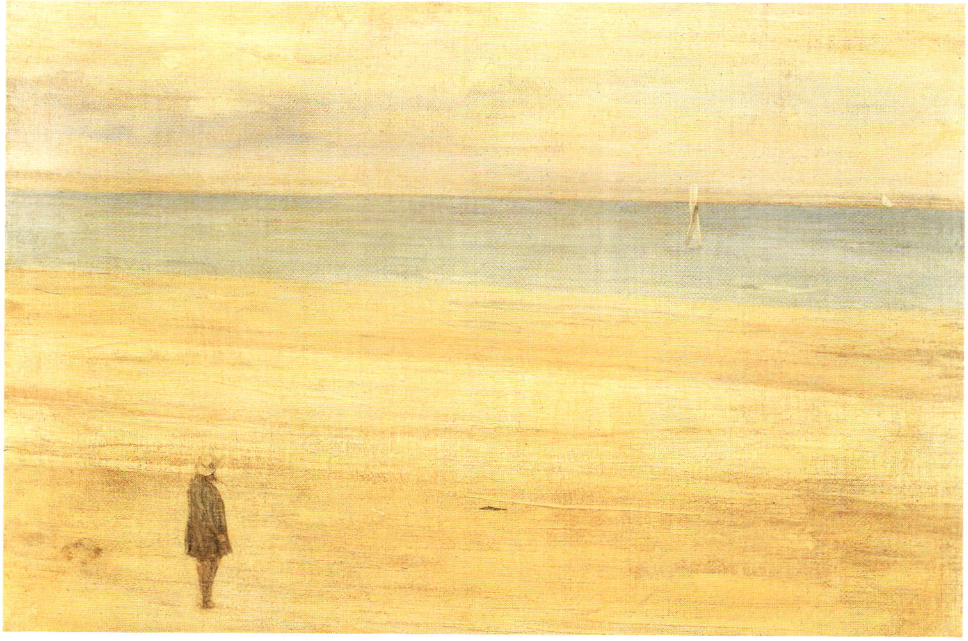

Fig. 46 James McNeill Whistler (1834–1903), *Harmony in Blue and Silver: Trouville*, 1865
Oil on canvas, 49.5 x 75.5 cm, Isabella Stewart Gardner Museum, Boston

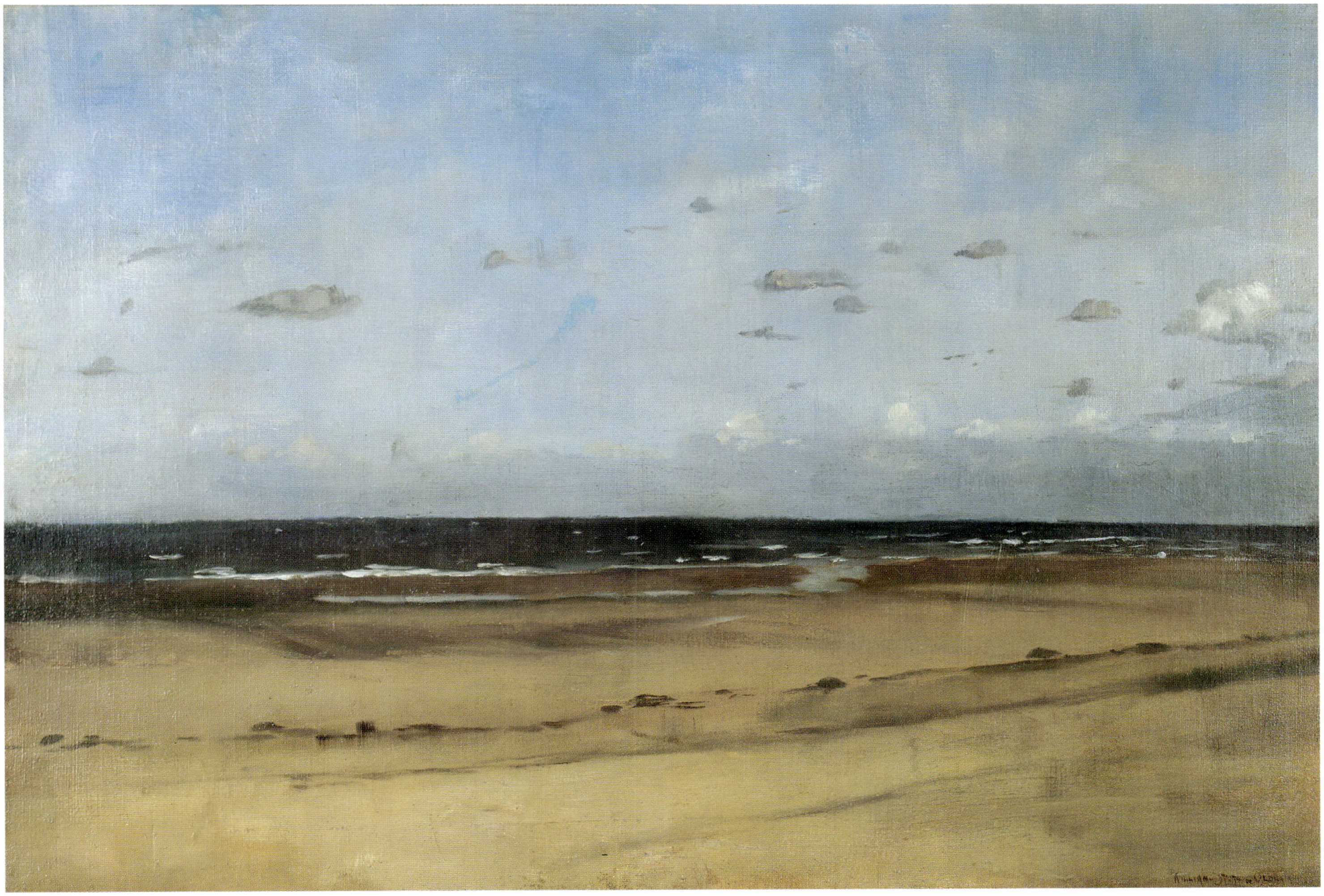

with titles such as *Marine Sunset* (fig. 45), *Beach at Low Tide* and *Beside the Sea*. What mattered to Degas in his landscapes was not topographical exactitude or anecdote, but the effects of light and atmosphere with colour. Like Whistler he wished to record the notes in nature's ever-changing harmonies. He worked in pastel to be able to respond quickly to the nuances of the atmosphere as the weather began to change. However, Degas's expansive and unpopulated landscapes are essentially realist and matter-of-fact and lack the self-conscious aestheticism of those by Whistler.

William Stott was introduced to Degas around 1883, probably by Whistler, and immediately started working in pastel, which was to become his preferred medium for preparatory studies and recreational landscapes. He would have been aware of Degas's coastal landscapes and also seen the minimalist seaside watercolours that Whistler showed at the Dowdeswell Gallery in London in 1884 after his return from a stay at St Ives with Walter Sickert and Mortimer Menpes. It is no surprise therefore that in his notebook, in the summer of 1884, Stott records a series of pastels with descriptions such as "*iii*) Tide rising; grey sky; green sea with big waves; *iv*) Blue sea; pools; sunny; *v*) Sunny sky; emerald sea; small waves".

For the next sixteen years until his death in 1900 Stott was to produce dozens of such studies. Some, such as *Sandpools* and *Little Bay* (cat. 24, 28), were used as background studies for larger pictures, but many were exhibited as works of art in their own right. His shoreline seascapes were all done within a mile of his house at Ravenglass. He made no attempt to identify the locations, as they were of little importance to him. What he was seeking in these exquisite, highly sensitive pastels was to record atmosphere and effect. It was 'art for art's sake' at its boldest and bravest. Stott was seeking beauty in form and light and colour. Walter Sickert considered the tiny panel paintings of Whistler his greatest achievement, and the equivalent might be said of Stott's small pastels with their careful orchestration and delicate finish. Like Monet, who became obsessed late in his life with the water-lilies in his garden, Stott became preoccupied with the challenge of capturing the changing patterns provided by the sea and shifting sand-dunes within sight of his home.

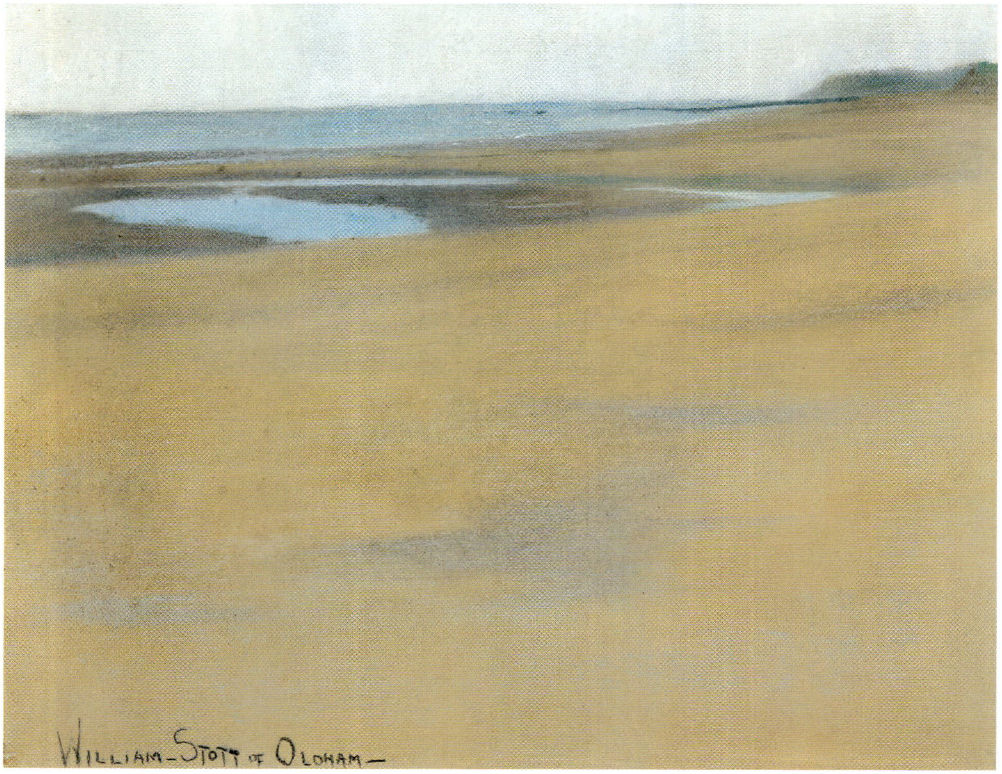

24 Sandpools

Signed *William Stott of Oldham*
Pastel, 24.1 × 31.7 cm (9½" × 12½")
Private collection

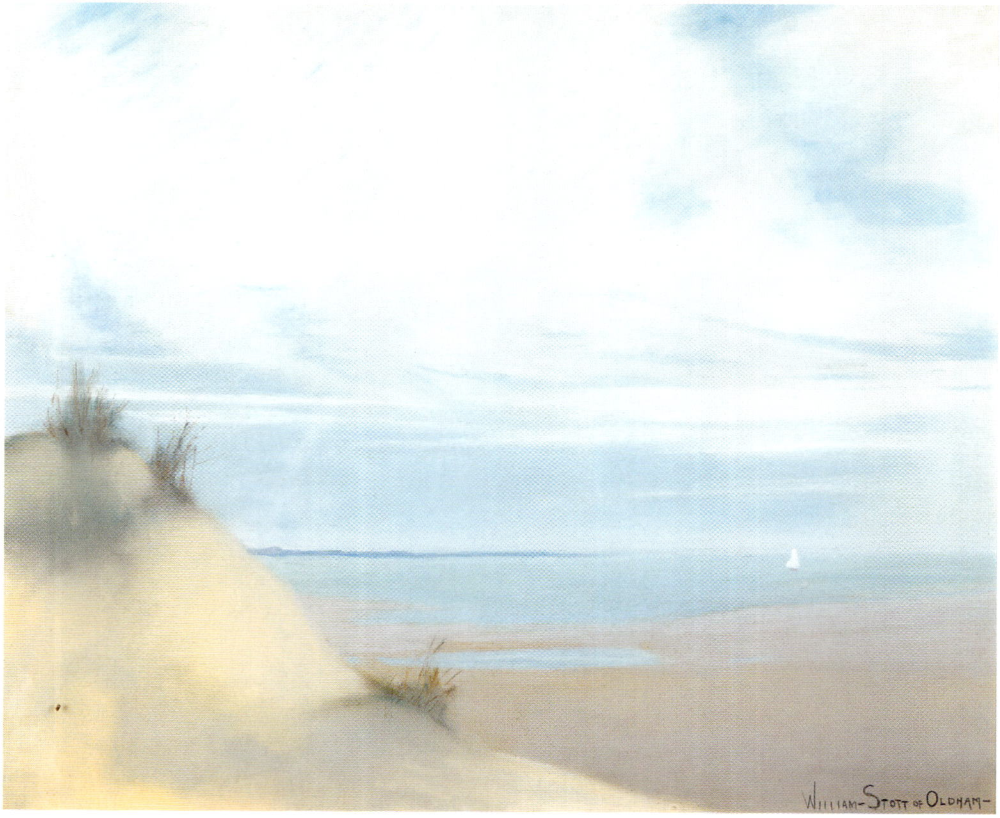

25 Sandhill

Signed *William Stott of Oldham*
Pastel, 41.9 × 50.8 cm (16½" × 20")
Private collection

26 Turquoise Sea

1885

Signed *William Stott of Oldham*

Oil on panel, 24.1 x 31.7 cm ($9^{1}/_{2}$" x $12^{1}/_{2}$")

Private collection

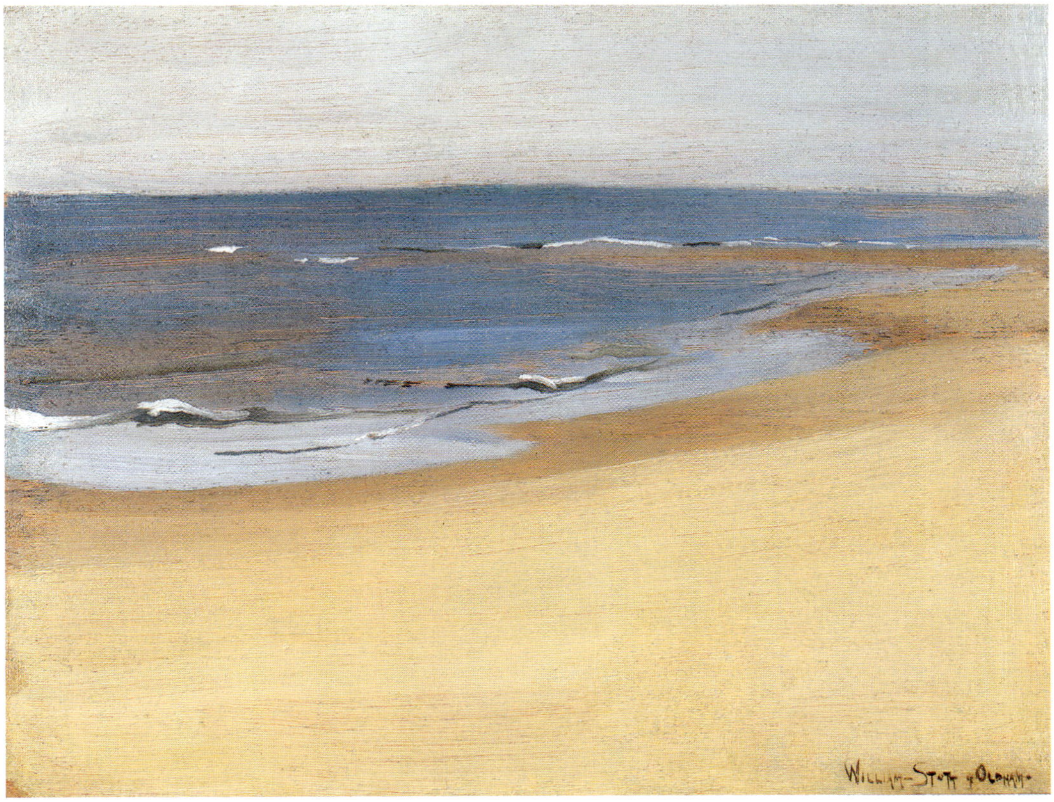

27 Sand-dunes

1884

Signed and dated *William Stott. 84*

Pastel, 24.1 x 31.7 cm ($9^{1}/_{2}$" x $12^{1}/_{2}$")

Private collection

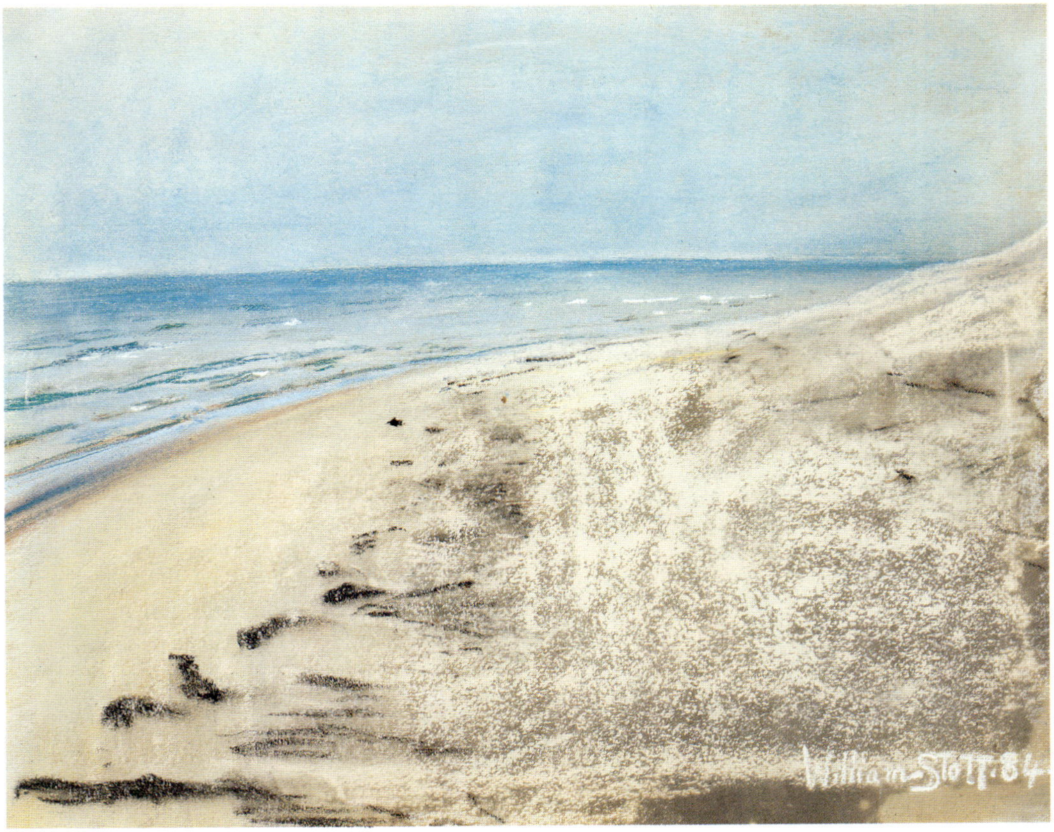

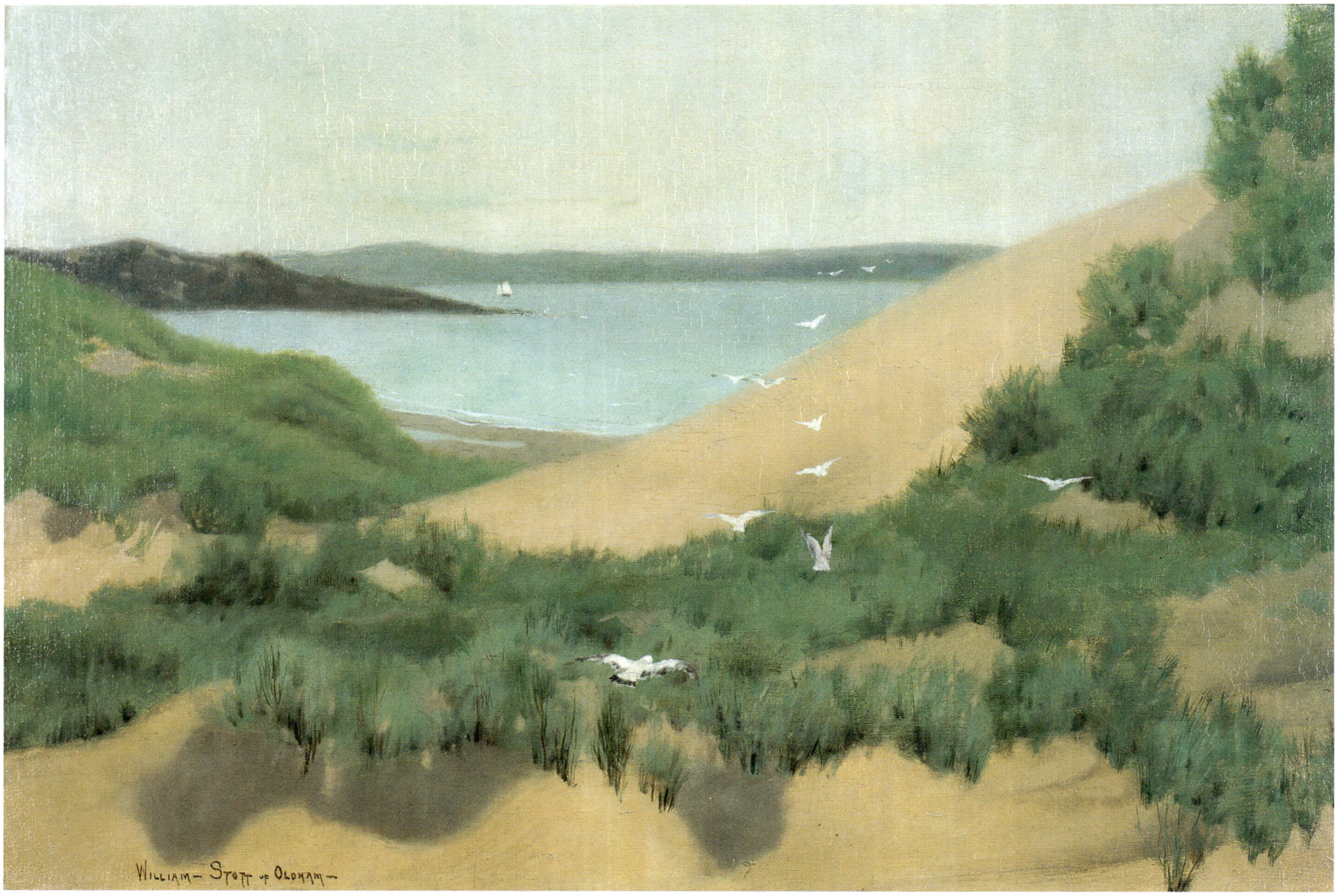

28 The Little Bay

Signed *William Stott of Oldham*
Oil on canvas, 48.3 × 73.7 cm (19" × 29")
Private collection

29 Returning Tide

ca. 1885
Unsigned
Pastel, 24.1 × 31.7 cm (9½" × 12½")
Private collection

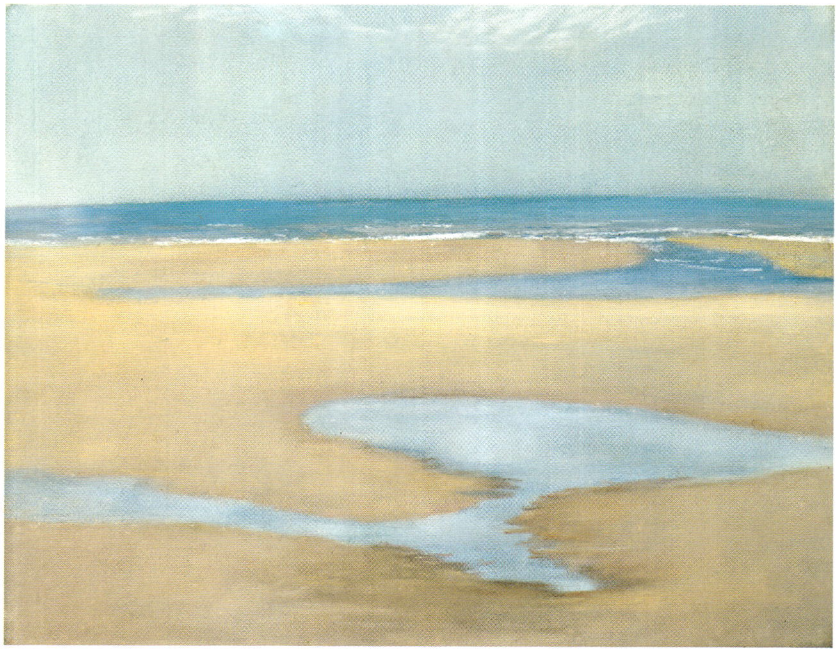

30 A Seascape

1884
Signed and dated *William Stott. 1884*
Pastel, 24.1 x 31.7 cm (9$^1/_2$" x 12$^1/_2$")
Gallery Oldham

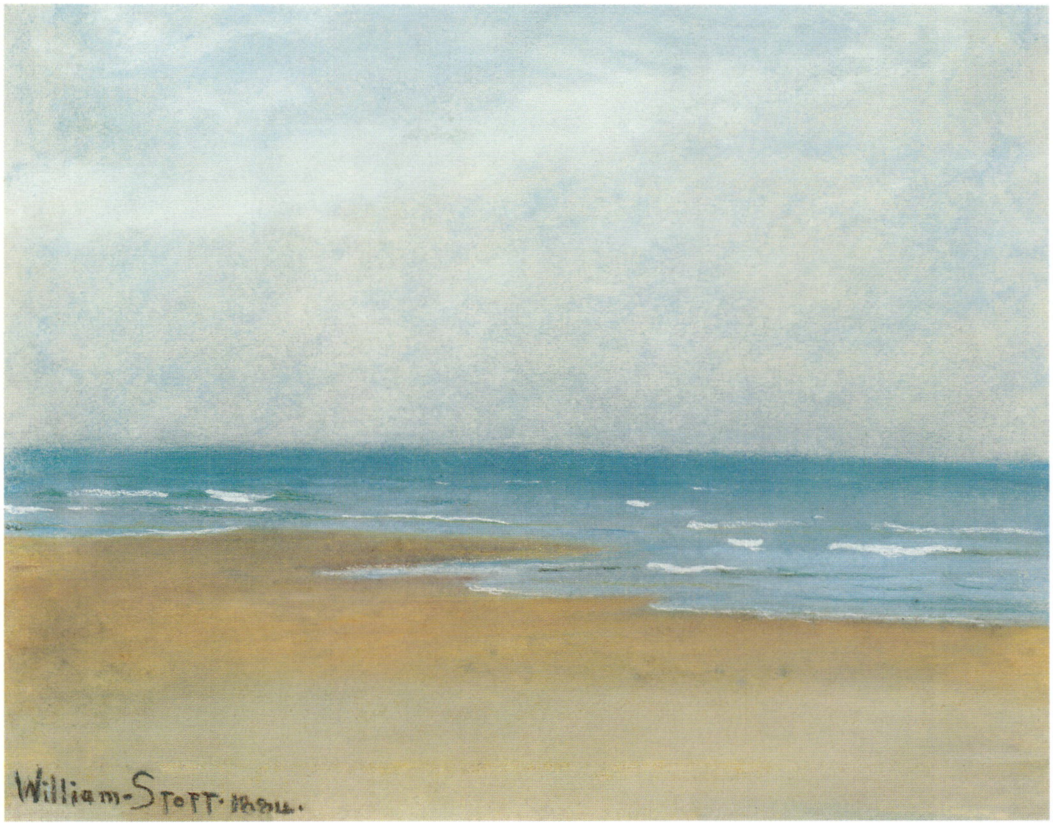

31 Sparkling Sea

ca. 1884
Signed *William Stott of Oldham*
Pastel, 24.1 x 31.7 cm (9$^1/_2$" x 12$^1/_2$")
Private collection

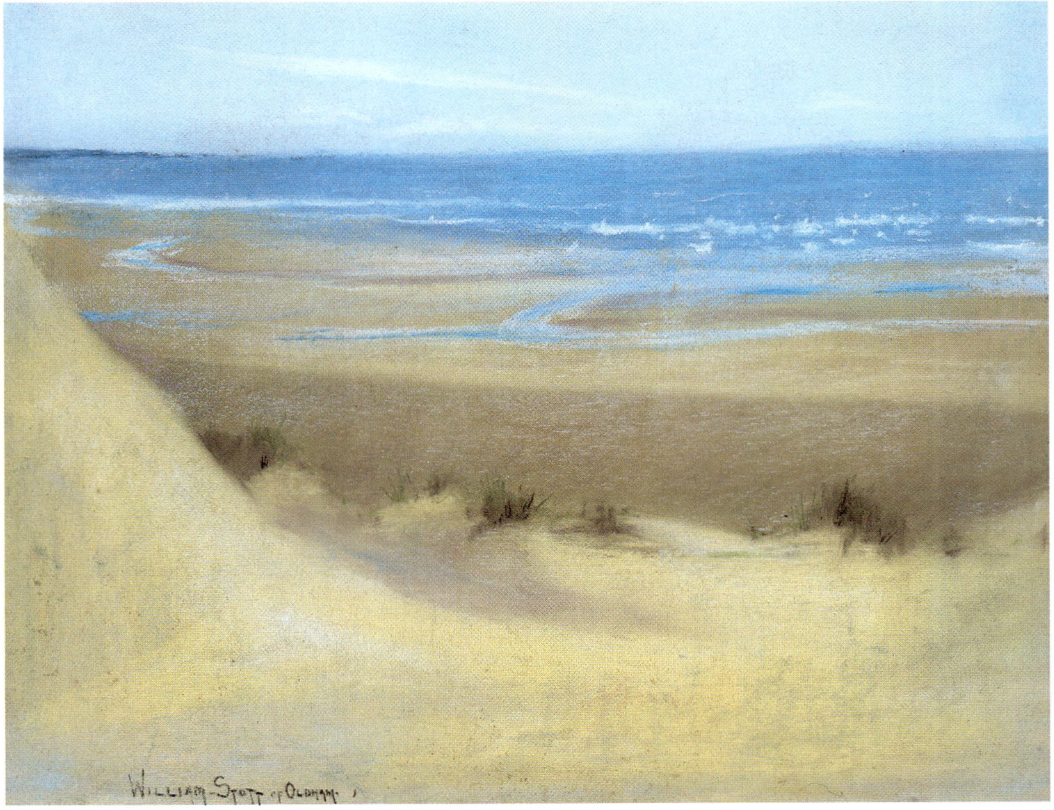

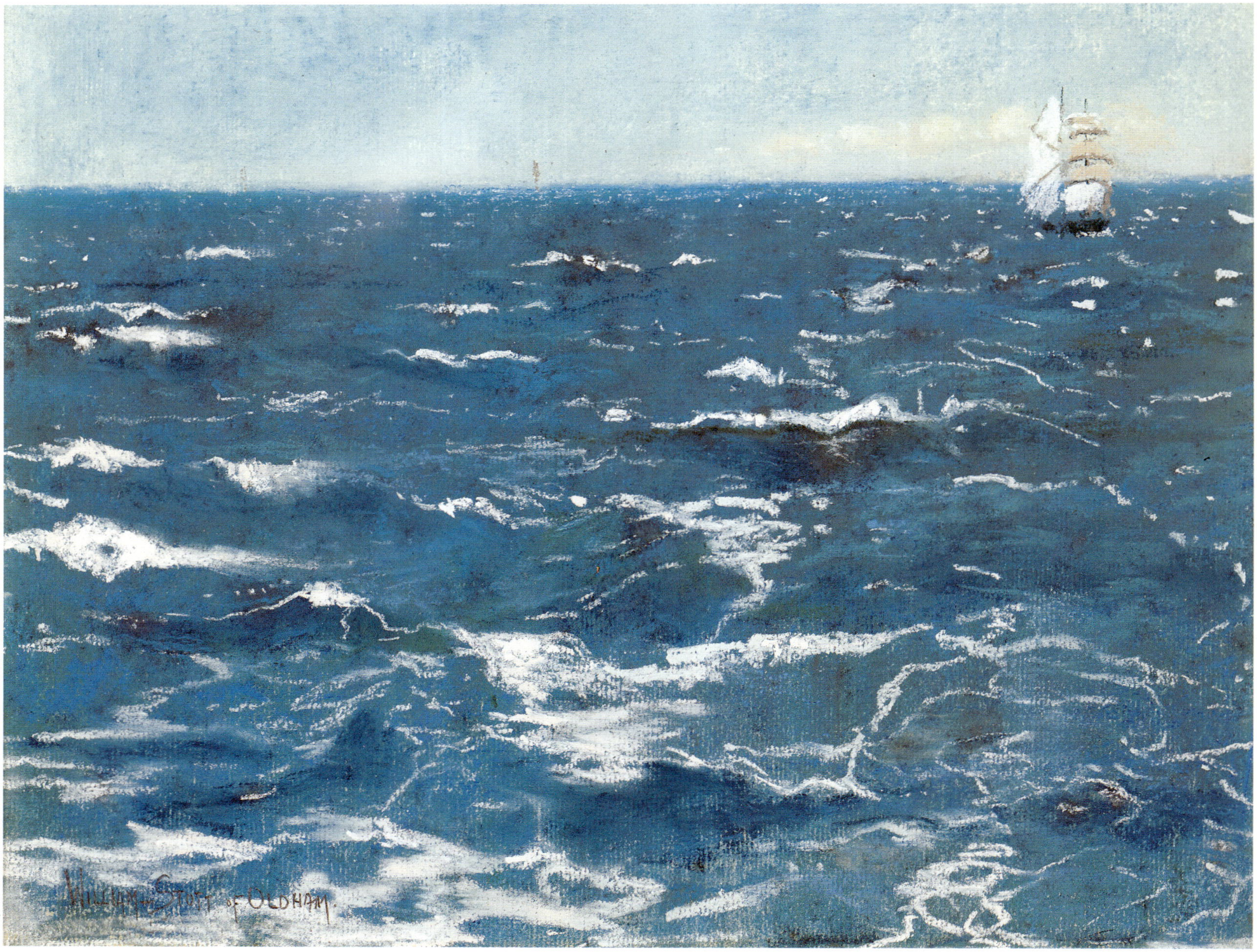

32 Choppy Sea

ca. 1896

Signed *William Stott of Oldham*

Pastel, 23.5 x 31.1 cm (9¼" x 12¼")

Private collection

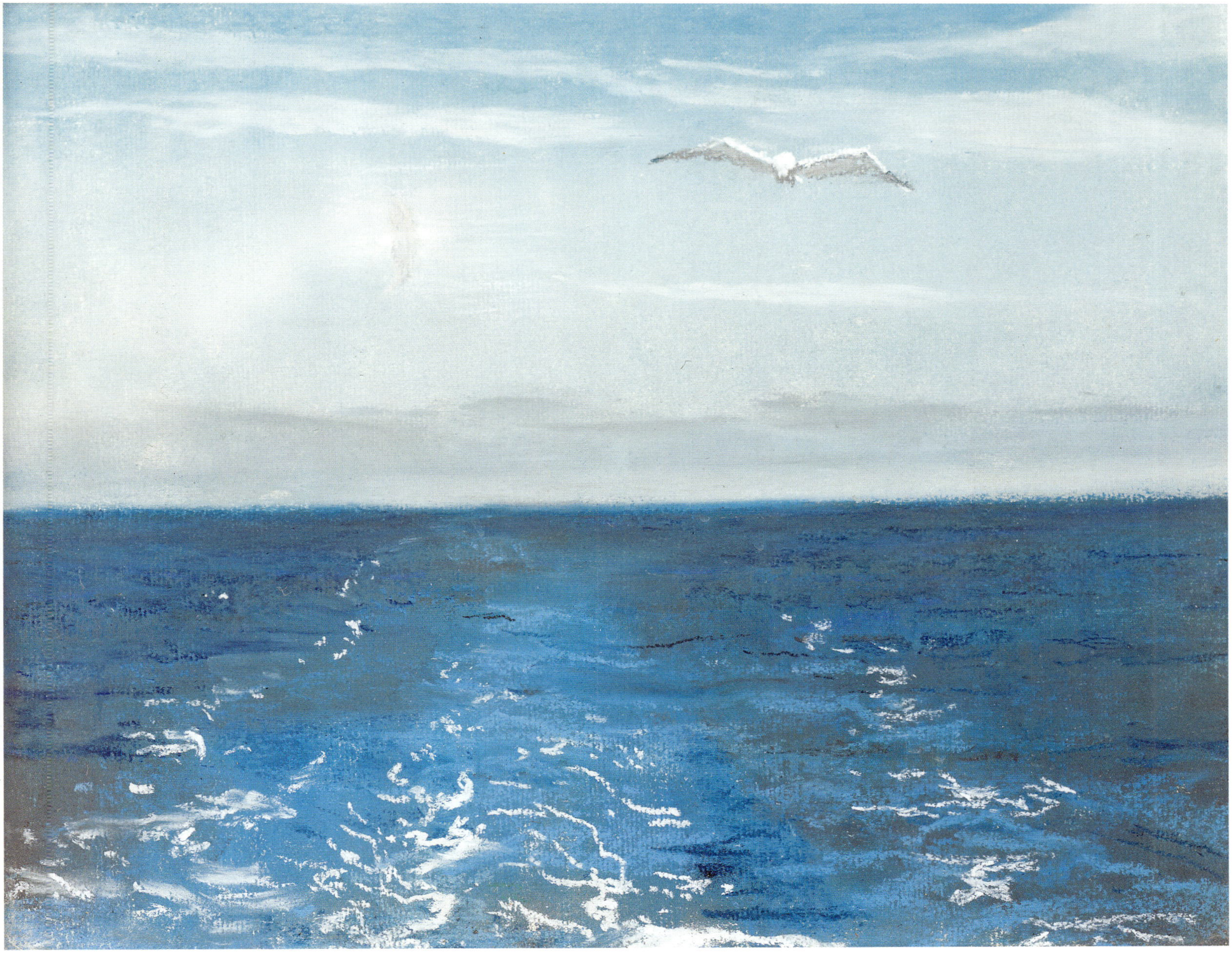

33 Seagulls Astern

ca. 1896

Unsigned

Pastel, 23.5 x 31.7 cm (9 1/4" x 12 1/2")

Private collection

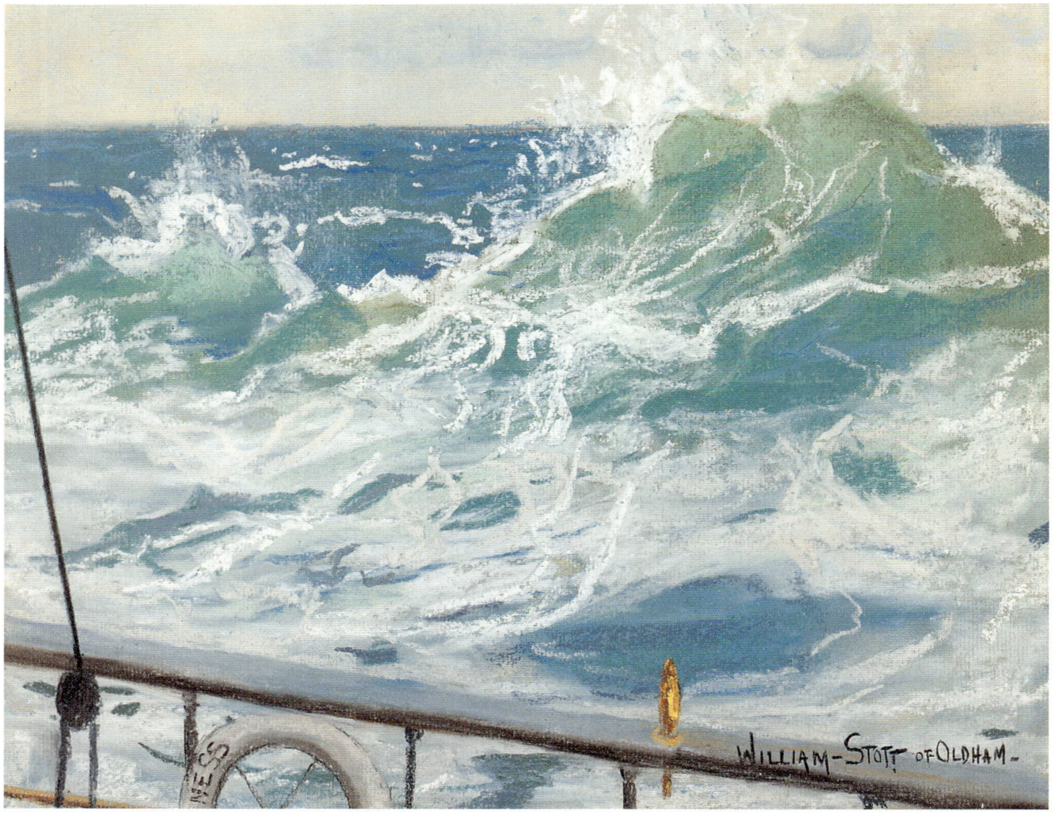

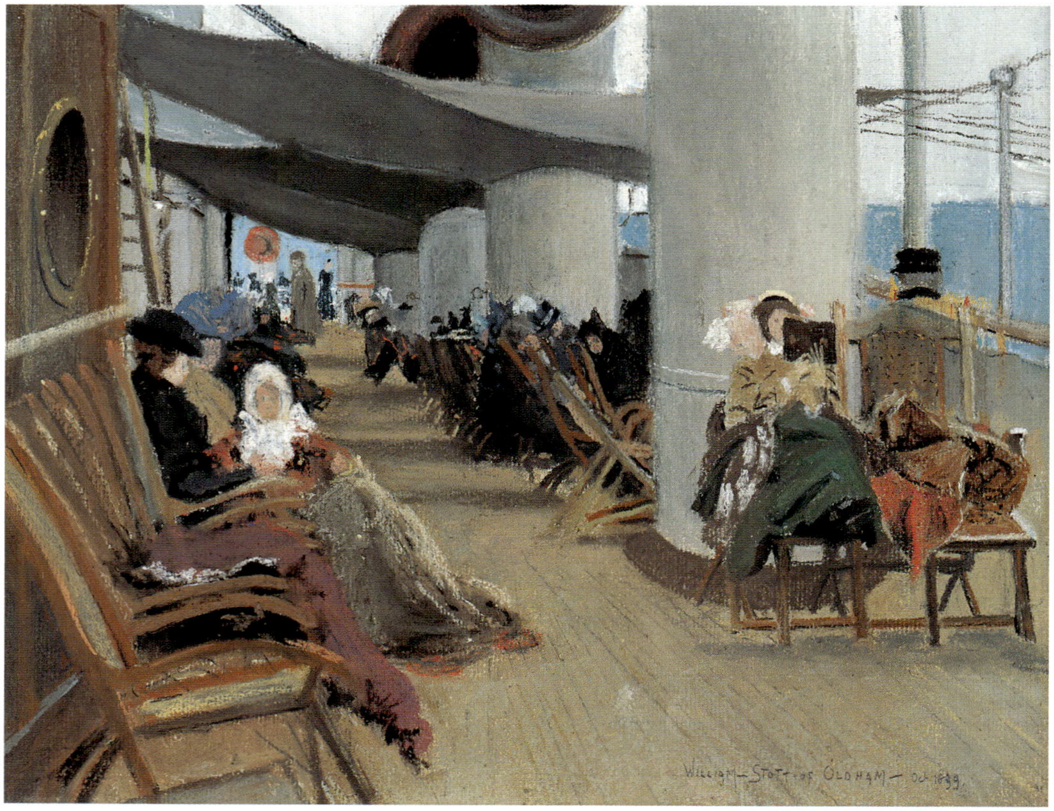

34 Sunlit Wave

ca. 1896
Signed *William Stott of Oldham*
Pastel, 24.1 × 31.7 cm (9½" × 12½")
Private collection

35 S.S. Umbria

ca. 1897
Signed *William Stott of Oldham*
Pastel, 31.7 × 38.1 cm (12½" × 15½")
Private collection

In his latter years Stott took numerous short sea voyages around the coast of Britain for the sake of his health. He normally made his frequent trips to Glasgow by steamer and when he died he was returning to Belfast from Southampton in order to catch the daily packet-boat back to Barrow, which was a short distance from his home in Ravenglass. These frequent trips by sea enabled him to perfect his skill of depicting through the medium of pastel the movement of water and the play of light on its surface. Works such as *Choppy Sea* (cat. 32), *Wake of a Ship* (cat. 36) and *Seagulls Astern* (cat. 33), although seemingly repetitive, repay careful study because of their sheer technical skill. In most of these works Stott eliminates the foreground, excludes reference to human intervention and, as in his Alpine studies (see cat. 56–64), focuses the viewer on the patterns, colours and inspiring moods of nature. In the *S.S. Umbria*, uniquely in this series, the ship and its passengers are the subject, and this exquisite little pastel makes us wish Stott had given us further genteel observations of his fellow voyagers.

The *S.S. Umbria*, the last Cunarder with auxiliary sail, was launched in 1884 and plied between Liverpool and New York until laid up in 1908. It is most likely that Stott disembarked at Queenstown (Cork), where she called to take on Irish passengers, as there is no record of him ever visiting America.

36 Wake of a Ship

ca. 1896
Signed *William Stott of Oldham*
Pastel, 24.1 x 31.7 cm (9½" x 12½")
Private collection

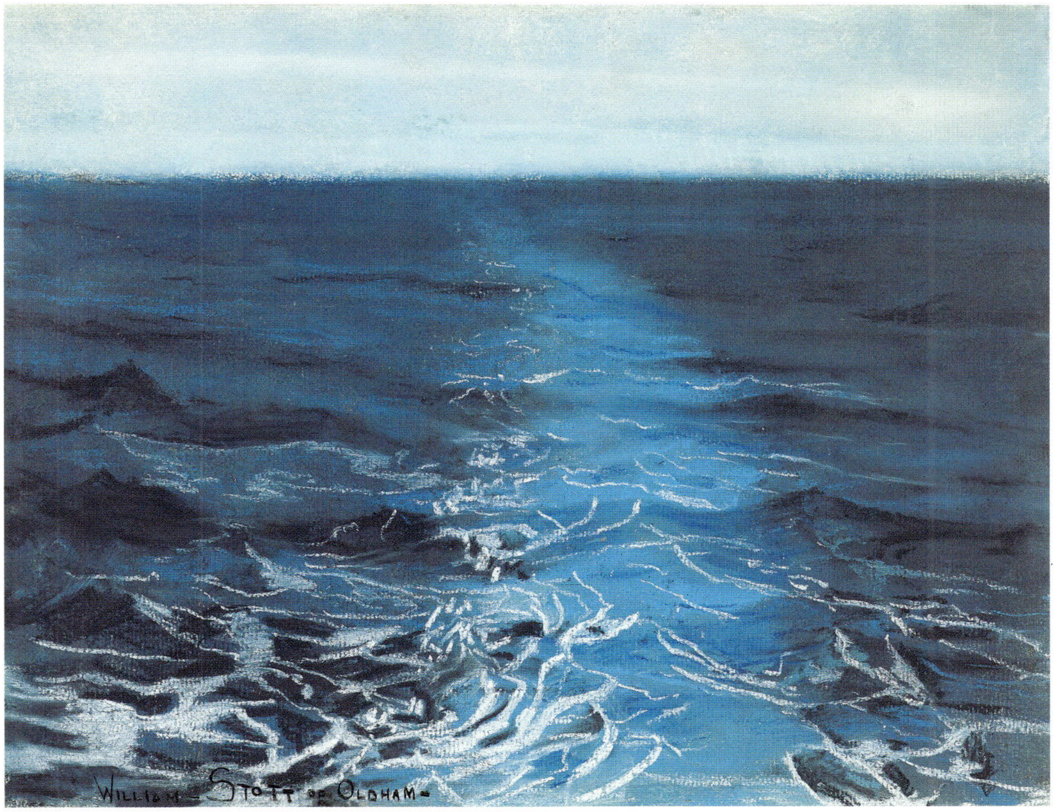

37 North Breeze

ca. 1885
Signed *William Stott of Oldham*
Pastel, 22.8 x 30.8 cm (9" x 12")
Gallery Oldham

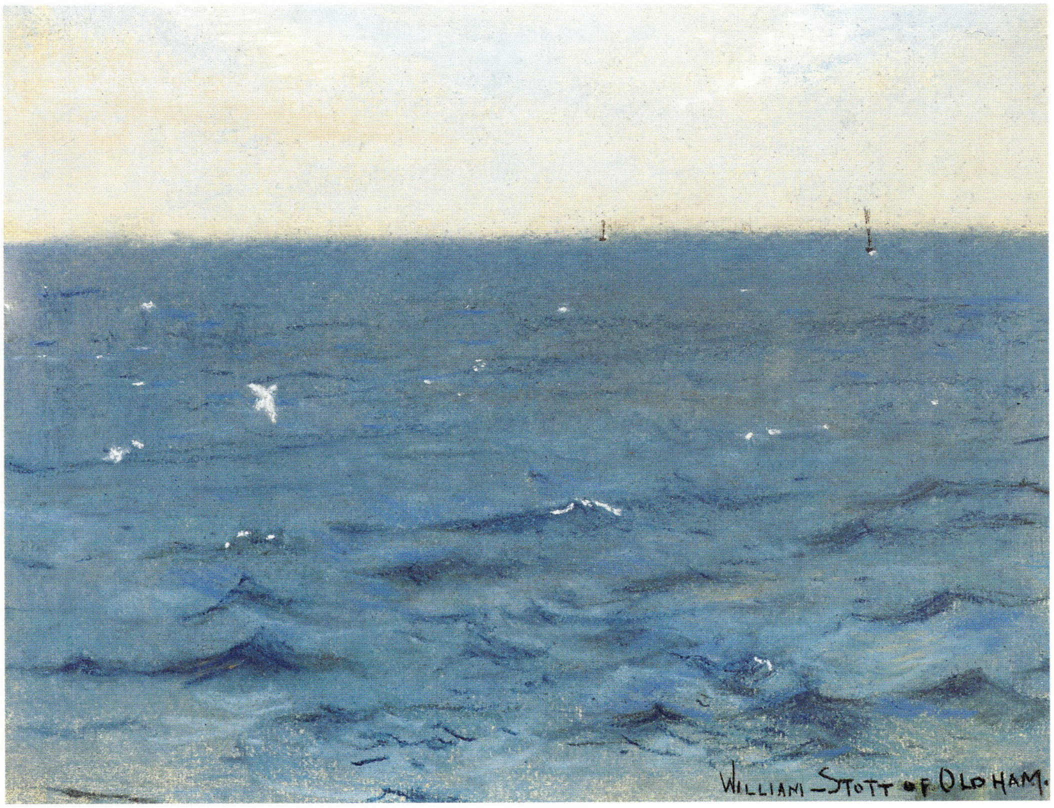

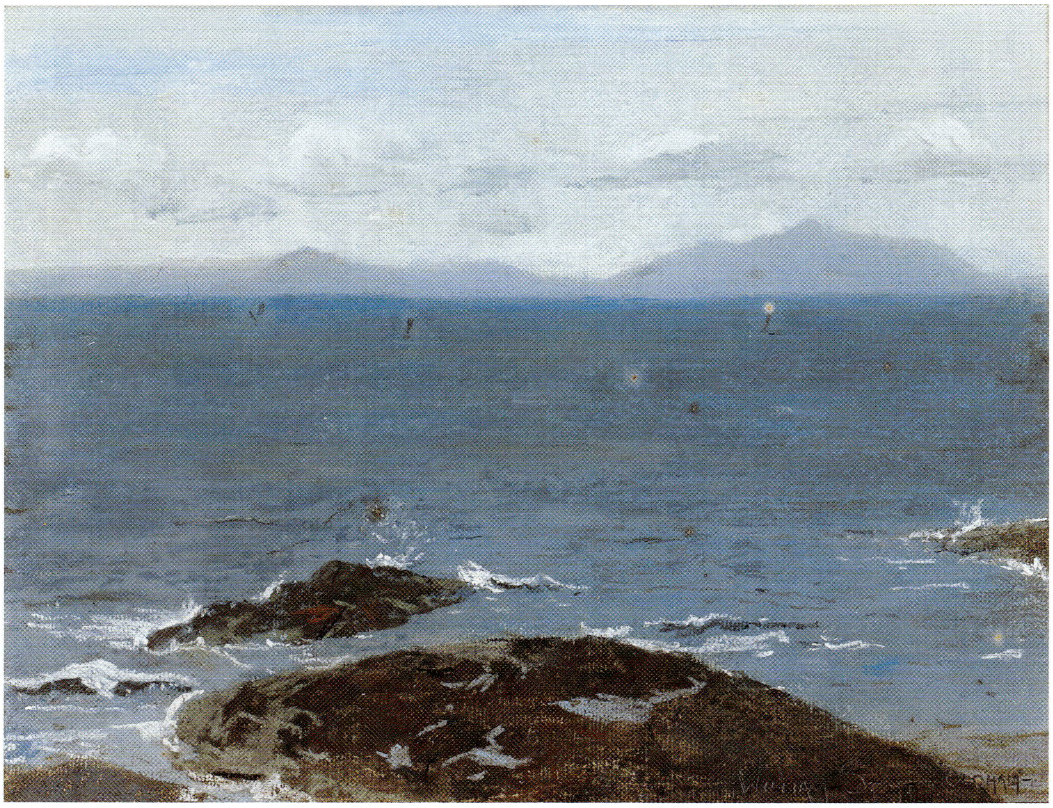

38 Arran

ca. 1893
Signed *William Stott of Oldham*
Pastel, 24.1 x 31.7 cm
Private collection

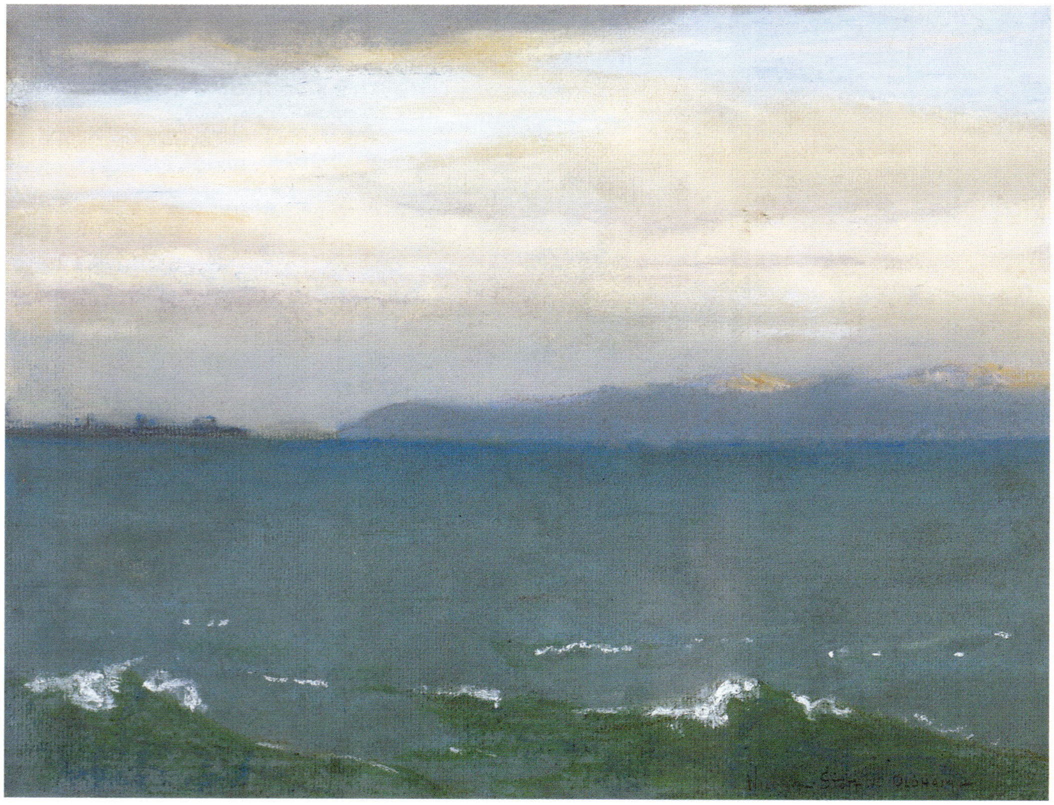

39 Seascape with Distant Mountains

ca. 1893
Signed *William Stott of Oldham*
Pastel, 23.5 x 31.1 cm (9 1/4" x 12 1/4")
Private collection

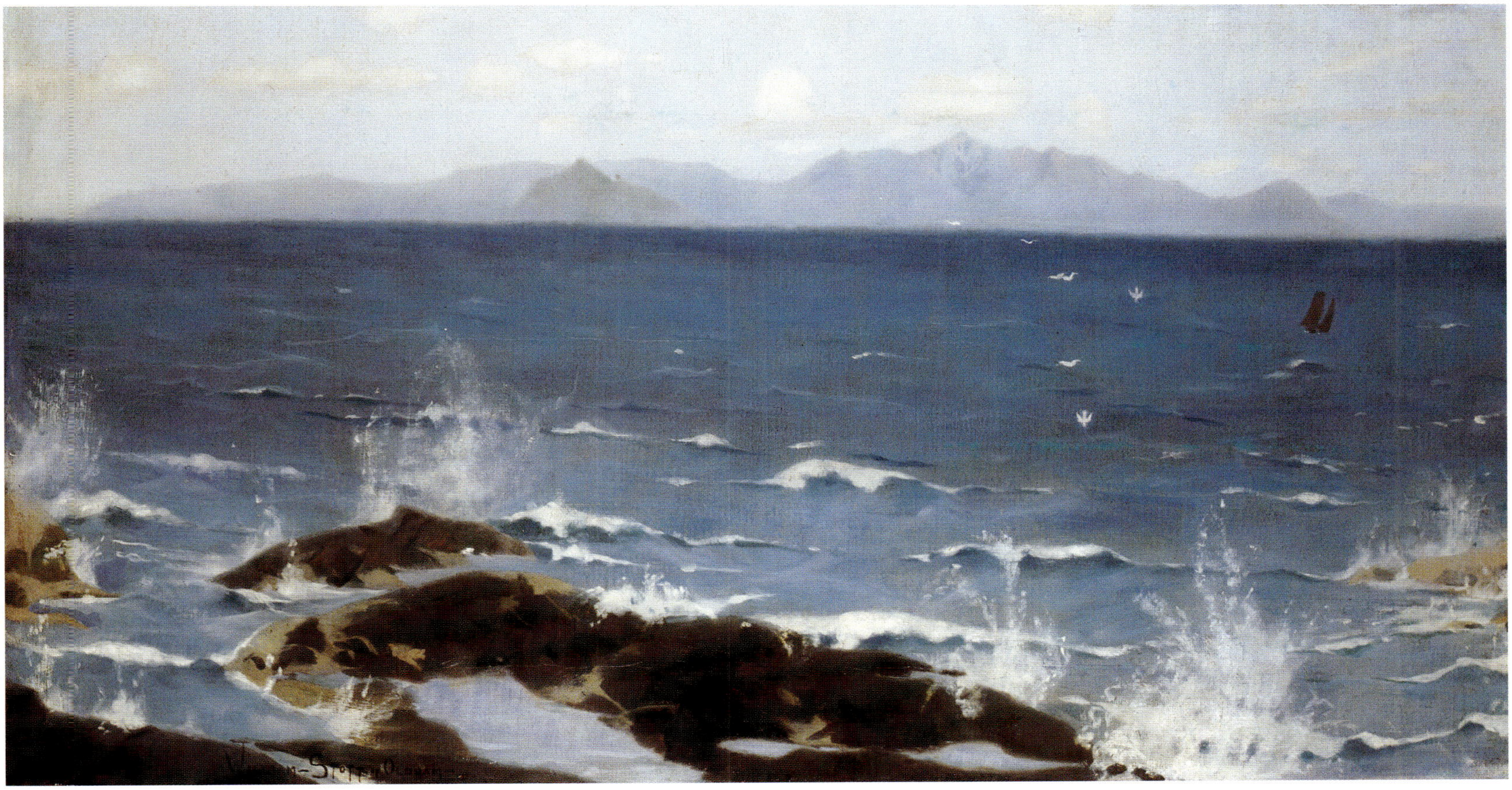

40 Memory of an Island

1895
Signed *William Stott of Oldham*
Oil on canvas, 67.3 × 128.3 cm (26½" × 50½")
Dundee Art Gallery

Memory of an Island was painted as souvenir of a happy summer Stott and his wife and son spent with his great friend the artist Tom Millie Dow and his family on the Isle of Arran in 1893. He worked it up from a number of pastel sketches (cat. 38, 39) in the autumn of 1895 and sent it to the Royal Academy in 1896. It was shown at the Paris Salon in 1896 and at some stage it was given to Tom Millie Dow as a reminder of the holiday the two families spent together.

The unspecific title and the sense of mystery that pervades the distant mountainous island gives the picture a dream-like quality. The vast expanse of blue sea with the groundswell breaking into spray on the rocks in front of the viewer adds to the feeling of remoteness and inaccessibility. Stott has succeeded in representing the bleak and rugged Isle of Arran as some far-off Shangri-La.

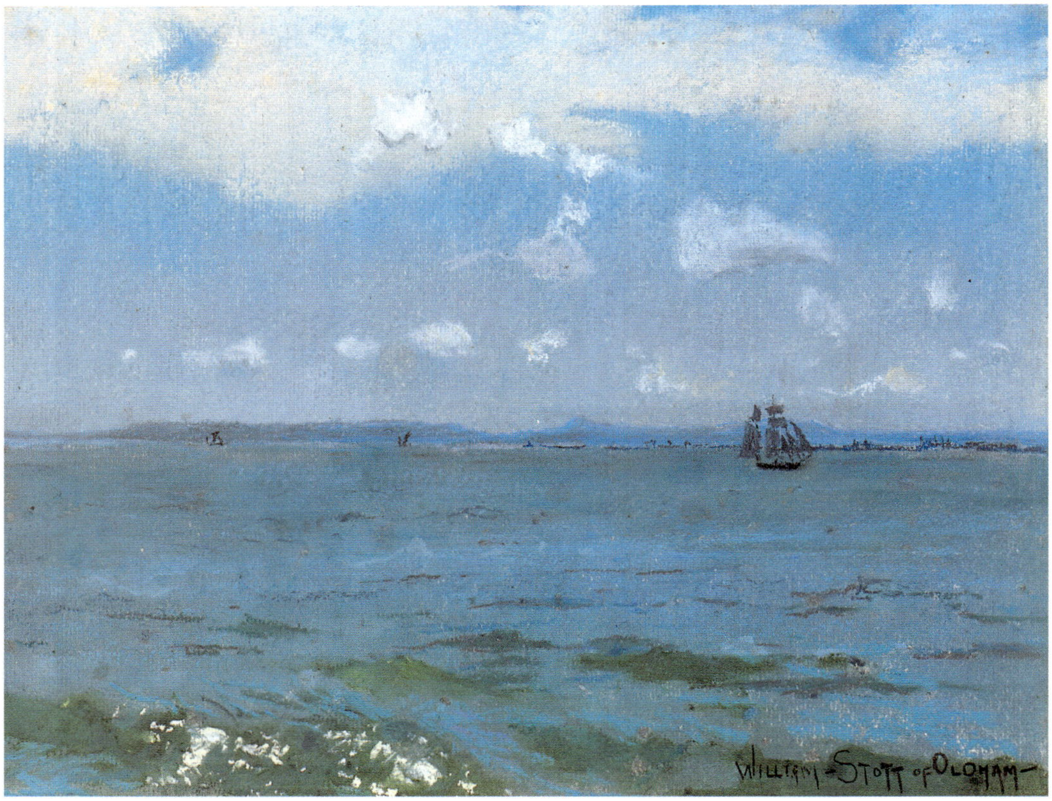

41 Below Gravesend

ca. 1897

Signed *William Stott of Oldham*

Pastel, 24.1 x 31.7 (9½" x 12½")

Private collection

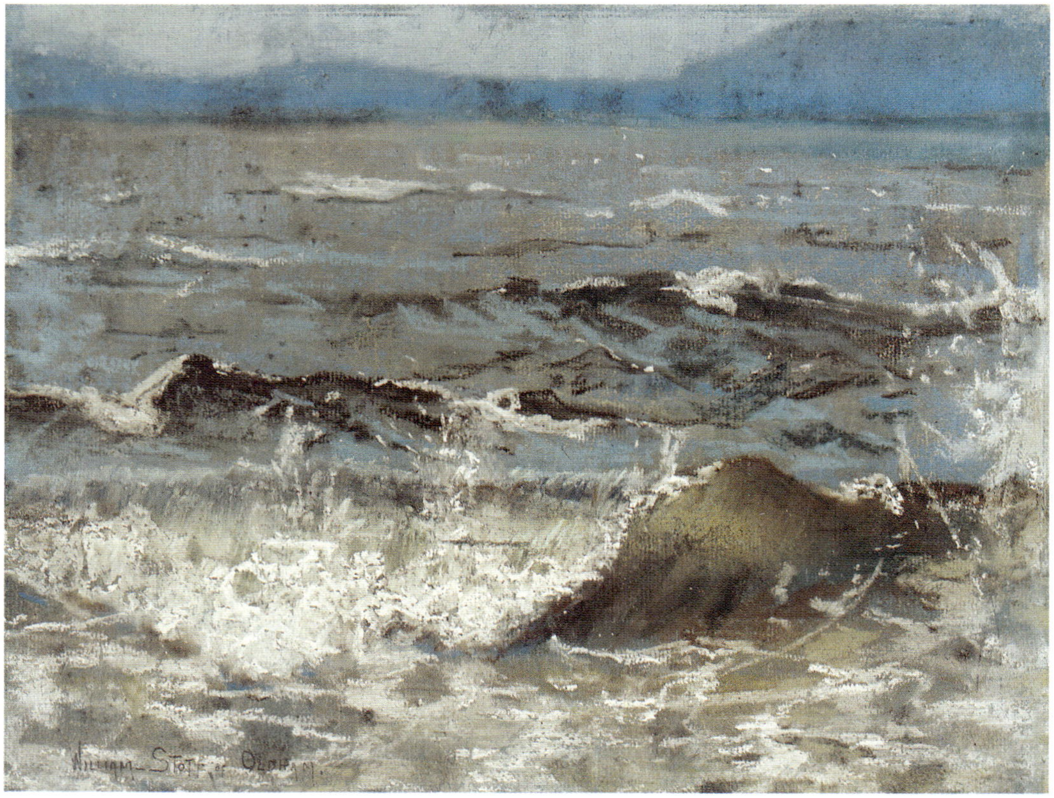

42 Breaking Wave

ca. 1893

Signed *William Stott of Oldham*

Pastel, 24.7 x 33 cm (9¾" x 13")

Bristol Museums and Art Gallery

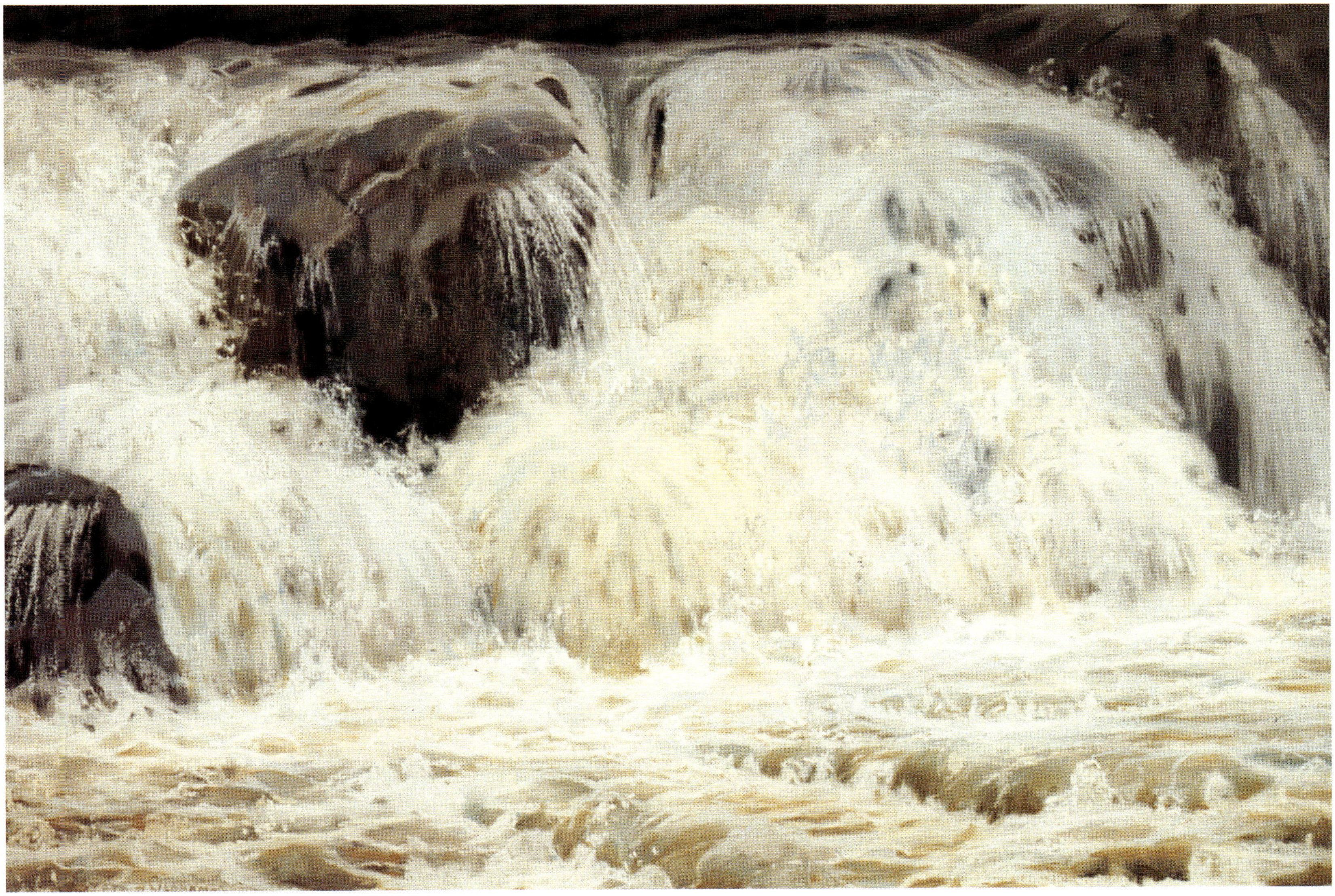

Torrents

43 A Freshet

ca. 1888–89
Signed *William Stott of Oldham*
Pastel, with opaque watercolour, 47 x 74.9 cm
(18½" x 29½")
Gallery Oldham

A freshet is a rush of water resulting from heavy rain or melting snow. In *A Freshet* and its companion pictures of mountain torrents Stott gives a truly virtuoso display of the art of the *pastelliste*. The movement and power of the fast-flowing water is caught with consummate skill. With pastel he also uses opaque watercolour, which is difficult to work, as it dries very fast and mistakes cannot be rectified. All these works were completed on his visit to Switzerland in 1888. He records in his notebook sketches of several "torrents" on the Lutschine river which runs down from Lauterbrunnen, "the valley of waterfalls", but only the Schwarzer Wasserfall (literally, 'the black waterfall') is positively identified.

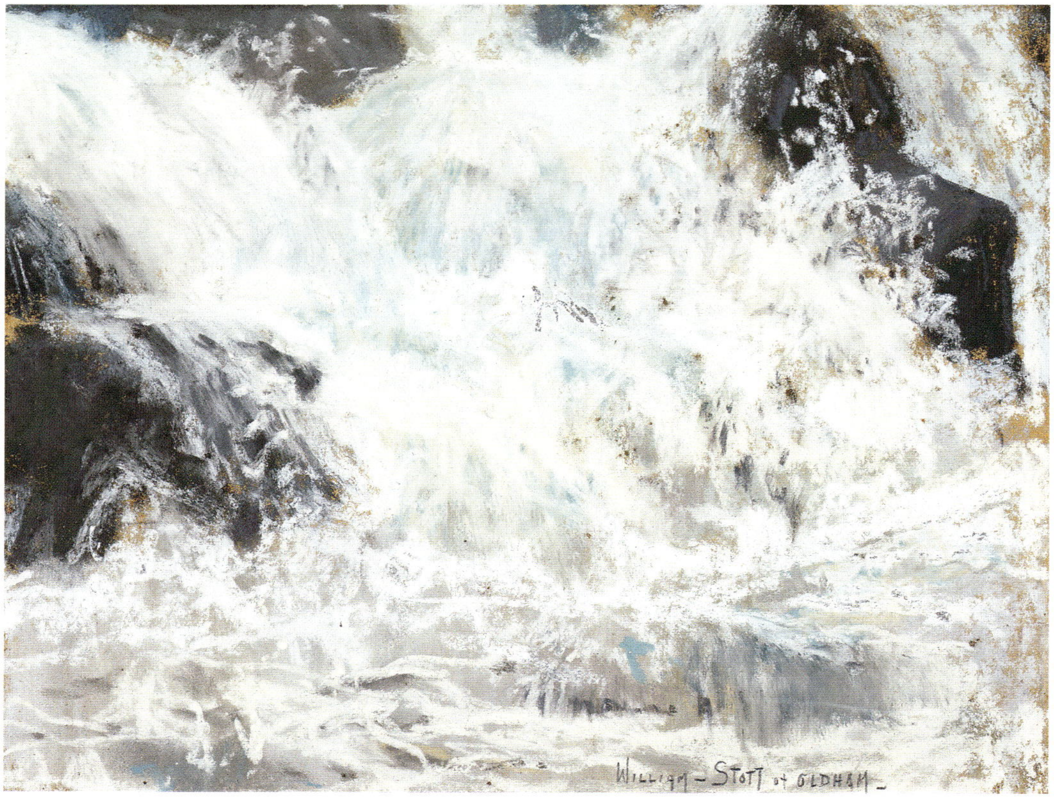

44 Sparklets

1888

Signed *William Stott of Oldham*

Pastel, 24.1 × 31.7 cm (9½" × 12½")

Private collection

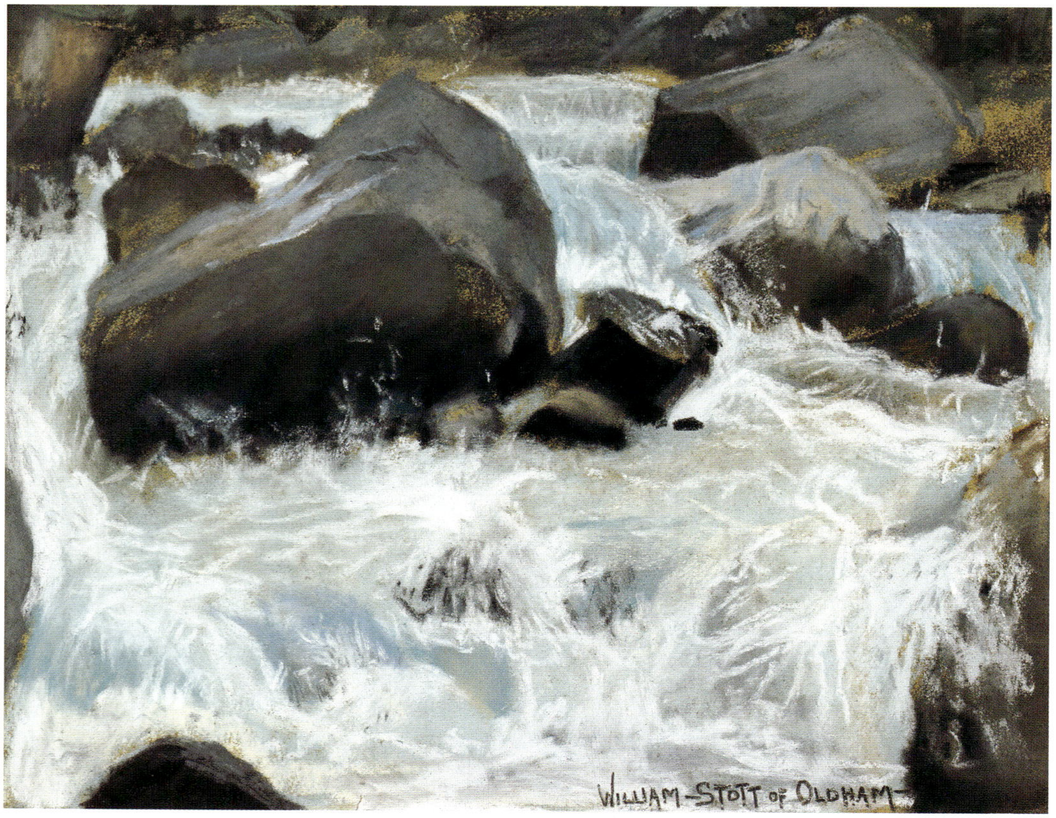

45 White Torrent

1888

Signed *William Stott of Oldham*

Pastel, 24.1 × 31.7 cm (9½" × 12½")

Private collection

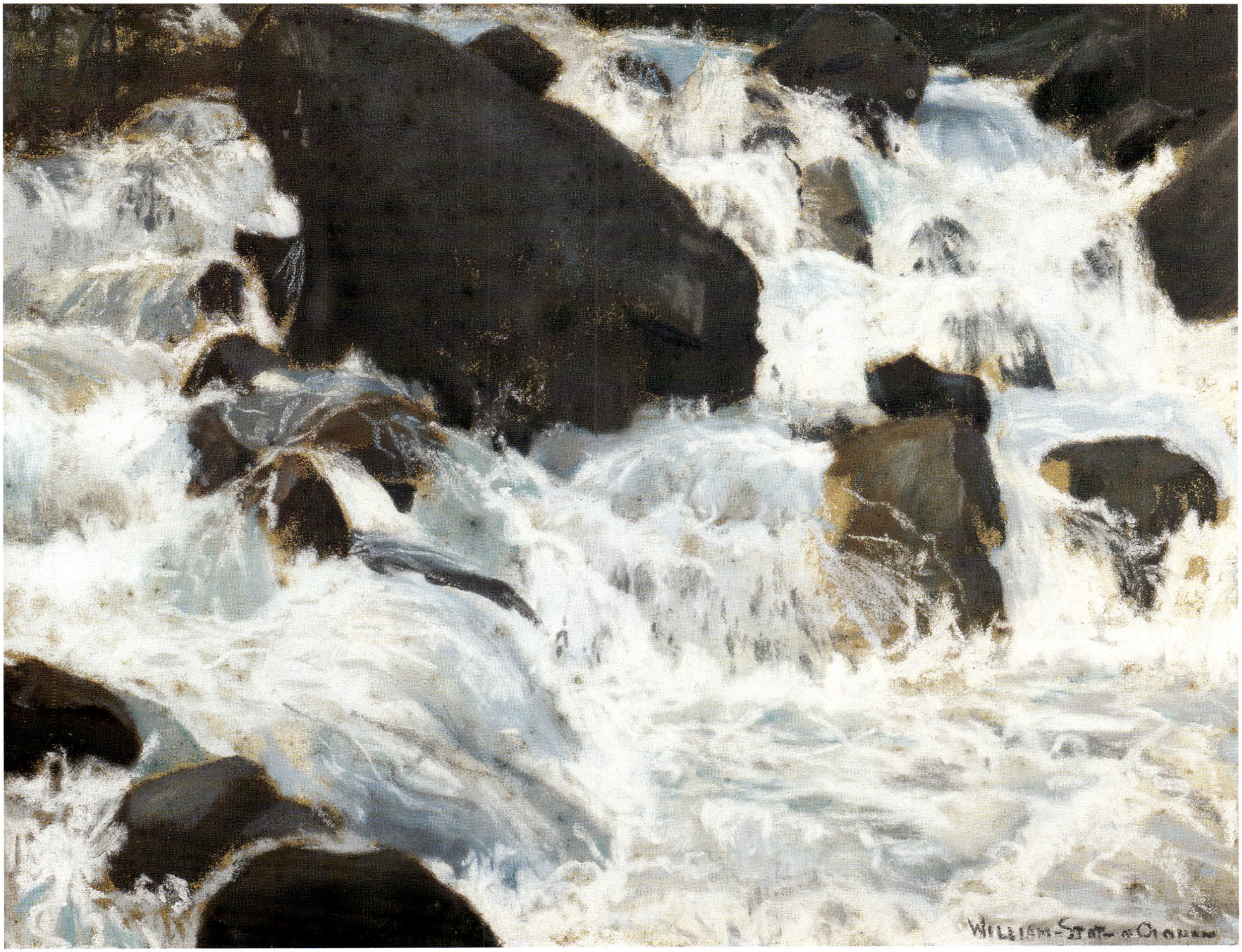

46 Schwarzer Wasserfall

1888

Signed *William Stott of Oldham*

Pastel, 24.1 × 30.8 cm (9 1/2" × 12")

Private collection

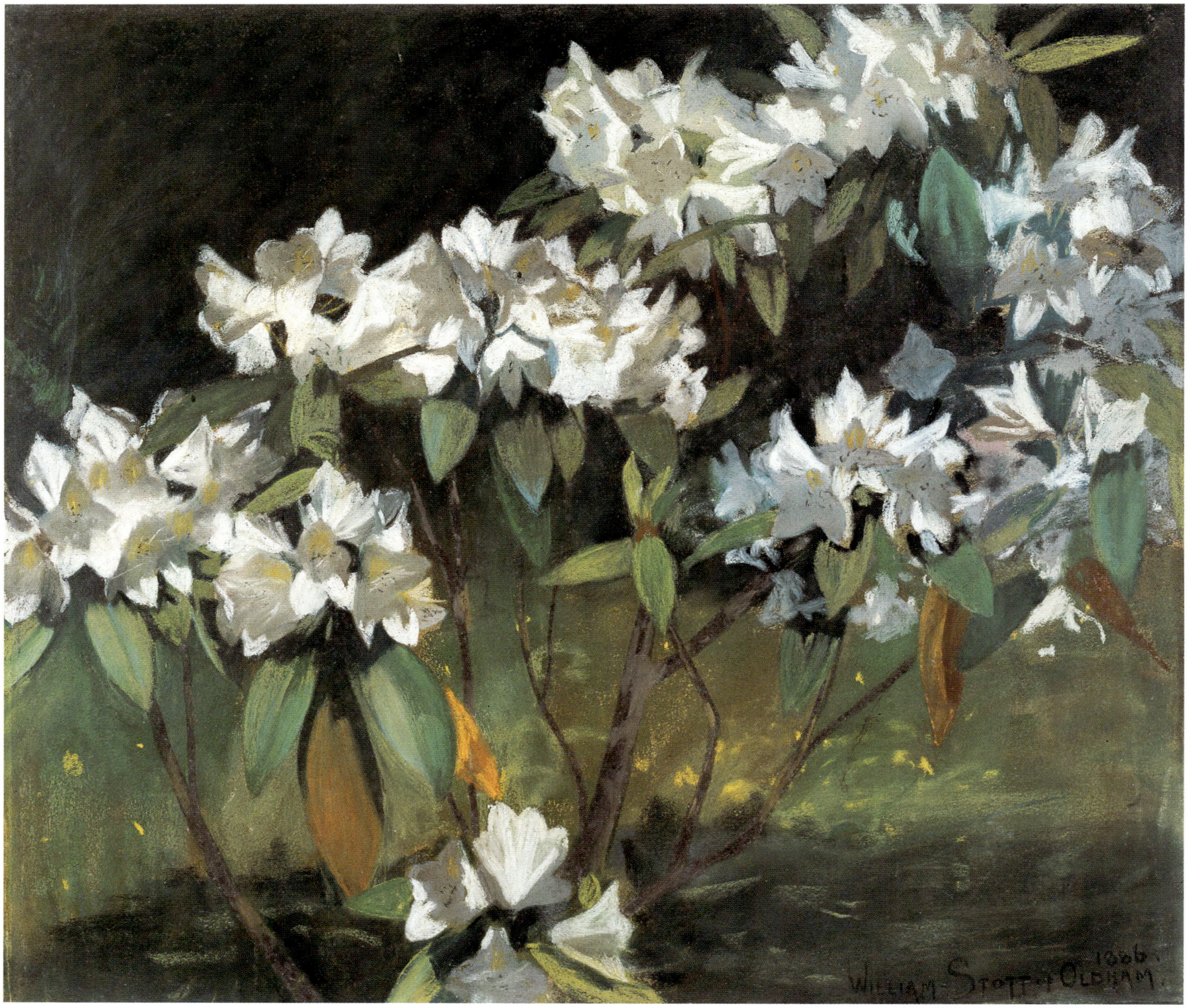

47 White Rhododendrons

1886
Signed and dated *William Stott of Oldham. 1886*
Pastel, with opaque watercolour, 45.7 x 53.3 cm
(18" x 21")
Private collection

48 Hollyhocks (Fairy Tales)

1886
Signed *William Stott of Oldham*
Oil on canvas, 121.9 x 76.2 cm (48" x 30")
Gallery Oldham

Hollyhocks is a transitional picture, perhaps even an experimental one. In his notebook Stott records, in the summer of 1886, "study of large hollyhocks – Fairy Tales (Oil)". On the same page he also notes, "Pastel large – first draught of Fairie Wood (destroyed)" and "Study of underwood for 'Nymph' (Oil)". Clearly, he was exploring new ideas, new techniques, new subject-matter that might release him from the handicap of being one of Whistler's acolytes and satisfy the fashionable demands of the Royal Academy.

We can detect in *Hollyhocks* a reference back to his earlier pictures from Grez-sur-

Loing, such as *Girl Knitting* and *Prince or Shepherd?* (cat. 8), which depicted solitary female figures in a mood of contemplation and at one with their surroundings. But Stott has moved very far from the realist mannerism of Bastien-Lepage which characterized those early works. As R.A.M. Stevenson put it in his article in *The Studio*, "During these five years Mr Stott has become less of a servant, more of a friend of nature. He dreams more; he decorates, he invents more" (October 1894, p. 14).

Thus *Hollyhocks* is a 'watershed' work which, with its bold use of colour, its decorative detail and its compositional harmony, marks a move forward into a world in which allegorical and mythological subjects were to be submerged in lush and lurid naturalism. *Hollyhocks* is unusual in Stott's oeuvre in that it shows 'nature' in the confines of a domestic garden, in which the contemporary figure of a young girl appears to be engrossed in her reading – presumably the allusion to "fairy tales".

This picture seems to presage a much later work, *Hide and Seek in the Garden of Epicurus* (cat. 67), which recalls *Hollyhocks* in its voluptuous foliage, hidden peacock and figures in perfect harmony with their natural surroundings. As in all his work, Stott strives for great accuracy in the foreground foliage and flowers, but *Hollyhocks* is painted through the eyes of an aesthete, not those of a botanist.

Though this work is listed as a "sketch" by Stott, it is possible he returned to it and developed it further for its only recorded showing in his lifetime, at the Liverpool Autumn show of 1899, where it was exhibited as *Faerie Stories* (no. 971). However, when shown at various memorial exhibitions after his death it once again had the title *Hollyhocks*.

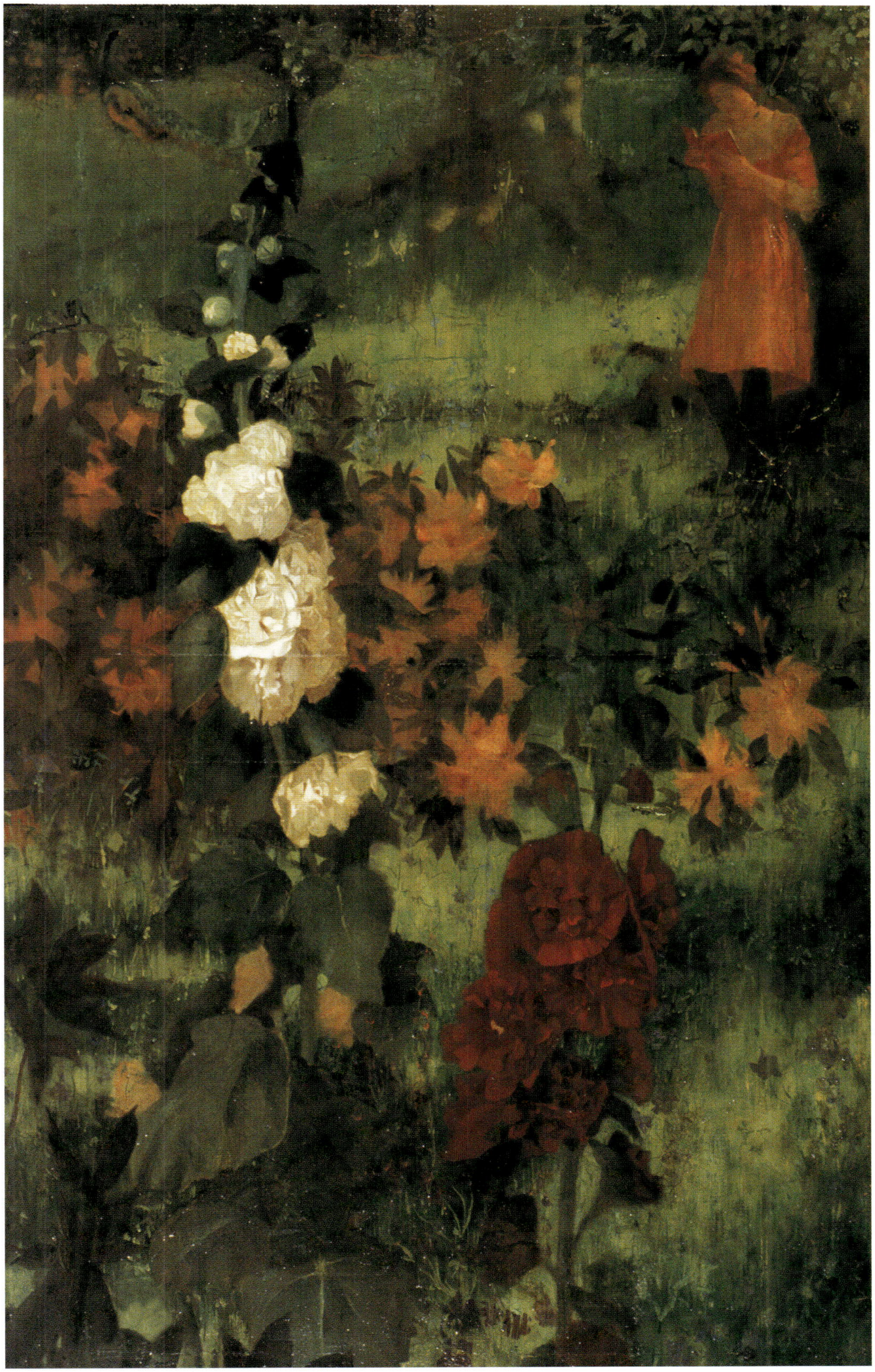

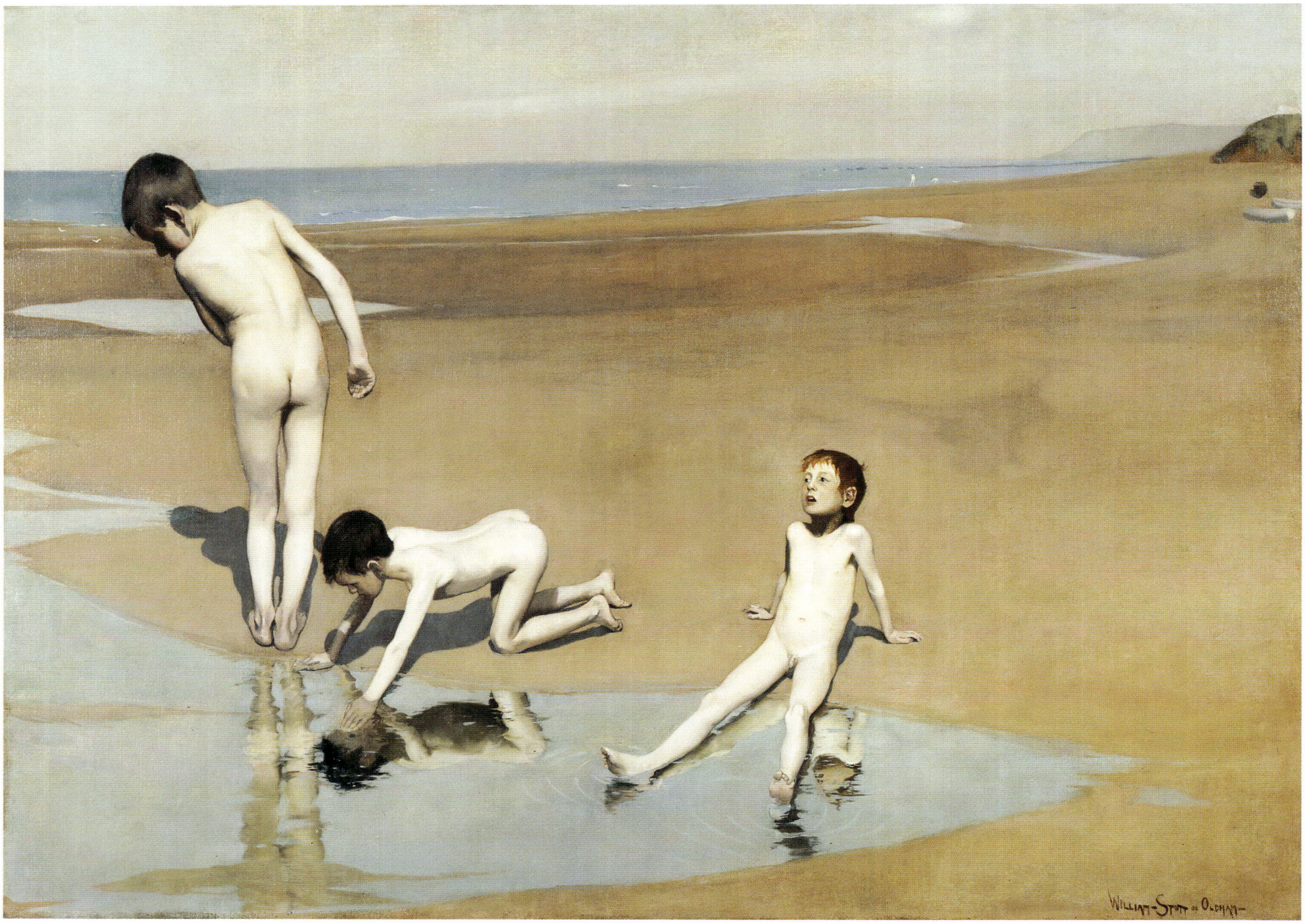

49 A Summer's Day

1886
Signed *William Stott of Oldham*
Oil on canvas, 132.7 × 189.2 cm (52¼" × 74½")
Manchester Art Gallery

Stott completed *A Summer's Day* in March 1886 and sent it off to the Salon in Paris, where it was shown without comment or controversy. But when it was shown later that year at the Society of British Artists it caused a furore among the London art critics both for its content and for its composition. Fifteen years later, after the artist's death, it was being referred to as a canvas "which will keep Stott's name alive" and a fine example of realist painting – which goes to show that fashions in art often take time to catch up with artists' intentions.

William Stott invested a great deal in *A Summer's Day*. He records several studies for the figures of the boys (see cat. 50, 51, 52) and a number of pastel sketches for the background, including *Sandpools* (cat. 24). R.A.M. Stevenson in his article in *The Studio* of 1894, before proceeding to be critical of *A Summer's Day*, acknowledged that it was "a favourite with its author" on account of the "the amount of serious work, of conscientious study that went into its making" (October 1894, p. 14). Many commentators see this work in the context of the rivalry that had existed between Stott and the American painter Alexander Harrison from their days together at Grez. In the 1885 Paris Salon Harrison had shown *Sea-side* (*Bords de Mer*, fig. 47), which also depicts a group of boys on a beach. Stott's response seems to have been immediate and something of a diversion from the path upon which his art had been developing at the time. It was to be his last realist canvas before he embarked on a series of works on allegorical and mythological themes.

A Summer's Day, with its uncluttered format and large horizontal sweeps of colour, does align Stott with Whistler's abstract values,

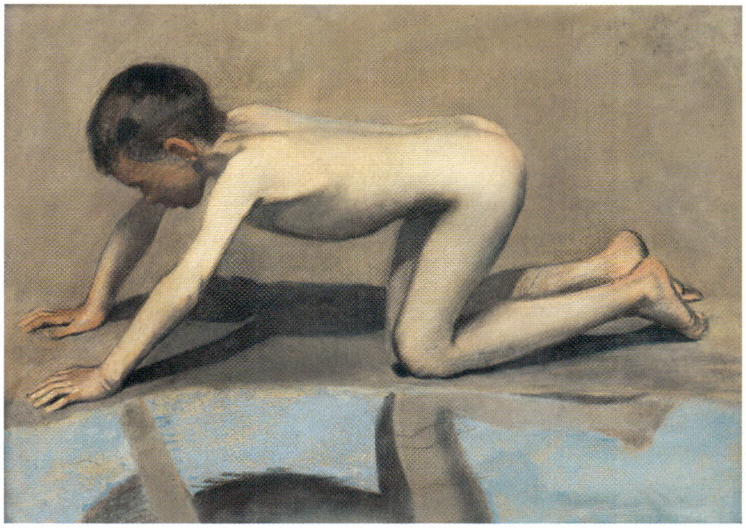

51 Study for A Summer's Day

ca. 1885–86
Unsigned
Pastel, 23.5 x 31.1 cm
(9¼" x 12¼)"
Private collection

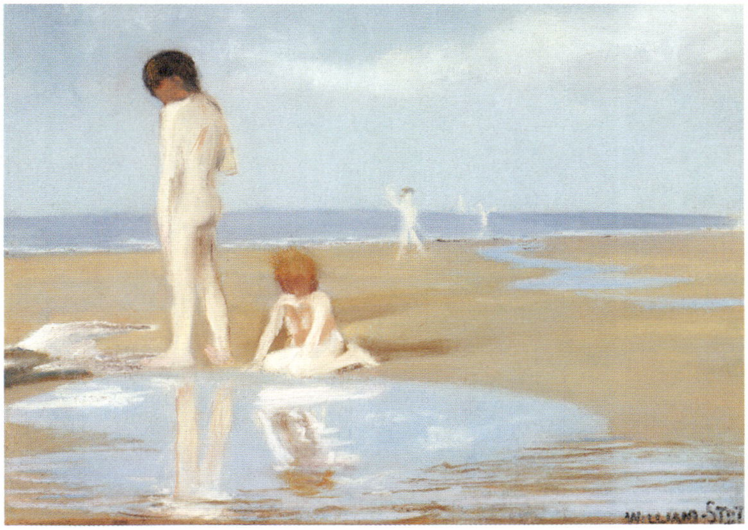

52 Study for A Summer's Day

ca. 1885–86
Signed *William Stott*
Pastel, 25.4 x 33 cm
(10" x 13")
Manchester Art Gallery

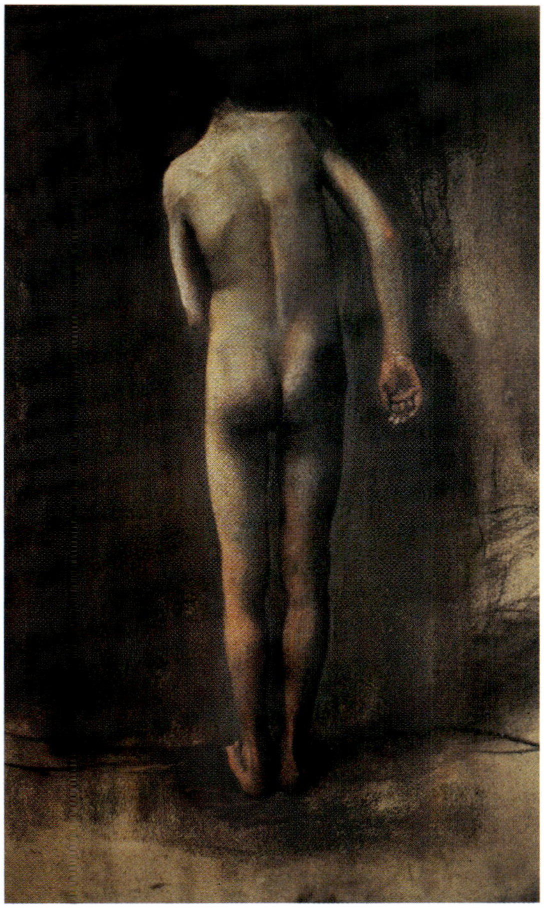

50 Study for A Summer's Day

ca. 1885–86
Unsigned
Pastel, 52,7 x 76.8 cm (20¾" x 30¼")
Atkinson Art Gallery, Southport

to which he was to remain faithful in all his pure landscape work. But the picture also has an uncomfortable quality for the viewer which, Stevenson explains, is due to the over-modelling of the figures: "The modelling is too intimate for the width of view embraced, and so the figures appear cold, frozen, and over-studied as separate objects". But Stevenson, a faithful admirer of Stott, put this "comparative failure" down to "an uncurbed delight in form and accurate draughtsmanship. … a fault which the artist in love with his work and jealous of his reputation, with difficulty amends …" (*ibid.*, p. 13).

The critics at the time of the Society of British Artists show in November 1886 were

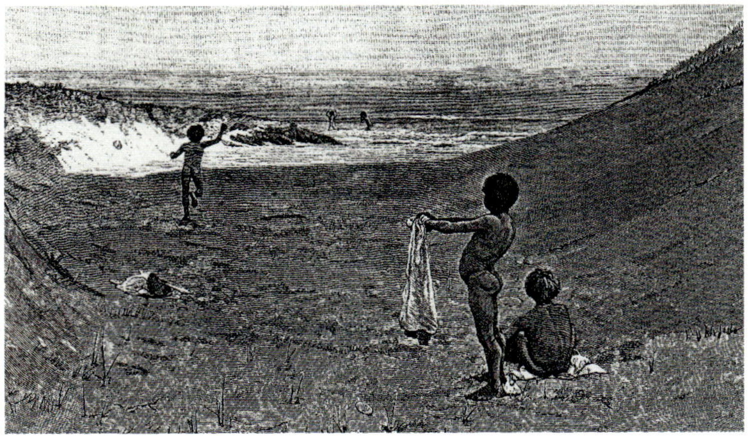

Fig. 47 Alexander Harrison (1853–1930)
Sea-side (*Bords de Mer*), 1885, Oil on canvas, destroyed

not so forgiving. *The Times* led the charge: "Mr William Stott ... distinguished himself by sending the largest, most expensive and least beautiful picture in the exhibition. In it there is a vast expanse of sand and sky, and there are three boys bathing. Apparently, they are constituted of something different from flesh, and the anatomy of the central boy passes understanding ... but still Mr Stott has his admirers ..." (17 November 1886). The *Daily News* was even more scathing: "If nature, if landscape and if boys with nothing on are as Mr Stott represents, one would prefer a different class of scenery, and be more tolerant of boys clothed and if possible in their right minds" (30 November 1886).

In spite of this slating by the critics *A Summer's Day* proved a popular picture with the public and was exhibited widely during Stott's lifetime (Paris, 1886; London, 1886; Liverpool, 1887; Manchester, 1888; Munich, 1892; Berlin, 1892; Glasgow, 1894; Brussels, 1895; St Petersburg, 1898). However, *A Summer's Day* was to be William Stott's last sally into realist art. Later in 1886 he began work on *The Nymph*, which, in its quest for absolute beauty, marks his entry into the arena of full-blooded Aestheticism.

53 Study for The Nymph

1885
Signed and dated *William Stott. 1885*
Pastel, 20.9 x 31.7 cm (8¼" x 12½")
Private collection

54 The Nymph

1886
Unsigned
Oil on canvas, 127 x 203.2 cm (50" x 80")
Glasgow Museums and Art Galleries

In the 1880s, when the Aesthetic Movement was in full swing, the portrayal of the nude as a paradigm of pure beauty had become not only acceptable but almost *de rigueur* for those who wished to enter the portals of the Royal Academy under its president Sir Frederick Leighton. It was Leighton's *Disrobing of Venus*, shown at the Royal Academy of 1867, that stimulated the 'renaissance' of the classical nude in Victorian painting. Leighton was the undisputed leader of the 'classical' strand of the Aesthetic Movement, which included such distinguished painters as George Watts, Lawrence Alma-Tadema, Edward Poynter and Albert Moore. As Christopher Wood has said, "... the election of Leighton to the Academy presidency in 1878 did give impetus to the general swing towards classical subjects, both among younger artists wanting to make their name and among older artists ready to trim their sails to the new artistic breezes blowing in from Italy and Greece" (*Victorian Painting*,

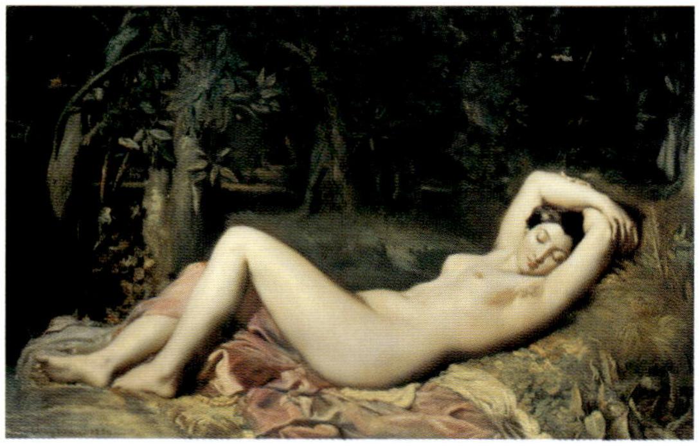

Fig. 48 Théodore Chassériau (1819–1856)
Sleeping Nymph (Baigneuse endormie près d'une source), 1850
Oil on canvas, 139.7 x 213.3 cm
Musée Calvet, Avignon

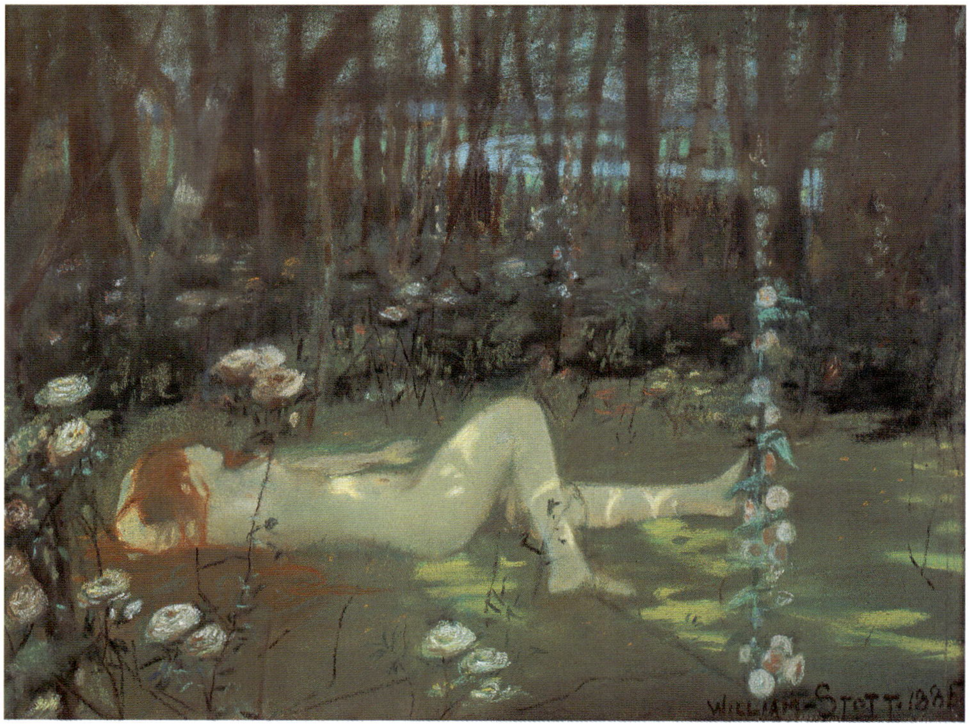

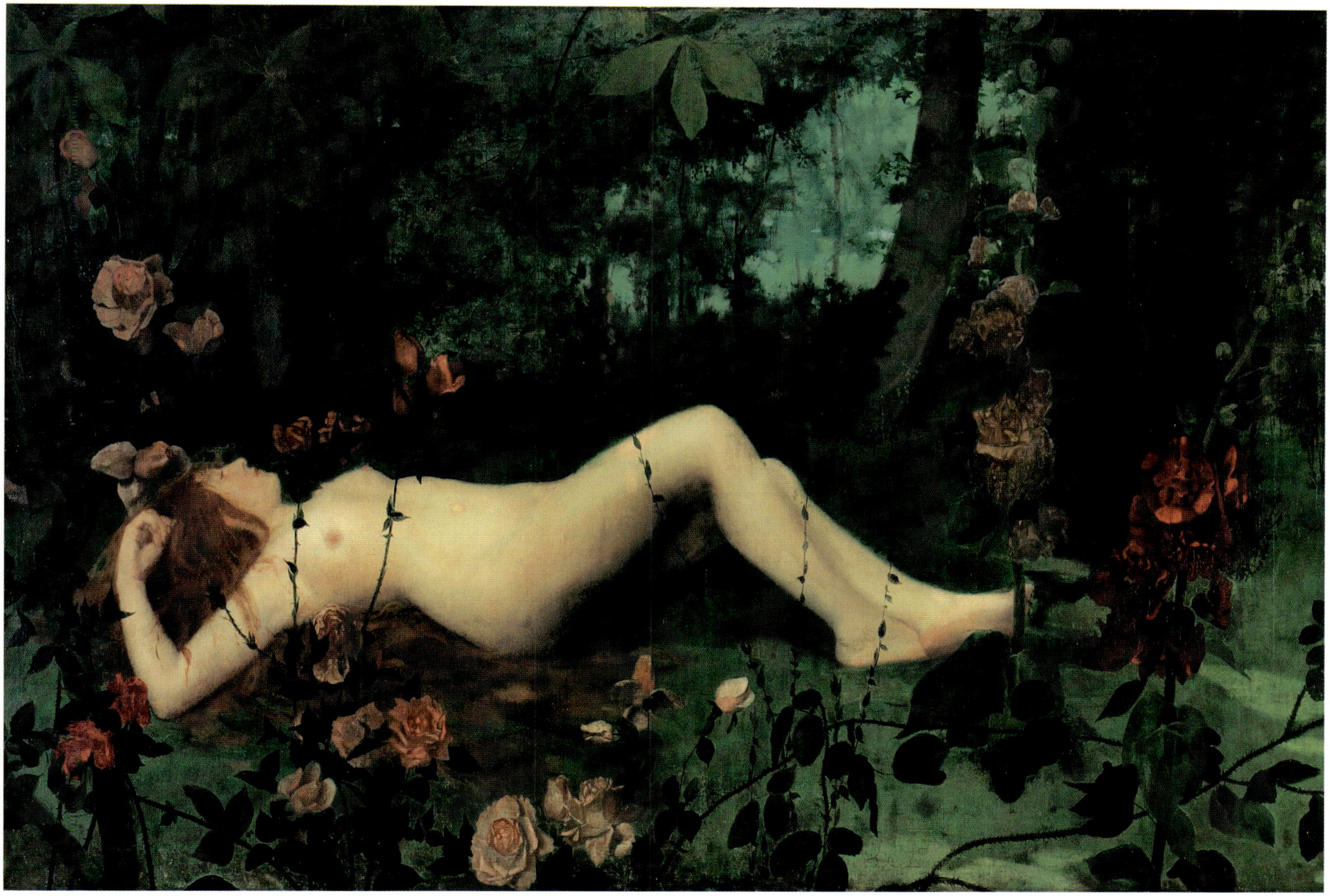

1999, p. 222). The aesthetic philosophy was by nature eclectic, "the aesthetic painter was in search of beauty, and whether he found it in Greek legend or in Arthurian legend was largely a matter of taste and temperament." (*ibid.*, p. 223). Associations with classical mythology, medieval allegory and legend helped to free the nude from any implications of impropriety and sexuality and gave a 'cover' for Victorian artists testing the boundaries of taste.

The Nymph was Stott's opening gambit in his attempt to move away from the stifling influence of Whistler and find acceptance with the art establishment as represented by the Royal Academy. The importance Stott attached to this work can be seen from the fact that he recorded several studies, beginning in 1885 (see cat. 53) and ending with a "full-sized cartoon". We also know from his notebook that he started drawing the outline in September 1886 and was still working on it at Christmas. *The Nymph* was most probably inspired by Puvis de Chavannes's *Tamaris* (*ca.* 1880), which Stott is likely to have seen in his studio in Paris. But the original inspiration for both pictures stems from the *SLeeping Nymph* (*Baigneuse endormie près d'une source*; fig. 47) by Théodore Chassériau, a painter greatly admired by Puvis and a painting widely used as a source by nineteenth-century artists.

Stott sent *The Nymph* to the 1887 spring show of the Society of British Artists. The critical reception was mixed. Some critics disliked it for its French provenance, but *The Times* offered encouragement to the artist: "At last Mr Stott seems to be condescending to the taste of those who ask in a picture for a little atmosphere and some beauty of line" (5 April 1887, p. 4). *The Nymph* proved to be a popular exhibition picture, being selected for the British Section at the 1889 Paris Exposition Universelle. Some commentators saw it as a great painting. R.A.M. Stevenson in his *Studio* article of 1894 saw it as "… one of the achievements of this century in colour as well as a true discovery in the placing, handling, and decorative adaptation of real nature". He continued, "The commonplace person accepts its truth, the visionary feels its strange vein of poetry, the decorator admires the amplitude of its lines and masses and the drowsy voluptuousness of its unity of colour" (*Studio*, October 1894, p. 14). And it seems Walter Sickert agreed: writing to *The Sun* in 1897 he recommended that Stott be elected to the Royal Academy, noting, "He has painted several masterpieces, which it does not fall to the lot of many painters to achieve in a lifetime …. His 'Wood Nymph' is a picture for the National Gallery" (*The Sun*, 10 February 1897). The immediate response to the picture in 1887 was sufficiently encouraging for William Stott to continue down the new path he had chosen, and in August that year he commenced work on his next attempt to court the art establishment, *The Birth of Venus* (cat. 55). It was to provoke a much stronger reaction!

55 The Birth of Venus

1887
Signed *William Stott of Oldham*
Oil on canvas, 187.9 x 187.9 cm (74" x 74")
Gallery Oldham

The Birth of Venus, sometimes exhibited as *Venus, Born of the Sea-Foam*, was to have been Stott's 'masterpiece', the work that would gain him attention by the English art establishment (the Royal Academy) and full membership of the Aesthetic Movement. It was a classical subject that countless artists had attempted, almost as a rite of passage. Its importance to him is indicated by the unusual exactitude of his notebook, which reads, "Begun August 24th 1887; finished November 8th 1887". It is a monumental work, larger than anything he had attempted before, and the circular format was itself designed to draw attention. For the first time Stott attached a quotation to the frame, in the manner of Dante Gabriel Rossetti and other Pre-Raphaelite painters, perhaps to add to its academic and aesthetic credibility. From the ancient Greek poet Hesiod's *Theogony*, it read: "Her, gods and men name Aphrodite, the foam-sprung goddess and fair-wreathed Cytherea".

The picture was certainly noticed, but not in the way which Stott hoped. It was slated almost unanimously by the critics as a failure. Furthermore, the model for Venus had been Maud Franklin, the long-term mistress of Whistler. The great man had not known that Maud was posing for Stott and the shock of seeing her naked at the 1887 winter exhibition of the Society of British Artists was only compounded by the vitriolic reviews the picture received – George Bernard Shaw describing Venus as looking like "an idiotic doll" (*The World*, 30 November 1887). The event led to the end of Whistler's relationship with both Maud and William Stott.

Not for the first, or last, time, Stott's intentions were misunderstood by the critics. Their views can be summed up by the report in *The Times*: "Candour again compels us to say that his ambition exceeds his ability …. The foam is hard and strange, but the treatment of the sea, in which there is good colour, is not unsuitable to the poetry of the subject. But the goddess herself – who that has ever advanced beyond Lempriere will think her Greek or divine? She is graceful, but not noble; and if she is Venus at all, she is merely Venus Pandemos. It is a great pity that the merits and high aims of the work should be thus brought to failure" (29 November 1887, p. 4). Even the normally supportive Alice Corkran, in her review of Stott's work in 1889, expressed the same sentiment: "What disappoints us is the Venus herself"; she went on to say that Stott had missed the "essential appeal" of the subject – "that of the suggestion of a spiritual beauty, of which the physical is but an emblem and token" (*Scottish Arts Review*, April 1889, p. 325).

Stott was challenging conventional notions surrounding the subject by representing a contemporary Venus in a naturalistic setting. Alexander Harrison, Stott's artistic sparring partner, had shown with success at the Salon the previous year, and in 1887 at the New English Art Club, his *In Arcadia*, which placed several nudes in the prosaic setting of a riverside orchard. To represent a nude subject on an epic scale naturalistically rather than according to classical conventions was something entirely radical for English audiences. Given his strong links with France, Stott would have been familiar with the work of Puvis de Chavannes, "a painter who saw no reason to compromise between naturalism and the poetic ideal" (Kenneth McConkey, unpublished Ms, 2003), and also the naturalist idylls of Jean-Charles Cazin, who often placed biblical and classical figures in contemporary settings.

Thus Stott's secular Venus was breaking the mould. Alison Smith regards it as "an ambitious fusion of myth and *plein-air* realism: employing the Renaissance tondo format, Stott presents a modern-day Venus whose streaming hair and open arms echo the undulations of the waves as they meet the shore" (*Exposed: The Victorian Nude,* Tate Britain, 2001, p. 222). It was clearly too 'modern-day' for most of the English critics. But in spite of its mauling from them, *The Birth of Venus* proved a popular exhibition picture both at home and abroad, and was shown at Ghent (1889), Munich (1891), Prague (1895) and Venice (1897), and at no fewer than seven different venues in Britain during Stott's lifetime.

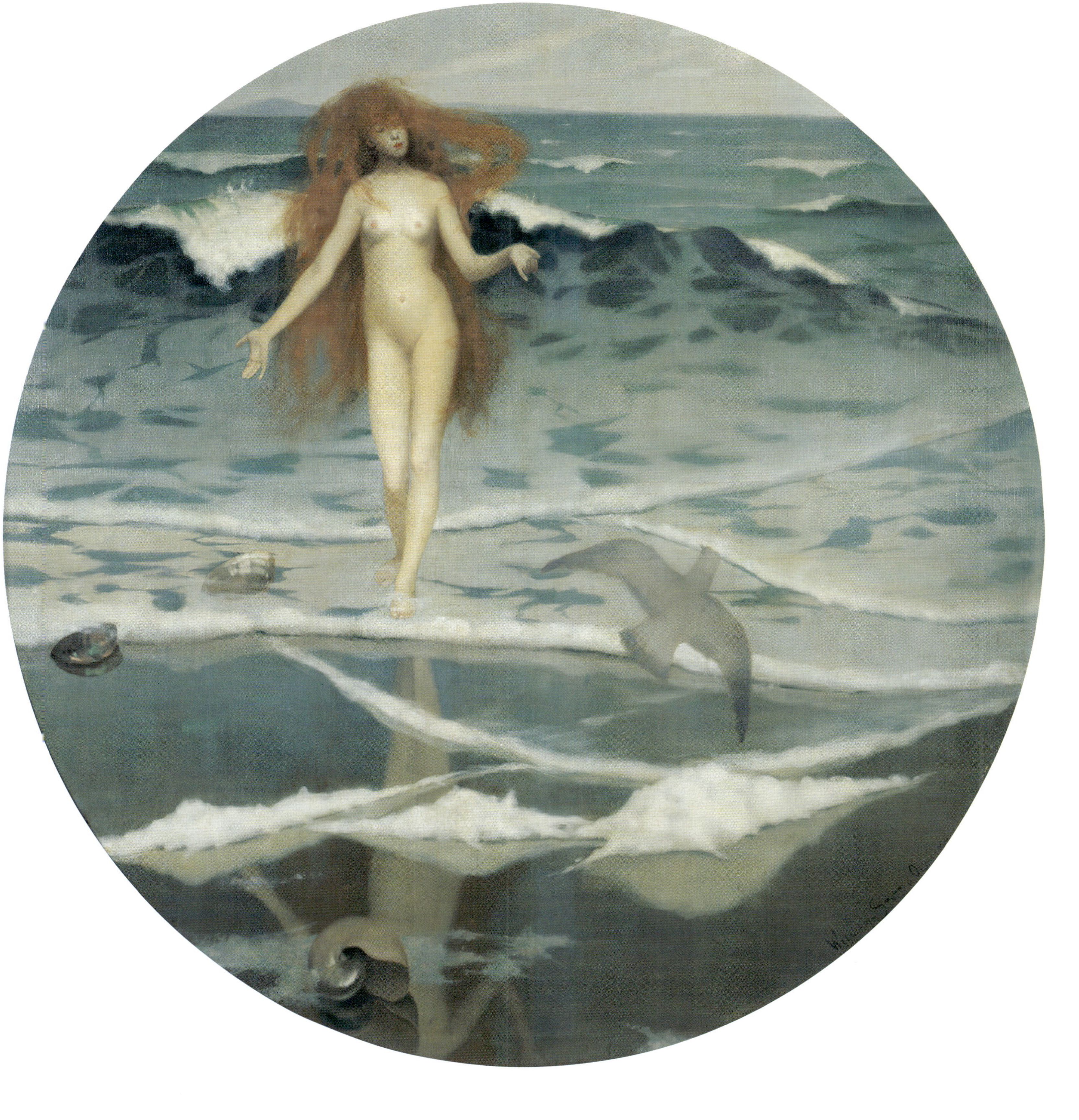

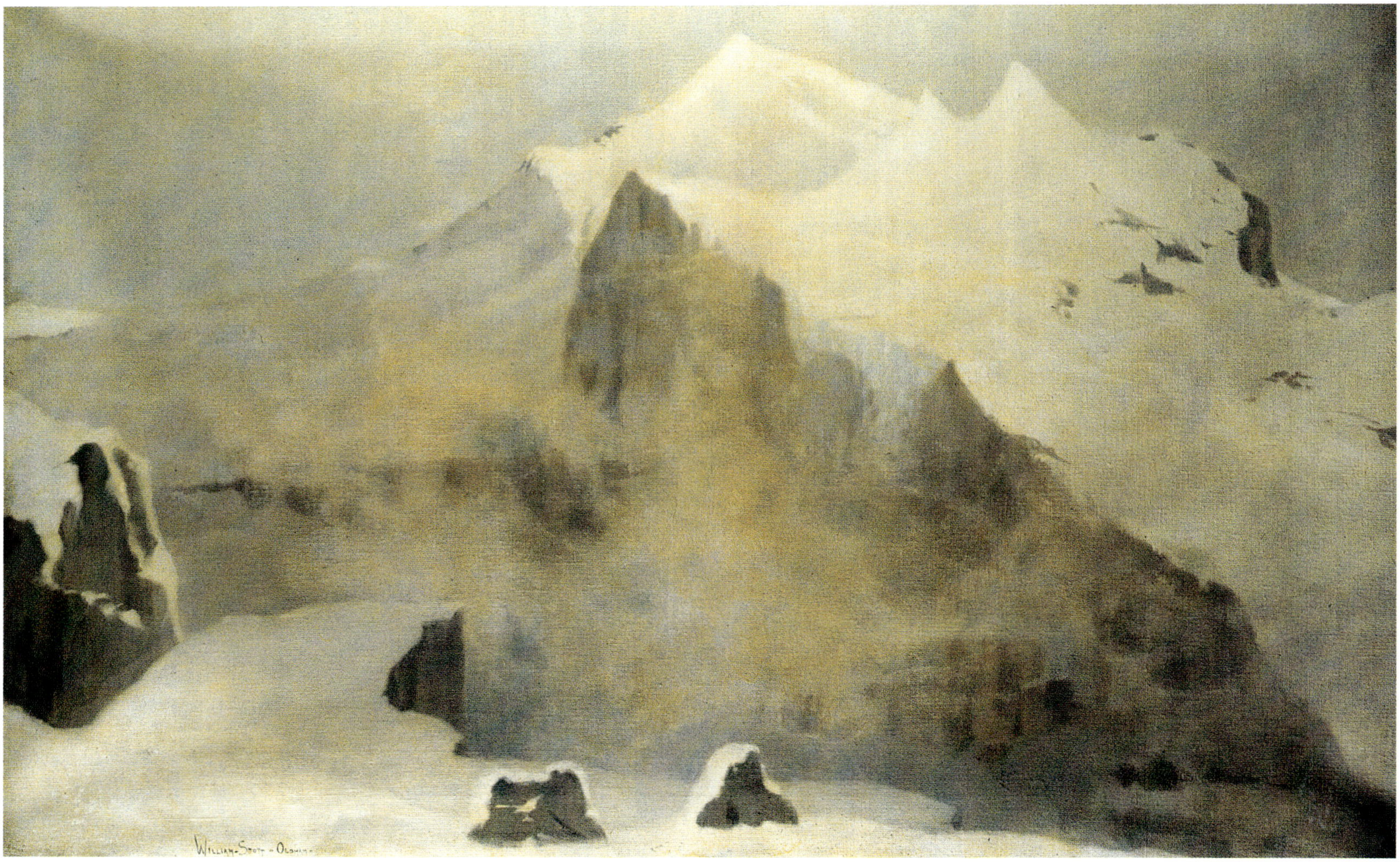

The Alps

56 Amethyst Cloud – Jungfrau

1888
Signed *William Stott of Oldham*
Oil on canvas, 91.4 x 152.4 cm (36" x 60")
Kirkcaldy Art Gallery

In the summer and autumn of 1888 Stott spent a prolific period of four months in the Swiss Alps, where he completed over thirty pastels and small oil-sketches on panel of mountain scenes, waterfalls and torrents. In October he was based at Wengen above the Lauterbrunnen Valley in the Bernese Oberland. While staying there he recorded in his notebook a pastel entitled *Jungfrau* and added later, "nearly same as Amethyst Cloud". On his return to Ravenglass he began working on a number of exhibition-size oil-paintings based on these pastels. *Amethyst Cloud: Jungfrau* was one of the first, and he recorded starting the painting on 13 December and completing it on 21 December. It was shown at the Manchester Academy of Arts spring show in 1889 and thereafter exhibited widely in his lifetime, as far afield as Munich, Prague and Stockholm. It was shown at the Paris Salon in 1893. After Stott's death in 1900 *Amethyst Cloud* was given by his widow to Tom Millie Dow, his friend and painting companion (see cat. 13), perhaps in memory of the time they spent together in Switzerland in the summer of 1888. The painting was given to Kirkcaldy Art Gallery by Florence Dow in 1926.

It seems that in visiting the Alps Stott was influenced by Ruskin's passion for the 'gloom and glory' of mountain scenery and his encouragement in his book *Modern Painters* (1860) to all artists to go to Switzerland. But although Stott's alpine views match the

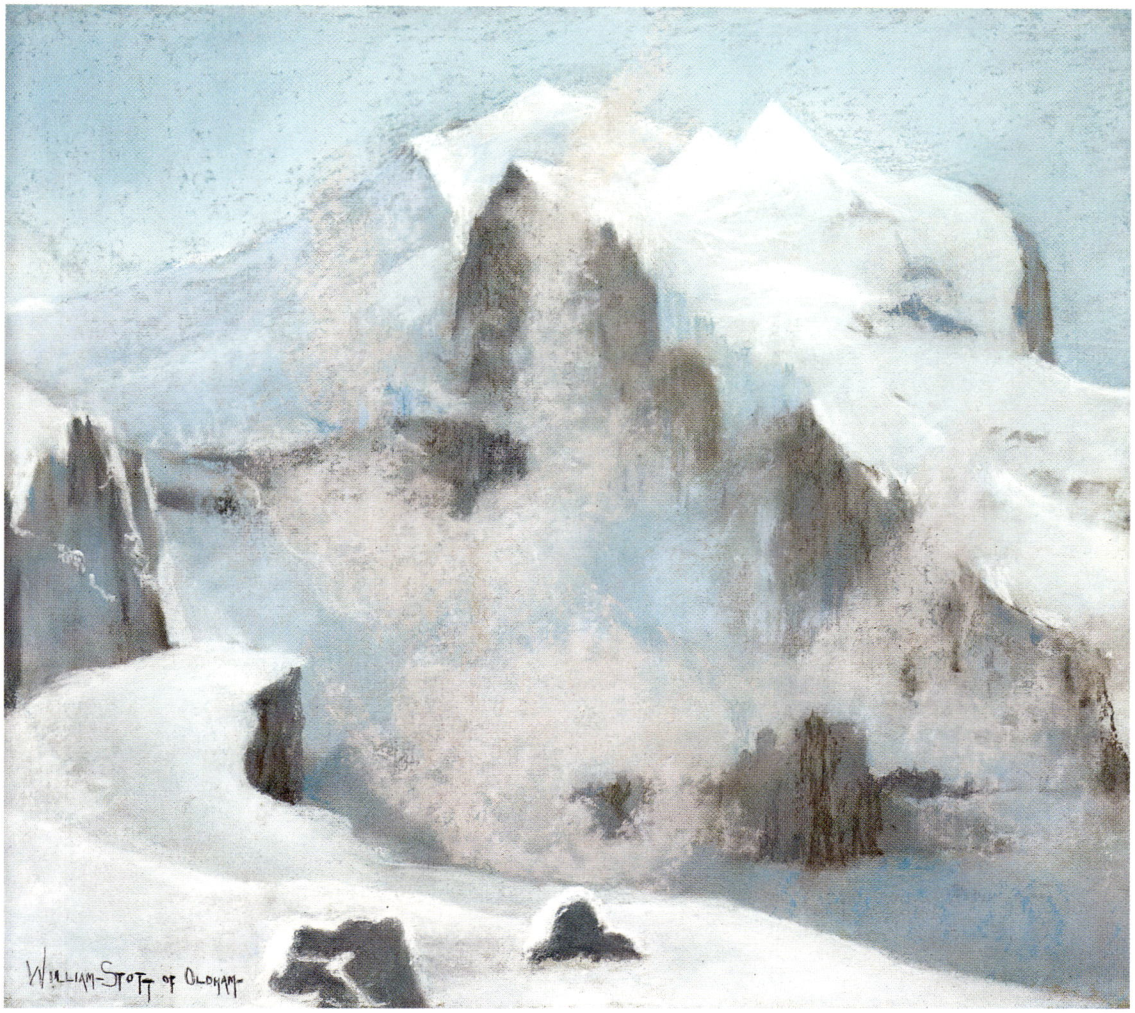

'sublime' quality found in those of J.M.W. Turner, a painter Ruskin greatly admired, they lack the human dimension found in Turner's works such as *Snow Storm: Hannibal and his Army crossing the Alps* (Tate, London). Stott depicts a heavenly solitude unsullied by evidence of the tourists who were beginning to invade the region at the time. In Alice Corkran's words, "He has brought back impressions of a charmed scene of incomparable whiteness and gleam" (*Scottish Arts Review*, April 1889, p. 325). Further praise came from R.A.M. Stevenson in *The Studio* of October 1894 (p. 15): "I know few pictures more subtle in colour than Mr Stott's large, soft and luminous views of stony peaks and white visionary glaciers. Alpine drawings, sketches, hard studies and wonderful photographs we have seen in plenty; but … Mr Stott's canvases are probably the most successful of all attempts hitherto made."

57 An Alpine Peak

1888
Signed *William Stott of Oldham*
Pastel, 45.7 x 52.7 cm (18" x 20 3/4")
Private collection

This large pastel was completed by Stott in December 1888 at Ravenglass after his return from Switzerland. He based it on a smaller pastel he had executed *en plein air* in October of the Jungfrau from Wengen, and in turn used it as a study for the large oil-painting *Amethyst Cloud: Jungfrau* (cat. 56). In 1896 he gave the large pastel to Sir Thomas Hall Caine (1853–1931), a novelist and journalist who wrote an effusive introduction to the catalogue for the one-man show Stott held at the Goupil

Gallery, London, in April of that year. He began, "I would say at the outset that the distinguishing characteristic of the paintings gathered together for this exhibition is their poetic imagination," and he went on to single out *Amethyst Cloud* as an outstanding canvas, "with its awesome majesty, its stark whiteness, its sense of a scene aloof from all human interest and beyond the touch of the little hand of man …". He ended by saying, "In these canvases, I think the spirit of Keats is expressed as it has never been expressed before – Keats in his love of beauty and in his love of colour, Keats in his power of vision and his delight in dream" (*Envoi*, in *Pictures by William Stott of Oldham*, The Goupil Gallery, April–May 1896).

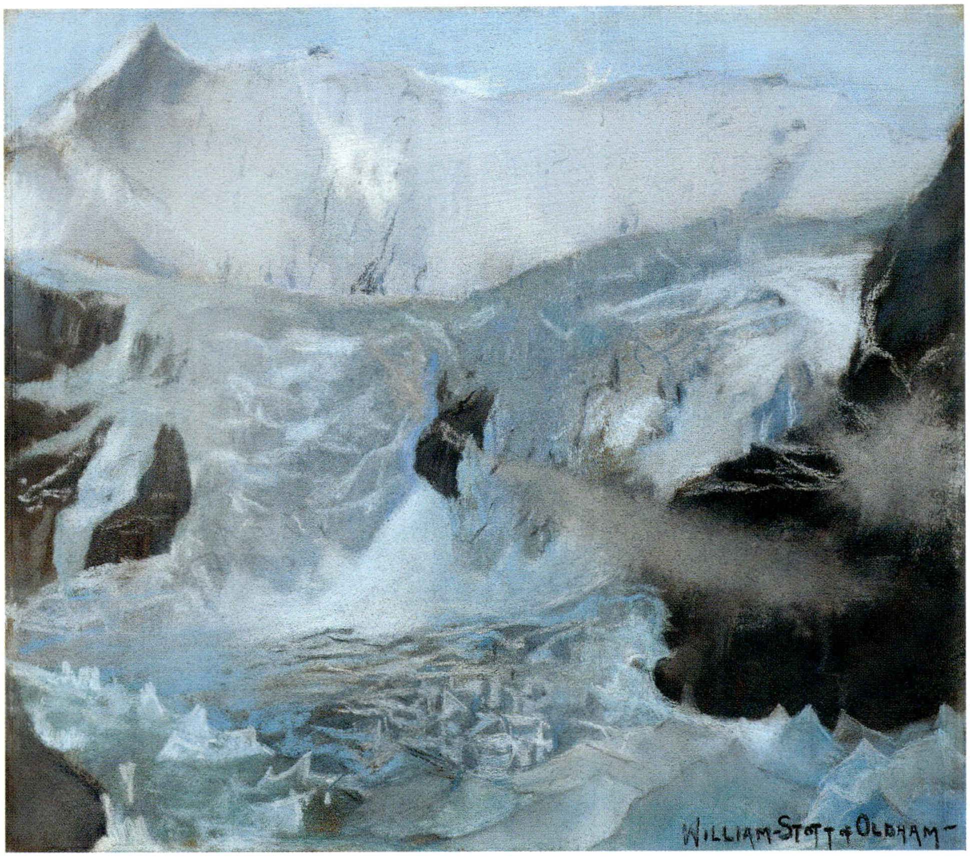

58 The Fischerhorn Glacier
1888
Signed *William Stott of Oldham*
Pastel, 24.7 x 32.4 cm (9¾" x 12¾")
The National Galleries of Scotland

59 The White Mountain
1888
Signed *William Stott of Oldham*
Oil on canvas, 94.6 x 144.8 cm (37¼" x 57")
Gallery Oldham

After Stott's death there was an uncommon consensus among the critics that his Alpine scenes represented some of his most accomplished and individual work. Reviewing his memorial exhibition in London in 1901 a contributor to the *Magazine of Art* wrote, "He excels exactly in those works which the public is least likely to recognise: by his pictures of Alpine heights and Alpine snows, in which the vast stillness is rendered by the most delicate passages of dainty colour. Here we see an elegance and refinement not too common nowadays …" (December 1901, p. 82).

Kenneth McConkey has written, "The important distinction between Stott's paintings and those of earlier painters of Alpine scenes

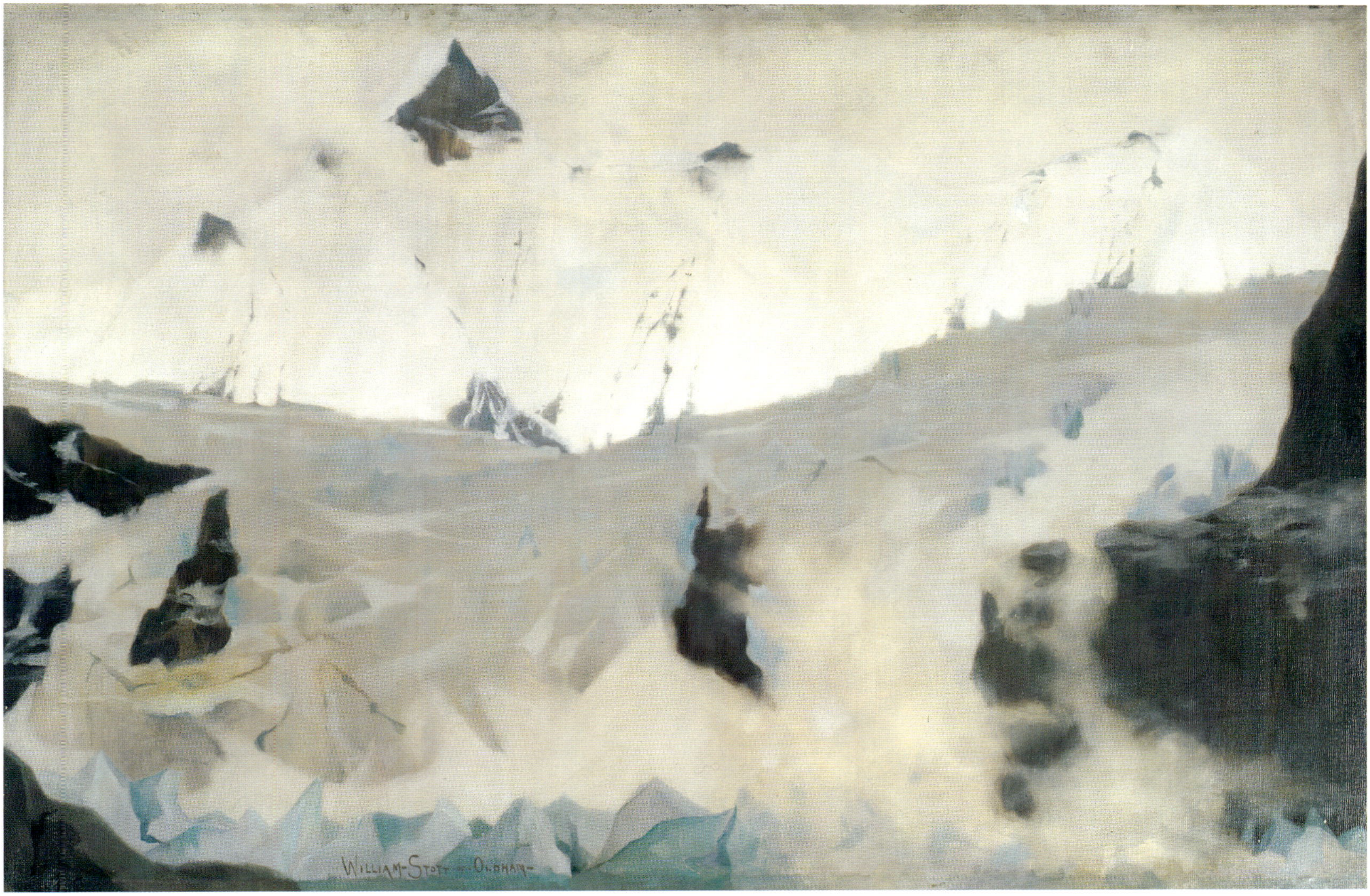

… was that he took an airborne view, while they led the viewer into the space of the picture using pathways from the immediate foreground … [Stott] placed himself in extreme conditions, viewing the frieze of mountain peaks from a high position. There is no foreground and thus an immediate sense of spatial relationship to the immensity is denied. No groups of holiday-makers, hill-walkers or skiers take us into these spaces and forms" (Kenneth McConkey, unpublished Ms, 2003).

In 1888, while in the Swiss Alps, Stott produced over thirty *plein-air* sketches, mainly in pastel. On his return to England he began to work up a number of these sketches into large exhibition oil-paintings. *The White Mountain* was the first of these and was developed from a pastel originally entitled "Eismeer and Mountain (lilac) 'Fischerhorn'" (cat. 58). It is a view of the Fischerhorn mountain in the Bernese Oberland. But Stott was not concerned with topographical accuracy, or, as R.A.M. Stevenson put it in his essay in *The Studio* of 1894, "… these pictures are not for the Alpine climber who wishes to retrace his perilous route. Mr Stott has chosen at any price to give us some of the beautiful qualities of the hills, and he steeps us in dreamy visions of delicate colour and exquisitely soft definition" (October, p. 15). In *The White Mountain*, with its emphasis on white harmonies, Stott achieves a poetic fusion of Whistler's aesthetic values which conveys a mystical and abstract quality.

Stott sent *White Mountain* to be exhibited at Les XX in Brussels in the spring of 1889. Thereafter it was a popular exhibition picture and was eventually shown at the Paris Salon in 1898. It was bought in 1902 by Oldham Corporation from his memorial exhibition at Manchester. The *Oldham Chronicle*, reporting the purchase, commented, "The committee are to be congratulated upon the choice of the 'White Mountain', a beautiful example of the artist's treatment of alpine scenery and atmosphere …. There is no doubt as to the charm of the picture and its intrinsic worth; it is one of the artist's best" (29 January 1902).

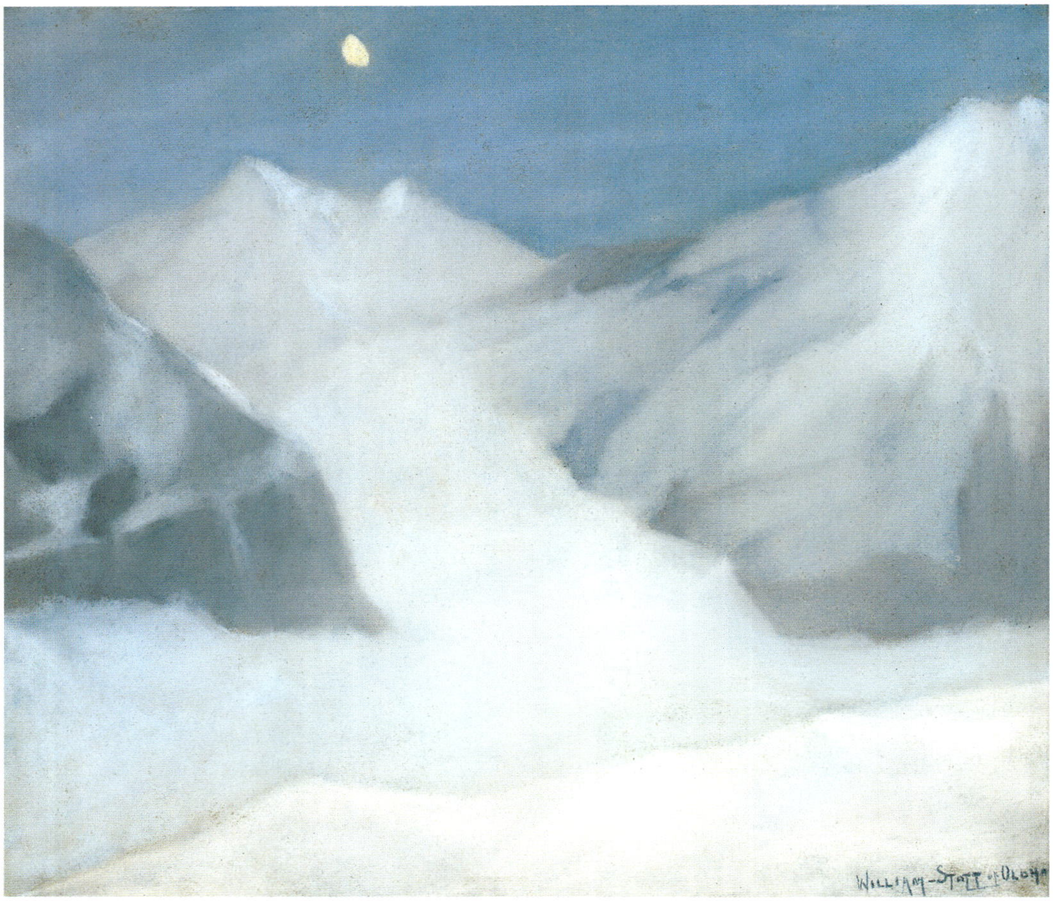

60 Mountain Peak by Moonlight

1888
Signed *William Stott of Oldham*
Pastel, 45.1 x 52.4 cm ($17\frac{3}{4}$" x $20\frac{3}{4}$")
Private collection

61 Alps by Night

ca. 1892
Signed *William Stott of Oldham*
Oil on canvas, 95.2 x 146.7 cm ($37\frac{1}{2}$" x $57\frac{3}{4}$")
Walker Art Gallery, Liverpool

We know that Stott camped out "among the frozen altitudes of the Jungfrau, and watched, through the night till dawn, the white world given over to the sway of the September moon" (Alice Corkran, *Scottish Arts Review*, April 1889, p. 325). His initial attempt to capture the scene was the pastel he recorded as "Moonlight 'White Glacier'" (cat. 60). However, in 1892 William Stott was invited to join the hanging committee for the Liverpool Autumn Exhibition (see fig. 34, p. 42) and, perhaps feeling obliged to produce a new, unexhibited painting, he worked this sketch up in oils into the *Alps by Night*. Interestingly, what was a straightforward topographical sketch turns into something altogether more abstract, dreamy and visionary, whether as a result of the passage of time, or as a deliberate attempt to offer a more Aesthetic interpretation.

Alice Corkran refers to William Stott's art as "drenched in a sort of Pantheism" (*ibid.*, p. 322), and Richard Whiteing in his tribute in the catalogue to Stott's London memorial exhibition in 1901 said of pictures such as *Alps by Night*, *Amethyst Cloud: Jungfrau* (cat. 56) and *White Mountain* (cat. 59) that they were "superb compositions breathing the very spirit of nature and bearing her message of dignity, repose and peace" (*William Stott and his Work, Pictures by William Stott of Oldham*, Royal Watercolour Society, October 1901).

Liverpool Corporation, after much controversy, decided to purchase *Alps by Night*. At that time the city was fortunate in having a forward-thinking Chairman of the Library, Museums and Arts Committee in Philip Henry Rathbone, who was the younger son of one of Liverpool's most distinguished and successful merchant families (see Edward Morris, *Victorian & Edwardian Paintings in the Walker Gallery and at Sudley House*, 1996, pp. 10–15). Rathbone dominated institutional art in Liverpool during the last thirty years of the century. His policy was to buy a limited number of paintings by young contemporary artists of promise, and under his regime Liverpool acquired outstanding early works of the Newlyn School, the New English Art Club and the Glasgow School.

In 1892 Rathbone persuaded the Committee to recommend the purchase from the Autumn Exhibition of Stott's *Alps by Night* and of *Summer* by E.A. Hornel, one of the 'Glasgow Boys'. The City Council referred the decision back to the Committee as they thought these paintings "were too experimental". Alderman Rathbone said he would resign if the purchase were not approved and such was his influence that he won the day.

George Moore, writing in *The Speaker* later in 1892 under the heading 'The Alderman in Art', derided the fact that such decisions were made by mere councillors. He reported, "Last month Liverpool County Council assembled to discuss the purchase of two pictures recommended by the art committee – 'Summer' by Mr Hornel; and 'The Higher

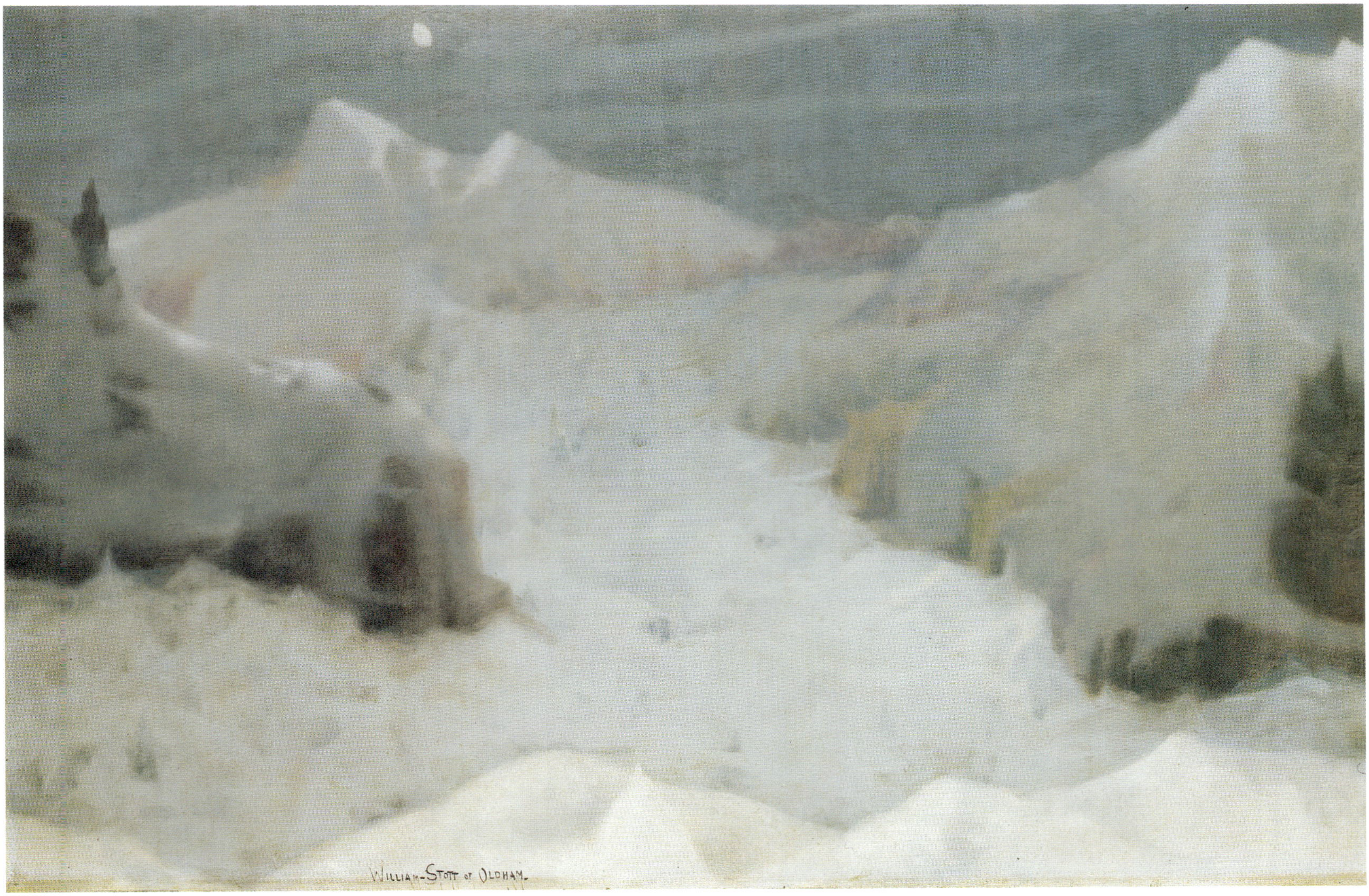

Alps' [*sic*] by Mr Stott of Oldham. The discussion that ensued is described by the Liverpool Daily Post as 'amusing'. It was ludicrous, and those who do not care a snap of the fingers about art might think it amusing. The joke was started by Mr Lynskey, who declared that the two pictures in question were mere daubs .... The next speaker was Mr Burgess. He could not imagine how anyone could recommend the purchase of such pictures. This does not surprise me. The Mr Burgesses of twenty-five years ago could not understand how anyone could buy Corots .... Then someone said – I think it was Mr Smith – that the pictures had horrified him: whereupon there was more laughter. Then a member proposed that they should have the pictures brought in, to which proposition another member objected, amid much laughter. Then Mr Daughan suggested that the chairman and vice-chairman should explain the meaning of the pictures to the council. More laughter and more County Council humour. The meeting was a typical meeting .... Next week I will show why a corporation cannot manage a picture gallery, and explain the advantages of a director" (22 October 1892, p. 497).

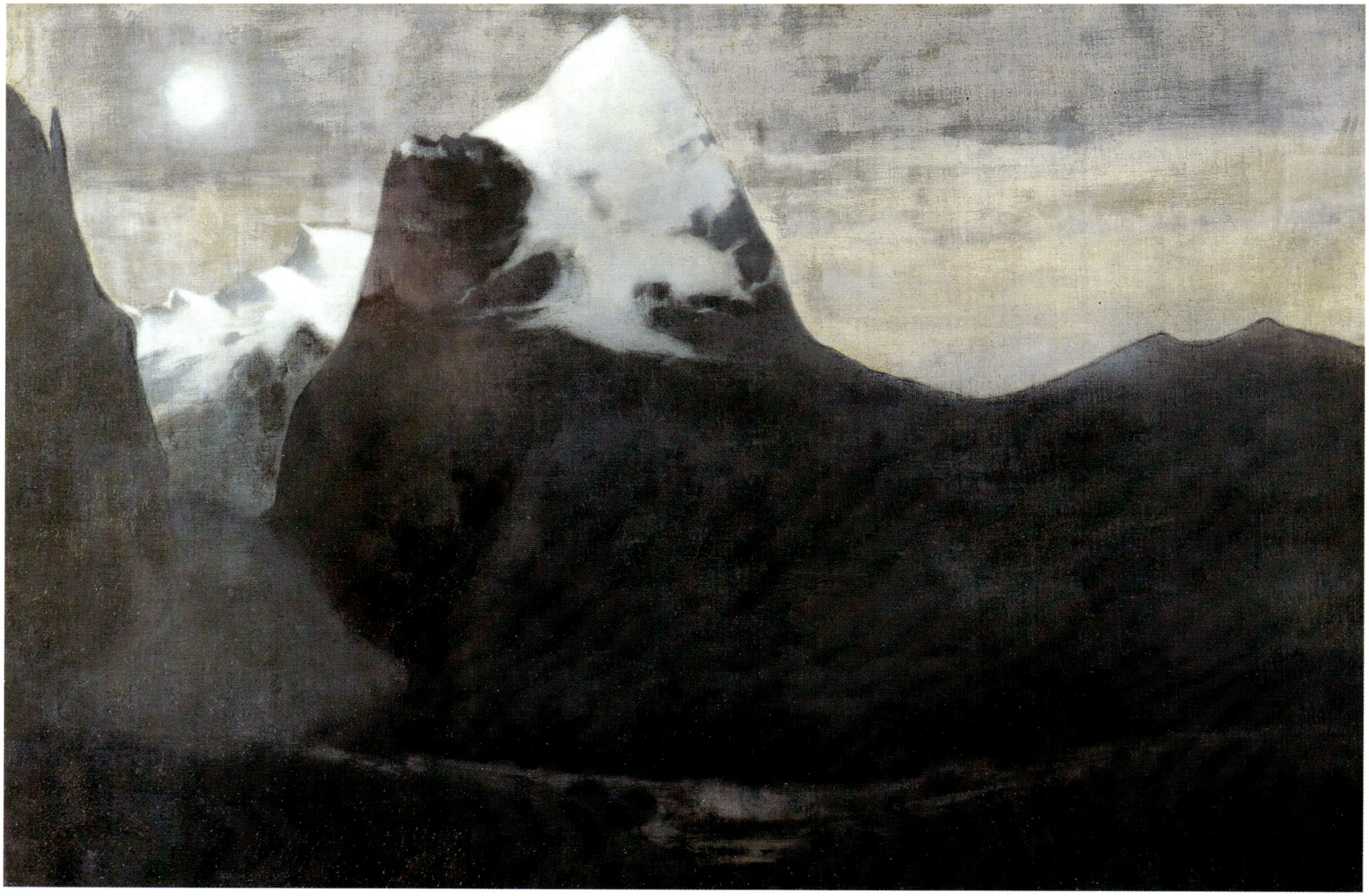

62 The Eiger

ca. 1889

Signed *William Stott of Oldham*

Oil on canvas, 94.6 x 149.2 cm (37¼" x 58¾")

Manchester Art Gallery

63 Ice River

1888
Signed *William Stott of Oldham*
Pastel, 22.8 x 31.1 cm (9" x $12^{1}/_{4}$")
The Whitworth Art Gallery, University of Manchester

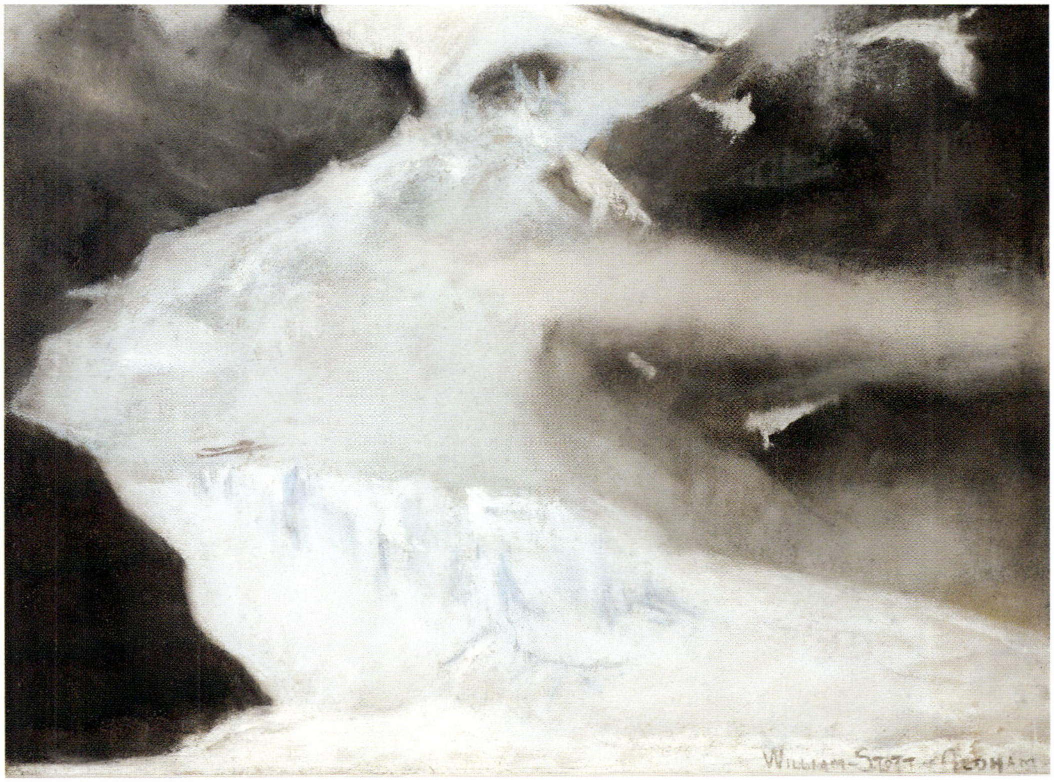

64 Turquoise Glacier

1888
Signed; detail only shown
Pastel, 44.4 x 52.1 cm ($17^{1}/_{2}$" x $20^{1}/_{2}$")
Atkinson Art Gallery, Southport

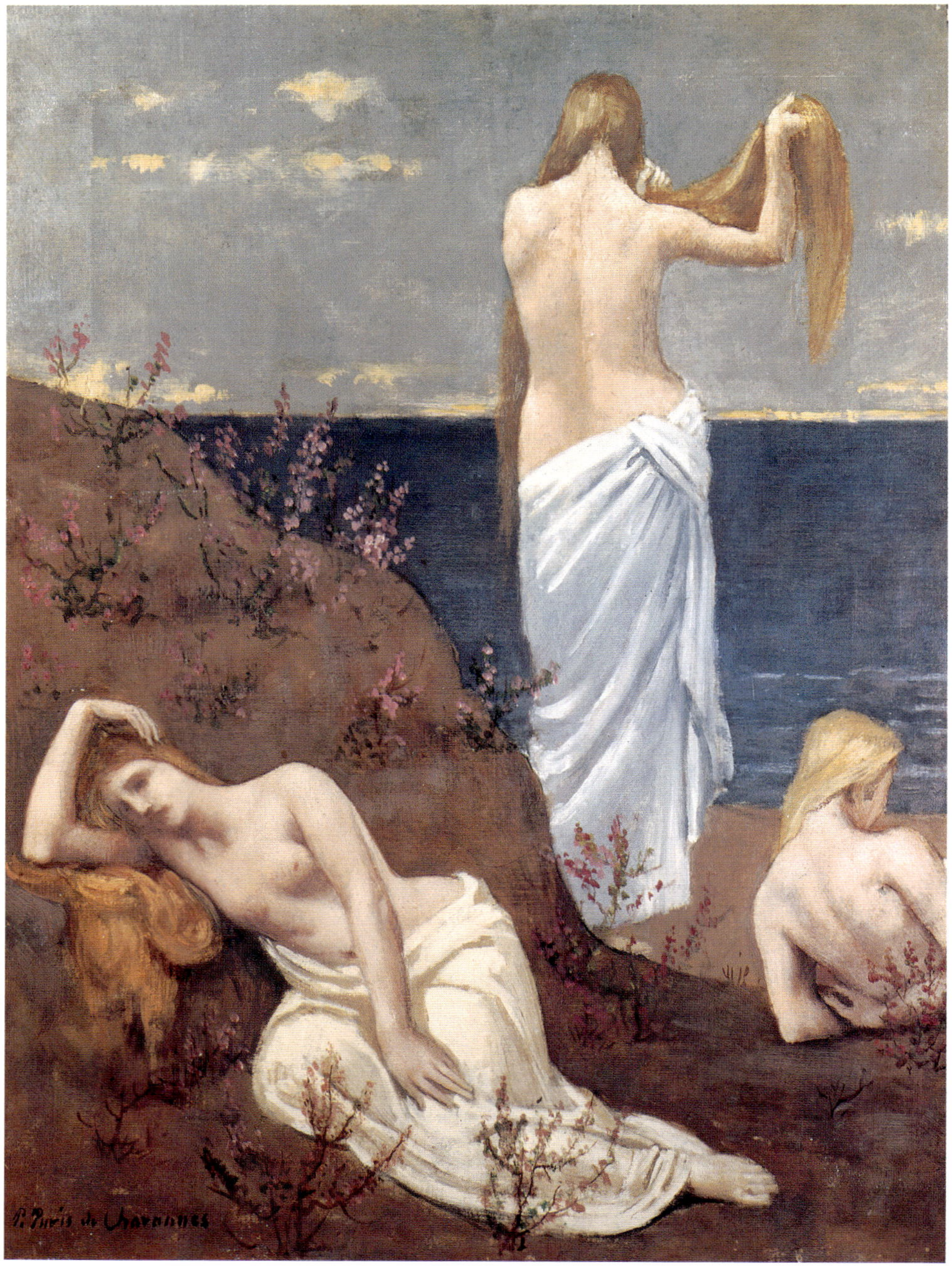

Fig. 49 Puvis de Chavannes (1824–1898)
Young Girls by the Sea (Jeunes filles au bord de la mer),
ca. 1879
Oil on panel, 205 × 154 cm
Musée d'Orsay, Paris

65 Idlers

ca. 1896
Signed *William Stott of Oldham*
Oil on canvas, 71.1 × 106.7 cm (28" × 42")
Private collection

This was one of Stott's more successful portrayals of the female figure. It seems to be a deliberate pastiche of *Young girls by the sea* (*Jeunes Filles au bord de la mer*; fig. 49) by one of Stott's artist heroes, the French Symbolist painter Puvis de Chavannes, even down to the small flowering shrubs superimposed against the figures and the prevailing mood of *ennui.*

In so doing Stott has performed a remarkable illusion. He has taken the familiar motifs of the Ravenglass foreshore and sand-dunes and transformed this bleak, wind-swept Cumbrian coastline into a believeable impression of the Aegean with Grecian maidens enjoying the Mediterranean sun. The classical buildings of an ancient city on the skyline add credence to this chimera.

Idlers seems to link Stott to the 'Olympians', a strand of Aestheticism promoted by the artists Sir Lawrence Alma-Tadema, Albert Moore, Sir Edward Poynter and Lord Leighton. Admiration for Greek and Roman culture was deeply ingrained in all aspects of Victorian life. Christopher Wood has written, "The Victorian vision of antiquity was a deeply romantic one; they looked back wistfully to the past as to a golden, far simpler, nobler and more inspiring world than their own. Their art was an expression of a desire to escape the ugliness, materialism and industrialism of their own age" (*Olympian Dreamers*, 1983, p. 17).

In *Idlers* Stott catches this contemplative nostalgia for a bygone age more successfully than in his other 'classical' works such as *The Happy Valley* (fig. 36, p. 44) and *Hide and Seek* (cat. 67). The picture was well received at the Royal Academy in 1896 and the *Art Journal* reproduced it full-page, commenting, "The picture is one that is bound sooner or later to be looked on as a masterpiece. The delicate treatment of this charming subject is well represented in our reproduction" (June 1896, p. 178).

It was shown at the Paris Salon in 1897 but was subsequently exhibited very little and remains in the family.

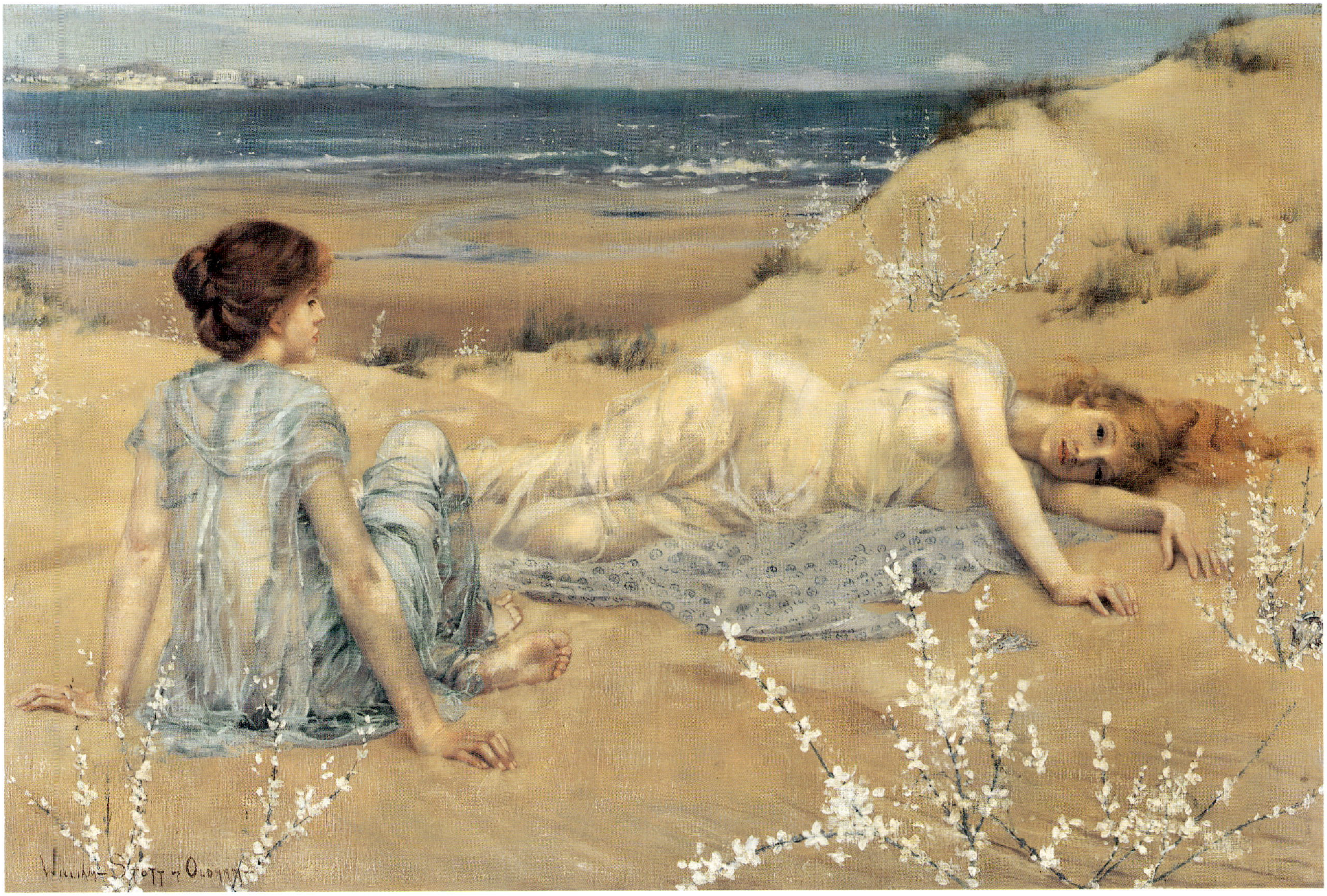
William Scott of Oldham

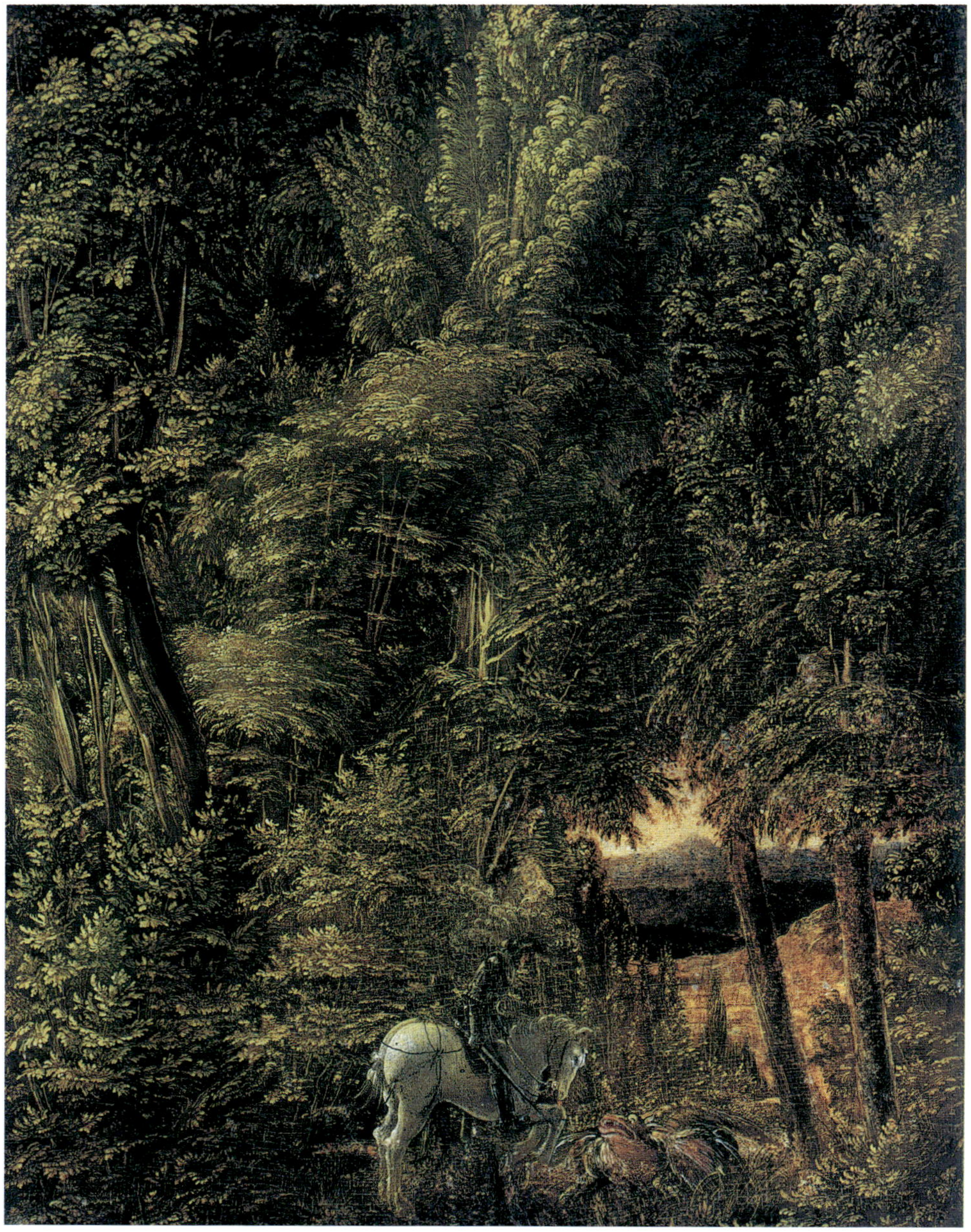

Fig. 50 Albrecht Altdorfer (*ca.* 1480–1538)
St George, 1511
Oil on panel
Alte Pinakothek, Munich

65 The Fairie Wood

1893
Signed *William Stott of Oldham*
Oil on canvas, 111.8 x 142.2 cm (44" x 56")
Atkinson Art Gallery, Southport

The revival of interest in medievalism in the second half of the nineteenth century led to a plethora of pictures on the walls of the Royal Academy depicting scenes from legend and the age of chivalry. This fascination was both reflected in, and promoted by, the work of the Pre-Raphaelite Brotherhood. The enchantment with this period was taken up later by numerous artists such as Sir Frank Dicksee, Frederick Sandys, Sir Edward Burne-Jones and J.W. Waterhouse, whose *Lady of Shalott* (1888; Tate, London) and *La Belle Dame sans Merci* (1893; Hessisches Landesmuseum, Darmstadt) illustrate the parallel interest in supporting literary sources. As well as the poetry of Keats and Tennyson, earlier works such as Spenser's *Faerie Queen*, an allegorical romance of chivalry, were enjoying a renewed popularity.

The Fairie Wood bears a striking similarity to Albrecht Altdorfer's *St George*, which Stott might have seen when his paintings were exhibited in Munich in 1892. The description of *St George* by Kenneth Clark in *Landscape into Art* could equally apply to *The Fairie Wood*. He wrote, "In it man, even though he be St George, almost disappears in the luxuriance of the forest. Trees fill every inch of the picture, not the orderly, decorative trees of tapestry landscape, with their gifts of fruit and blossom, but menacing, organic growth, ready to smother and strangle any intruder" (edn 1979, p. 75). In Stott's obsession with subordinating the human presence to a mere detail within the harmony of nature his anonymous knight is almost lost to the viewer behind the woodland screen. Painstaking care is taken with every leaf, every frond and every flower, and increasingly one feels in his later pictures, such as this, *The Awakening of the Spirit of the Rose* (fig. 35, p. 43), *Happy Valley* (fig. 36, p. 44) and *Hide and Seek* (cat. 67), that the foliage canopy is becoming the real subject.

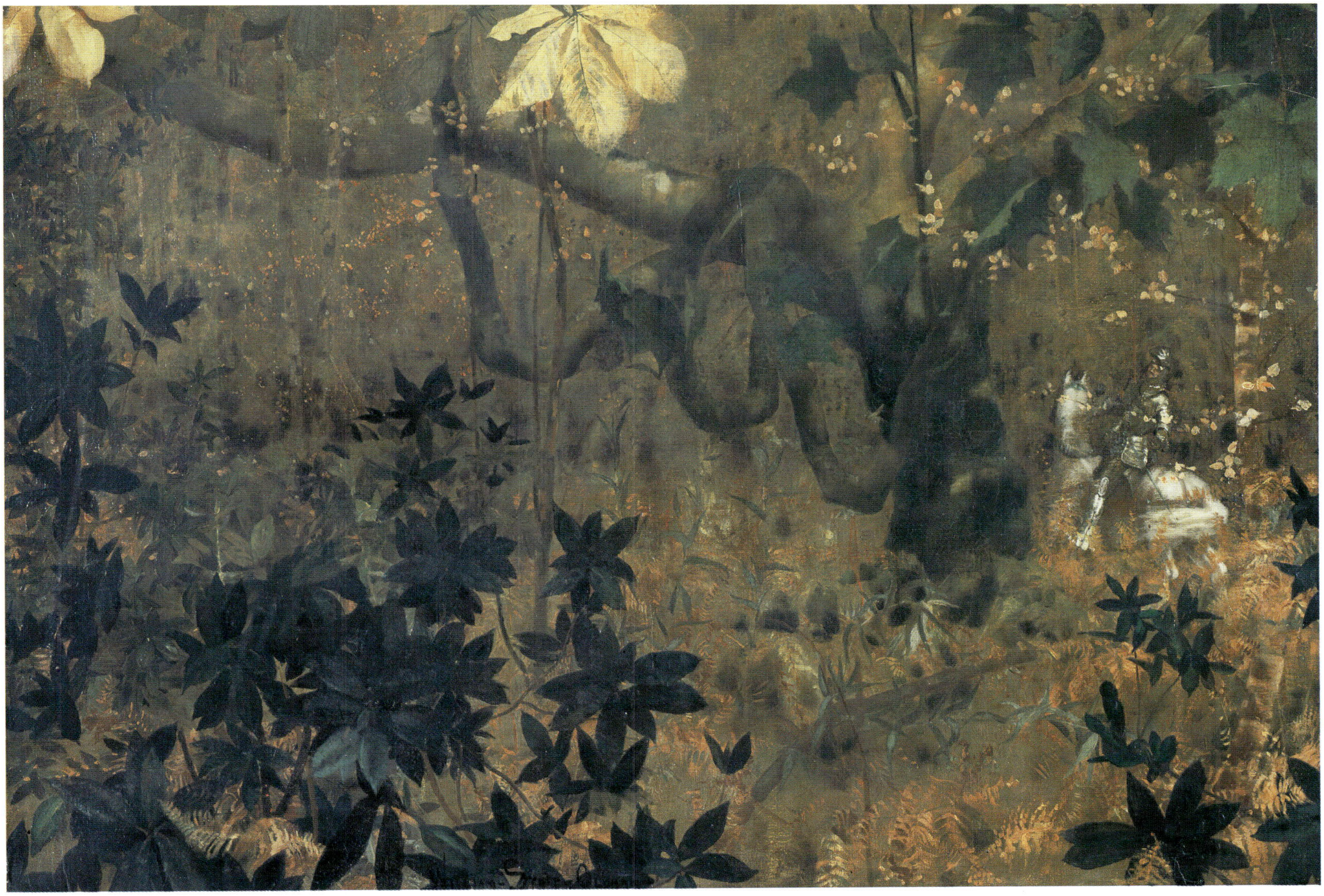

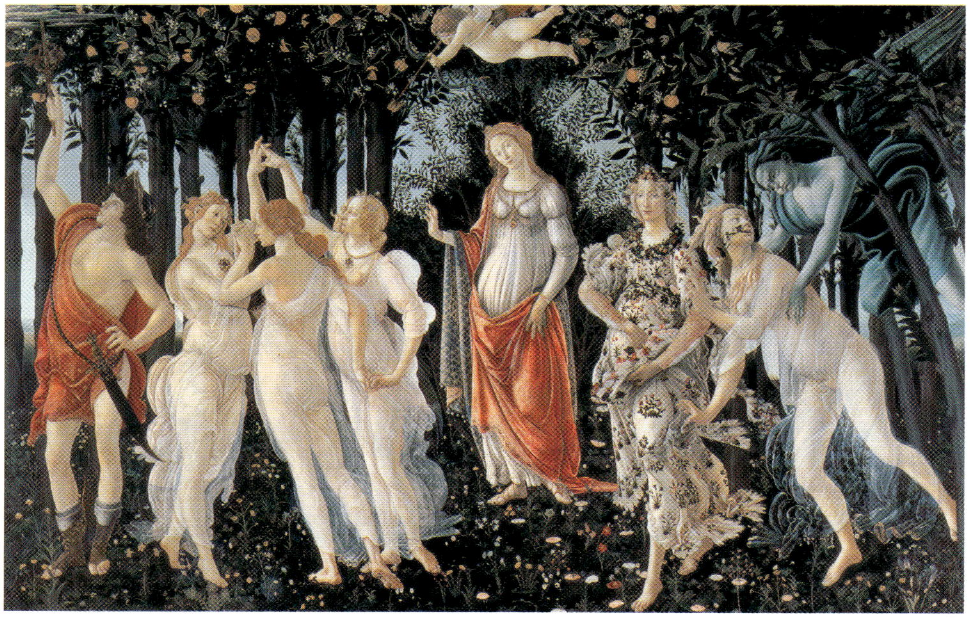

Fig. 51 Sandro Botticelli (1445—1510), *Primavera, ca.* 1478
Tempera on panel, 203 x 314 cm, Gallerie degli Uffizi, Florence

67 Hide and Seek in the Garden of Epicurus: Leontium and Ternissa

Signed *William Stott of Oldham*
Oil on canvas, 145.3 x 127 cm (69" x 50")
Gallery Oldham

This is Stott's last major work to have been shown at the Royal Academy. It was probably painted specifically for the Academy show of 1899; the following year Stott was dead. In some ways it can be seen as a valedictory work, as it seems to epitomize all that he stood for and tried to achieve in his latter years, but we do not know that he had any premonition of his early death.

The Greek philosopher Epicurus founded a system of moral philosophy in which he argued that pleasure was the basis of an ethical life. To Epicurus pleasure consisted of right living, which led to tranquillity of mind and body. He held intellectual pleasures superior to all others, and advocated the denial of more transient pleasures. This philosophy later became corrupted and the hedonism it proclaimed took on pejorative meaning which in some quarters was associated with decadence.

Epicurus had a house outside Athens with a large irrigated garden that provided a private and pleasurable space for his followers. The Garden of Epicurus thus became a symbol for the detachment and hedonism of the Epicurean School.

The teachings of Epicurus became central to the Aesthetic Movement in England during the last quarter of the nineteenth century, largely thanks to the writings of Walter Pater, seen by some as the apostle of Aestheticism. Setting a supreme value on the enjoyment of beauty, Pater promoted Epicurean philosophy in his novel *Marius the Epicurean* (1885), which was written to illustrate the highest ideal of the aesthetic life. In a previous book, *Studies in the History of the Renaissance* (1873), he had praised the idea of 'art for art's sake' and made the now famous remark, taken up by Whistler, that "all art constantly aspires towards the condition of music". The book also included a fulsome essay on the merits of the fifteenth-century Florentine painter Botticelli.

William Stott expressed his admiration for Botticelli in a speech to the Manchester Art Club in 1898, a year before *Hide and Seek* was painted. He said, "I have personally had as much delight in looking at Botticelli's pictures as I have had in pondering over the poems of Keats ..." (*Manchester Guardian*, 23 February 1898). The delicate, elongated figures in *Hide and Seek* are certainly reminiscent of Botticelli's fragile maidens (fig. 51). The painting, with its painstaking attention to detail and carefully posed figures enjoying the pleasures of the fabled garden, could be taken as a statement by Stott that he subscribed to the Epicurean philosophy. It is noteworthy that there is no Christian iconography in Stott's entire output of works, and it is very likely that, although he came from a highly religious family, he became a sceptic very early on, probably while still in Paris, and almost certainly under the influence of the writings of Walter Pater.

As was the case with all Stott's later works, the critics, while praising his use of colour, the ingenuity of his compositions and the skill and labour he lavished on "rendering each separate growth with all the care that drawing and palette can afford", always felt that he left something to be desired. A review in the *Magazine of Art* of December 1901 of his London memorial exhibition said, "There is something in his ideal creations that seems curiously artificial – in spite of their colour and treatment ...", and on *Hide and Seek* it commented, "While admitting the fine qualities, we cannot close our eyes to incorrect drawing ...". The conclusion of the anonymous reviewer was that "the artist's mental qualities were beyond his powers of accomplishment in poetry".

Hide and Seek was bought by Oldham Corporation for £350 at the memorial exhibition held in Manchester City Art Gallery in January 1902.

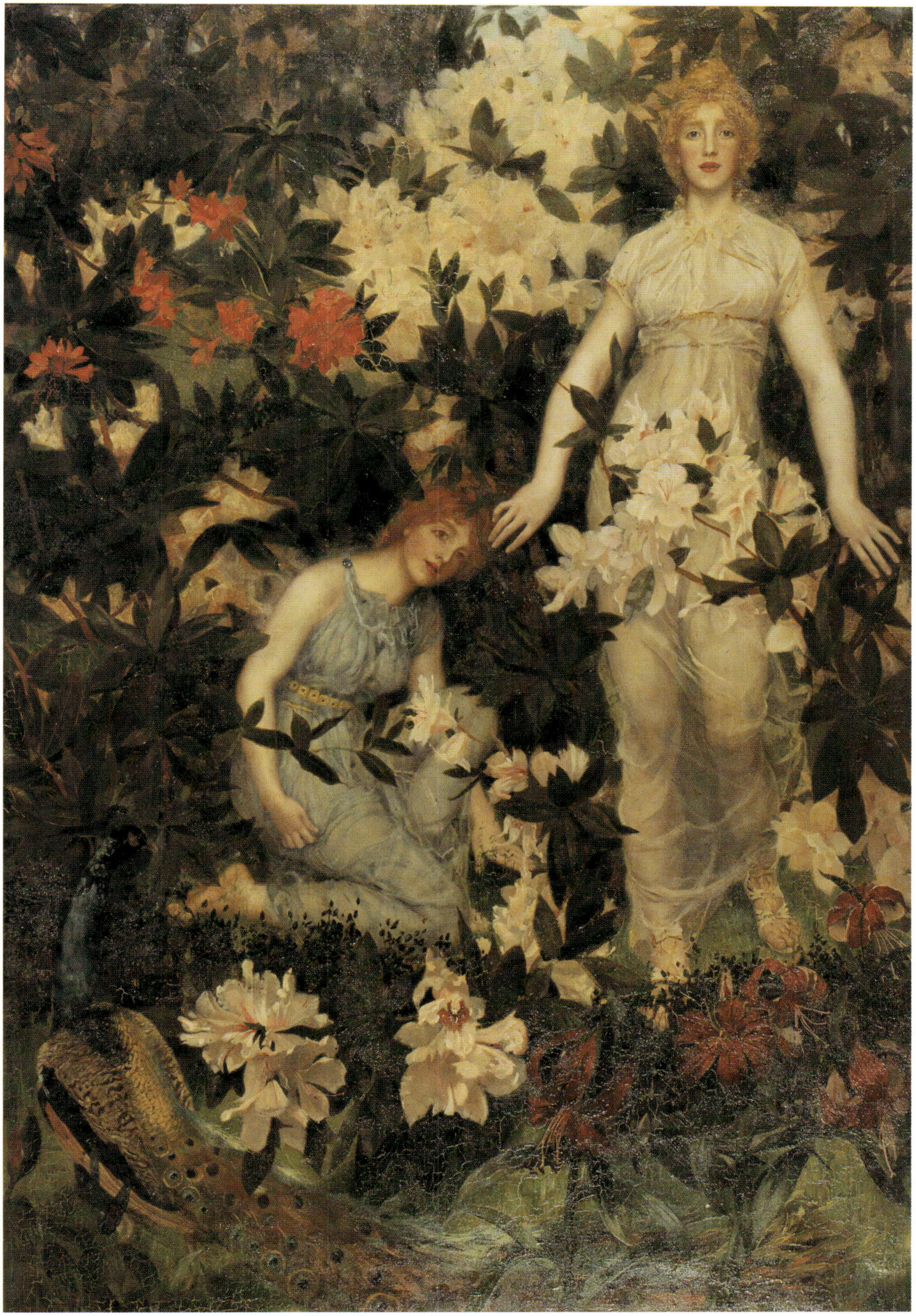

68 Tristram's Farewell

1898
Signed *William Stott of Oldham*
Pastel, with opaque watercolour, 63.5 × 47 cm
(25" × 18½")
Private collection

The Gothic revival in arts and architecture which swept through Europe in the nineteenth century brought a renewed interest in the age of chivalry, and poets and painters alike found inspiration in the legends of King Arthur. In England the Pre-Raphaelite Brotherhood of painters led the way with a mixture of romantic medievalism and Christian morality. This short-lived impetus soon gave way to the more relaxed pseudo-medievalism of the Aesthetic Movement and artists such as Edward Burne-Jones, Frank Dicksee and J.W. Waterhouse. There was also a renewed interest in early literary sources such as Thomas Malory's *Morte d'Arthur* and Edmund Spenser's *Faerie Queene*, which was reflected in the contemporary works of the poets Tennyson (*Idylls of the King*, 1859) and Swinburne (*Poems and Ballads*, 1866), the latter being a close acquaintance of both Whistler and Burne-Jones. In addition the music of Richard Wagner had a significant impact on the artists of the Aesthetic Movement in England and the Symbolist movement throughout Europe. His two operas *Tristan and Isolde* (1865) and *Parsifal* (1882) fuelled the prevailing appetite for Arthurian legend and romance.

This picture shows an episode in the story of Tristram (or Tristan) and Isolde (or Iseult). Tristram is sent to Ireland by his uncle Mark, king of Cornwall, to escort Isolde, the daughter of the king of Ireland, to whom Mark is betrothed, back to England. During the voyage they fall deeply and irretrievably in love. Isolde marries the king, who later discovers their relationship, and Tristram has to flee to Brittany. It is this scene of the lovers' hurried farewell that Stott has chosen to depict here. Subsequently Tristram falls ill in France and calls for Isolde, who sets sail from Cornwall to be with him. But she arrives too late and Tristram has died. Isolde then kills herself.

Stott's first painting on this theme was *Iseult* (or *Isolde*; untraced; fig. 52), which was

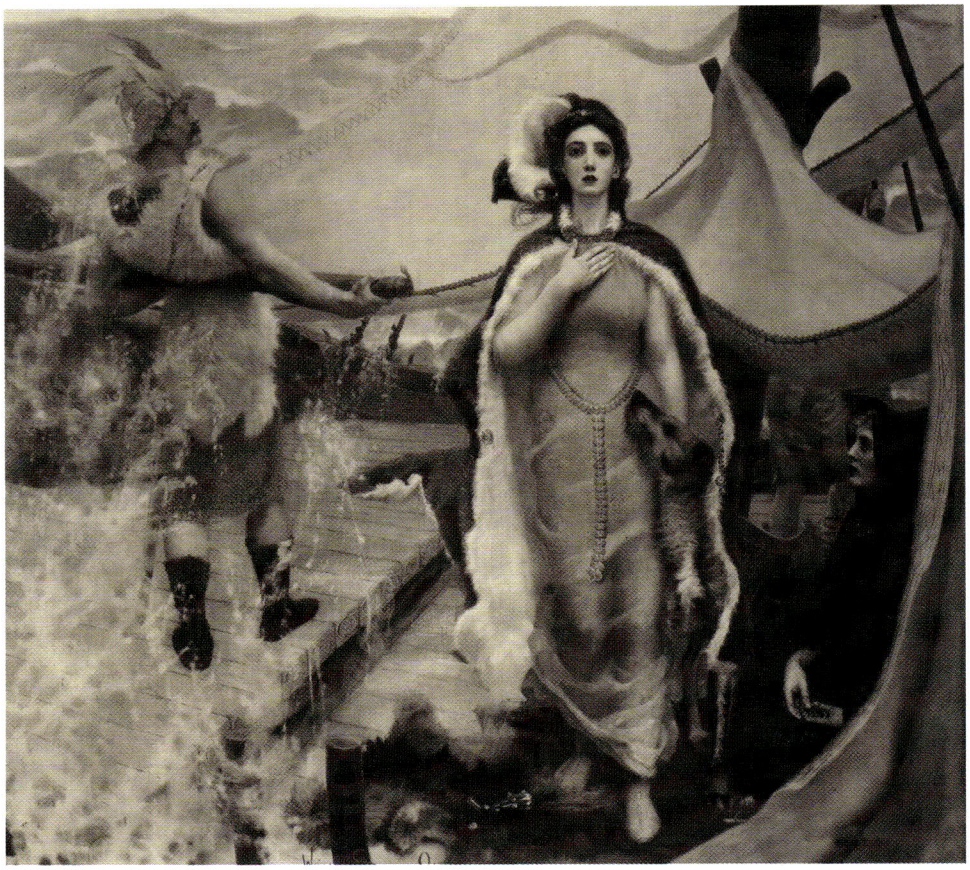

Fig. 52 William Stott of Oldham
Iseult (Isolde), 1891
Oil on canvas, untraced

completed in 1891, the year of his success in Munich, when *The Bathing Place* (fig. 17, p. 21) was medalled and bought by the Bavarian Government. It is possible that at that time he visited Bayreuth and paid homage to the spirit of Wagner. Certainly in the 1890s London was in the midst of a Wagner revival, with his operas being performed regularly and his standing within the Aesthetic Movement undiminished.

Iseult was a large exhibition oil depicting Isolde on a ship being conveyed by Tristram to Cornwall for her marriage to King Mark. Attached to the frame was a quotation from the *Morte d'Arthur*. It was shown at the Grafton Gallery in 1893 and the critics were scathing. D.S. MacColl in the *Spectator* wrote, "Mr Stott thinks his people are heroic and beautiful and means them to be so …. It is a disastrous failure by a painter who has elsewhere done good work" (25 February 1893). Perhaps bruised by the ridicule of the critics, Stott did not return to the subject for another seven years. It has to be said that *Tristram's Farewell*, although it is an adept composition, does not appear any more convincing than his previous attempt to depict these heroic characters.

Stott worked on *Tristram's Farewell* at Ravenglass in the autumn of 1898. Just why he returned to this Arthurian romance at this stage, after a series of classical tableaux, is a mystery. He was to die on a sea voyage to Ireland in February 1900 and this picture of the lovers bidding farewell before Tristram embarks on his last voyage to France does therefore lead one to speculate whether Stott had some premonition of the future. Did he cast himself in the role of the well-meaning, misunderstood and ultimately tragic Tristram?

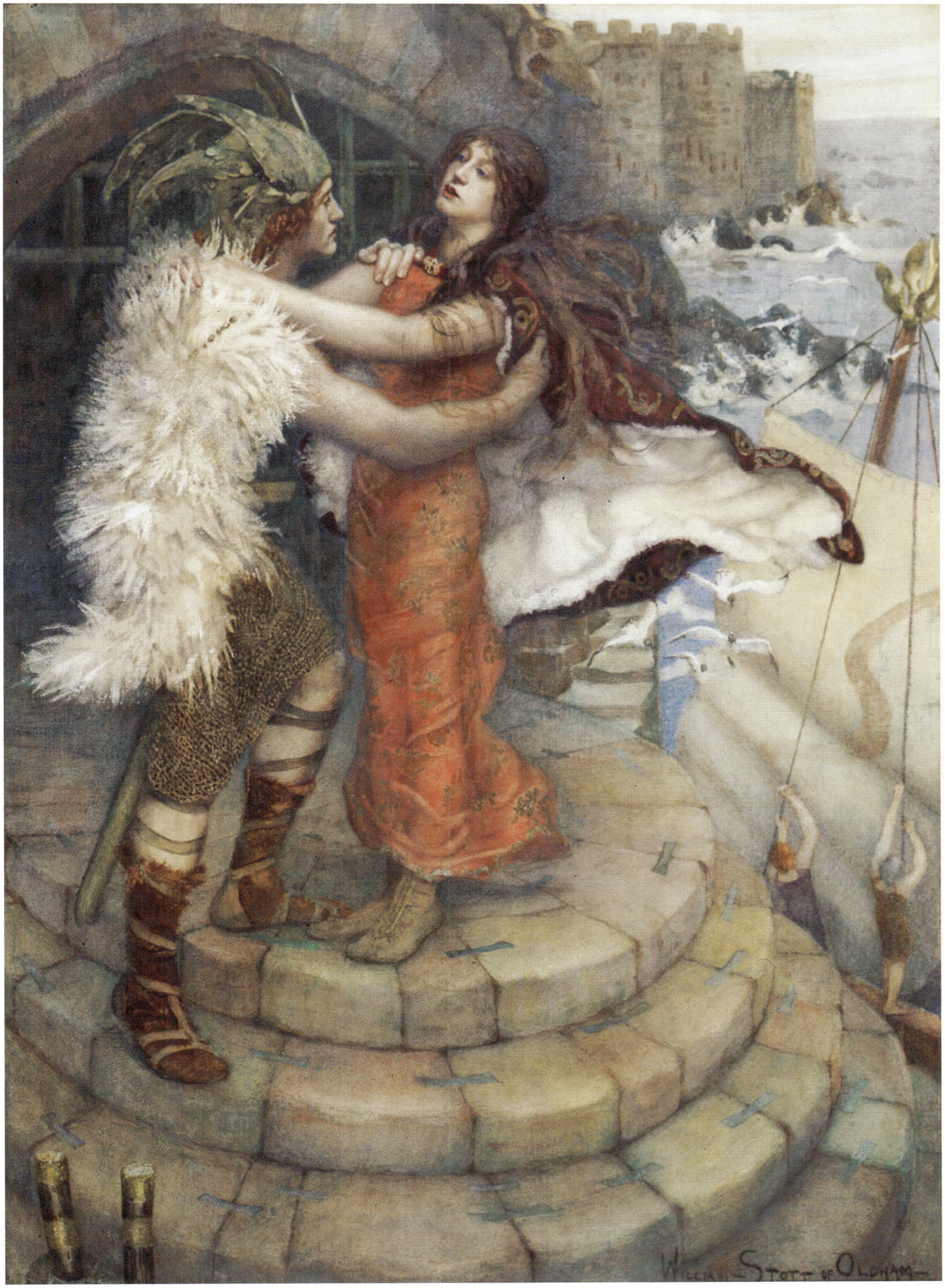
William Stott of Oldham

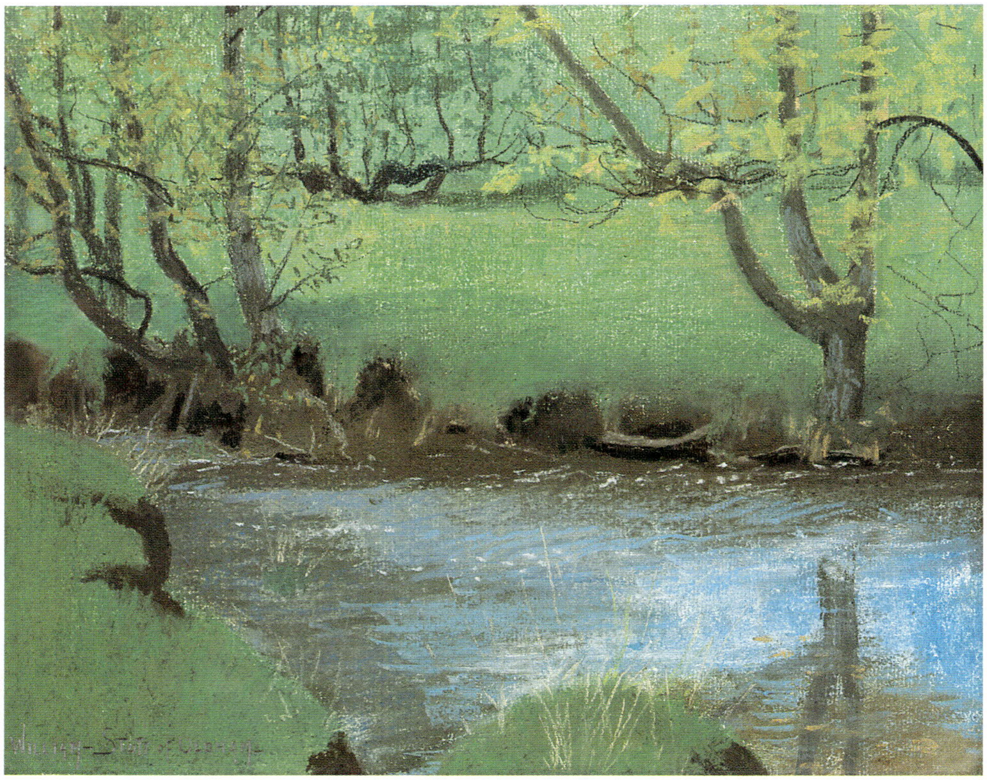

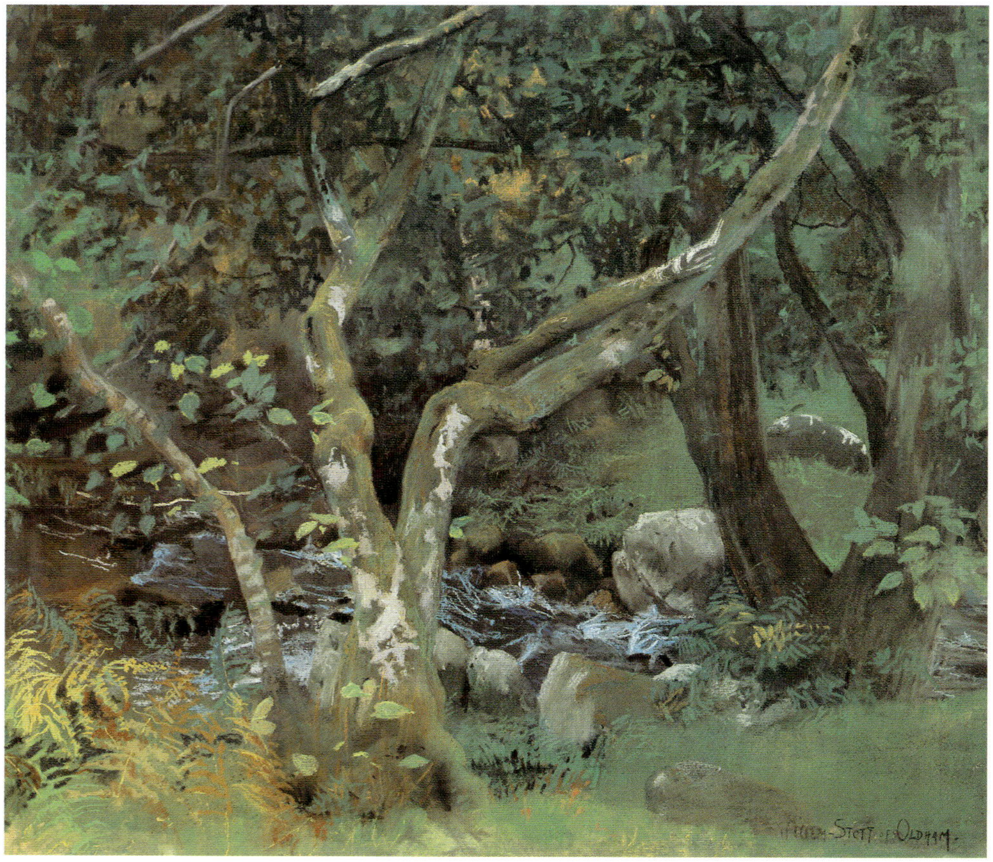

Cumbrian Landscapes

69 The Mill Stream

ca. 1886
Signed *William Stott of Oldham*
Pastel, 24.1 × 31.7 cm (9½" × 12½")
Private collection

70 Autumn Woodland

ca. 1889
Signed *William Stott of Oldham*
Pastel, 44.4 × 52.1 cm (17½" × 20½")
Private collection

From 1882 until his death in 1900 William Stott rented a house and studio at Ravenglass on the Cumbrian coast. In his latter years, although owning a house in London, he spent more and more time at Ravenglass, both for the sake of his health and for the inspiration he gained from the beauty and solitude of the area. Many of his major exhibition works were completed there and we know that in the 1890s he was bringing models up from London in order to finish canvases for the Royal Academy.

During the eighteen years he had a home in the little community of Ravenglass he produced numerous small landscape studies. All of these were done within two miles of his home and illustrate his engagement with the local community. Surprisingly, given its proximity, there is no evidence that Stott did any landscape drawing in the Lake District. Rather like Monet's absorption with the water-lillies in his garden, Stott's later landscapes show a preoccupation with the sites and scenes to be found on his doorstep. Not for him were the wide vistas, the popular picturesque motifs and the local characters. These intimate little landscapes are unpopulated and only rarely identified geographically. As in his seascapes, Stott is interested in the structure, colour harmonies and tonal values to be found in the scene before him, rather than recording the locale or its inhabitants. For him beauty lay in the colours and shades of the autumn woodland, the patterns formed by stooked corn against the skyline and the sparkle of the sun on the surface of water.

Stott became a well-liked and respected member of the small community at Ravenglass. It is said that he paid for the hard to be built at the sea-end of the village street to enable small coastal vessels to lay up and unload their cargo at low tide. In the Gallery Oldham archive there is a letter dated 1961 from an elderly gentleman who knew William Stott at Ravenglass. He writes, "He was a great swimmer and taught many of the village lads, of whom I was one, to swim ... as I knew him he was a man of great heart, a lover of the sea, woodland and young folks – generous to a fault." Stott was is buried in Muncaster churchyard, the parish church for Ravenglass. When he died the local newspaper reported under Ravenglass items, "Gloom was cast over our village early on Monday morning, when it was reported that Mrs Stott had received a telegram from Belfast to the effect that her husband had died" (*Cumberland Pacquet*, 1 March1900).

These landscapes count as some of William Stott's finest work and are a lasting testimony to his pantheistic belief in nature and delight in the beauty provided by its changing moods and seasons.

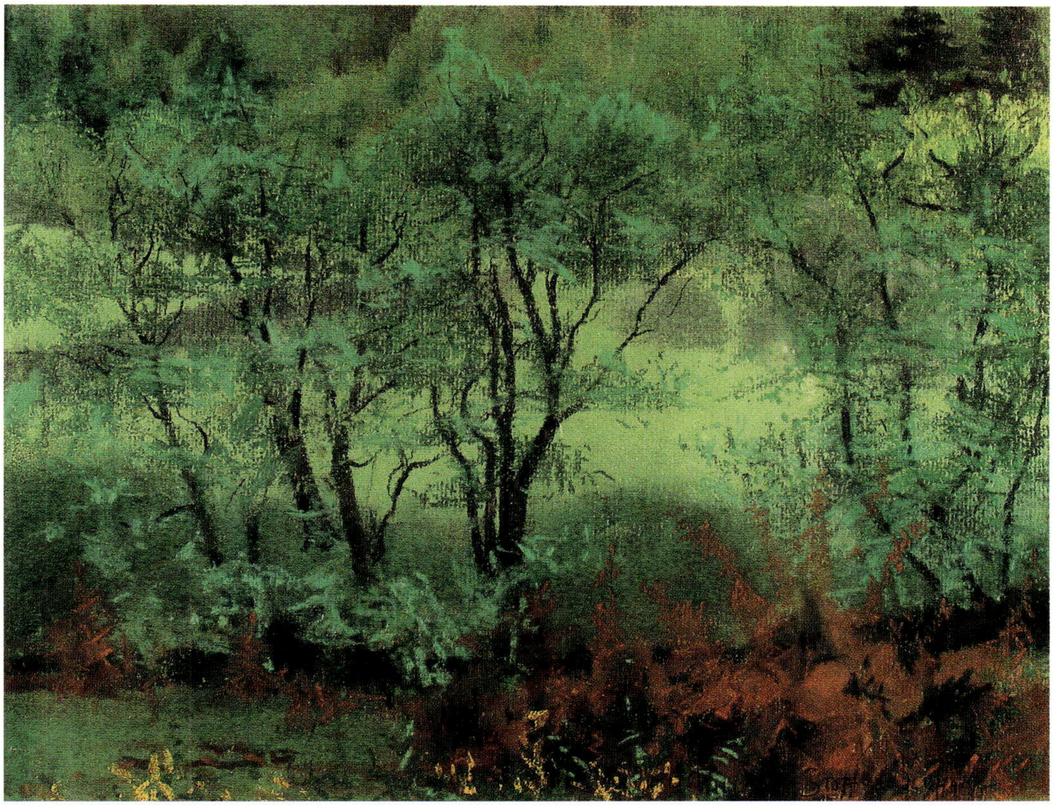

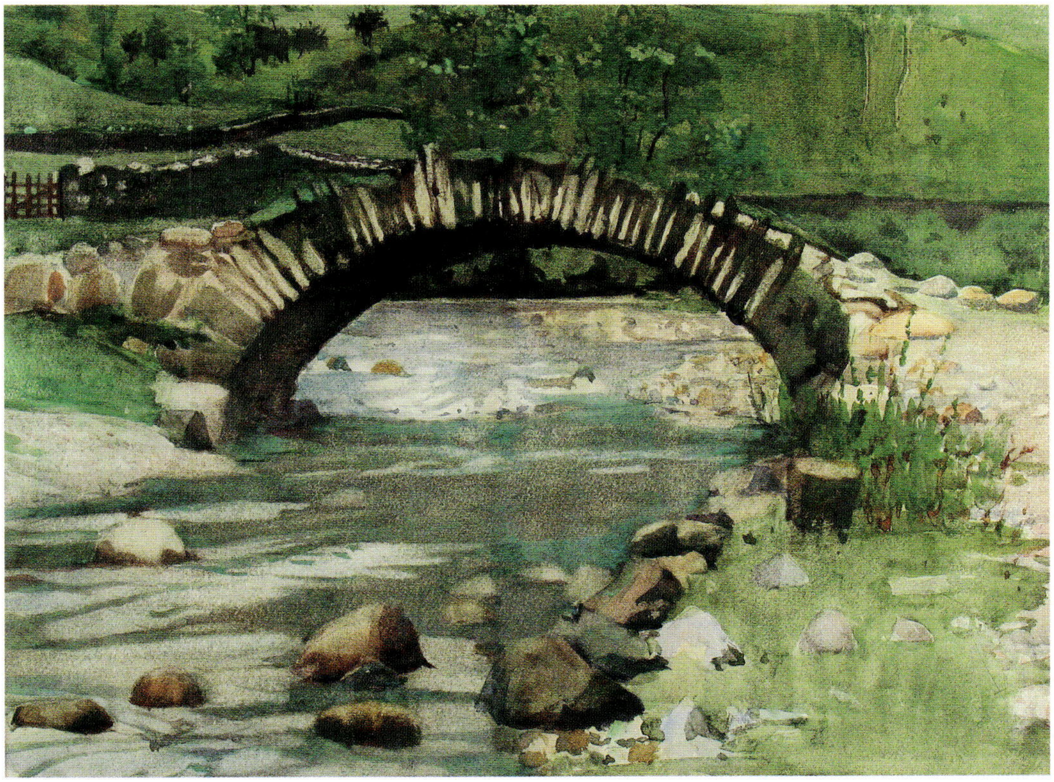

72 Woodland Scene, Brantrake

ca. 1895
Signed *William Stott of Oldham*
Pastel, 24.1 x 32.4 cm (9½" x 12¾")
Gallery Oldham

71 A Bridge

ca. 1896
Unsigned
Watercolour, 25.4 x 34.3 cm (10" x 13½")
Gallery Oldham

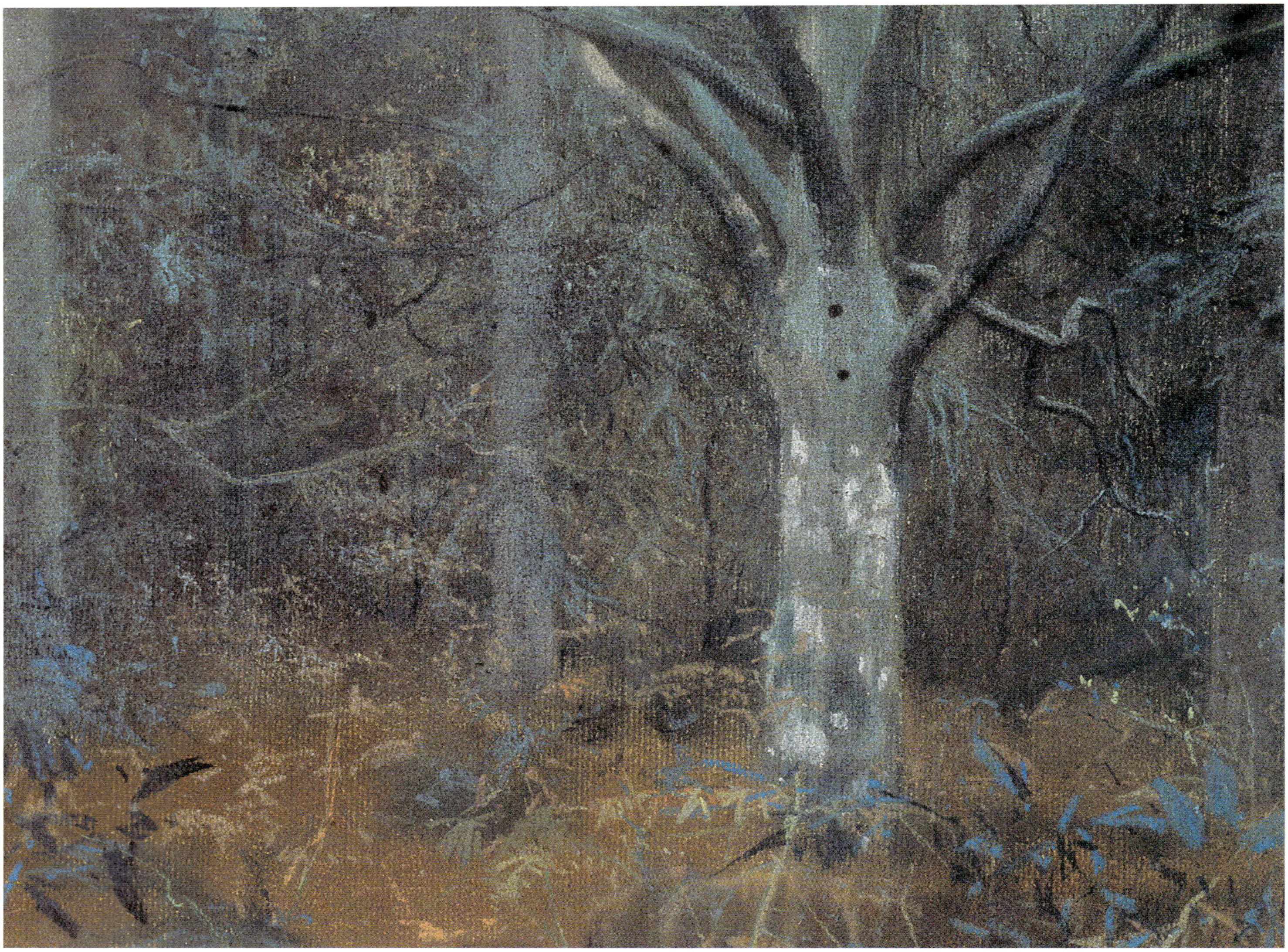

73 The Old Sycamore

ca. 1885

Signed *William Stott of Oldham*

Pastel, 24.1 × 32.4 cm (9 1/2" × 12 3/4")

Gallery Oldham

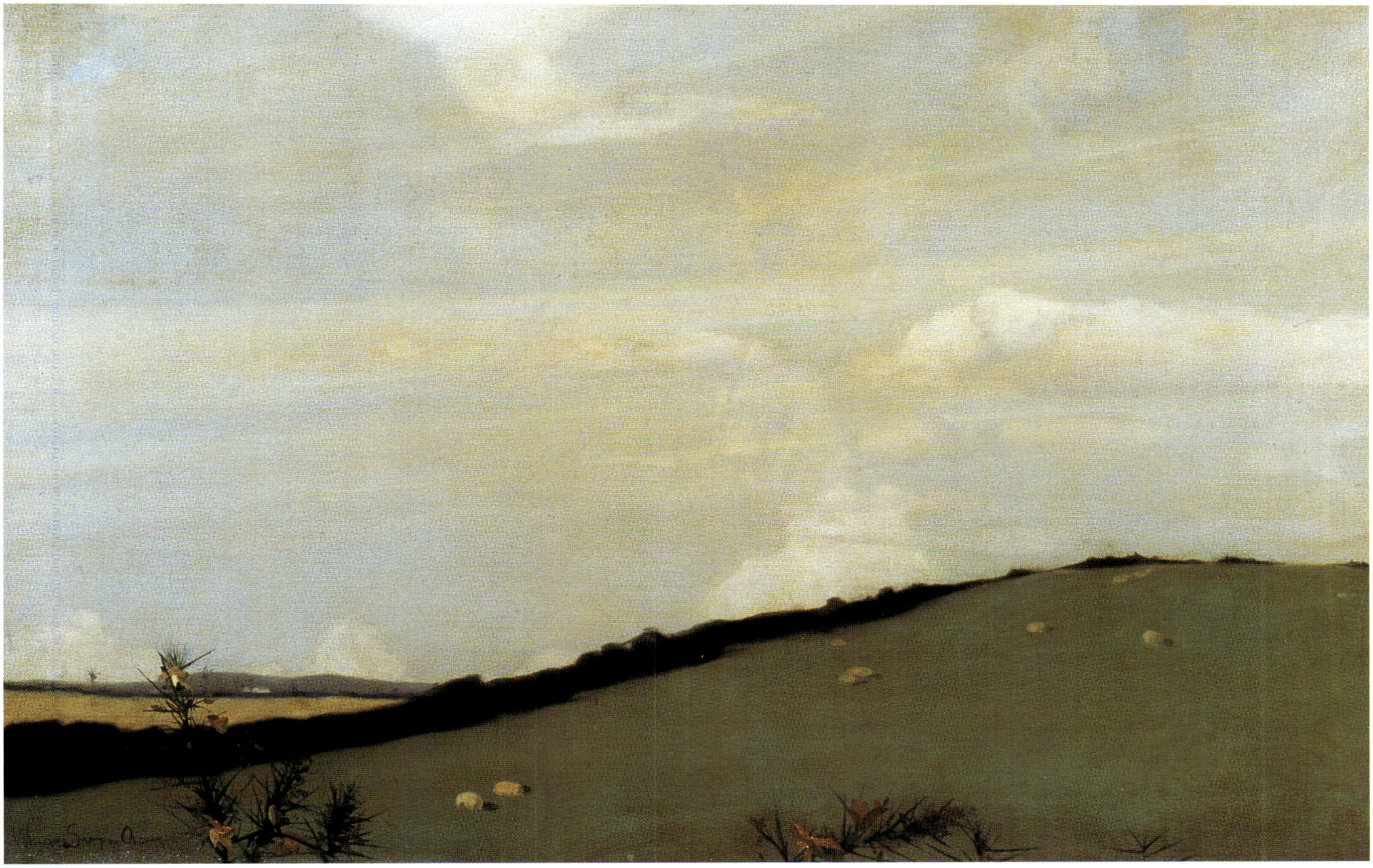

74 Pastoral

1886
Signed *William Stott of Oldham*
Oil on canvas, 64.8 × 106 cm (25 1/2" × 41 3/4")
Gallery Oldham

Pastoral was shown at the Society of British Artists spring exhibition in 1888 and it may well have been the picture that prompted one critic to remark, "A streak of blue above, and a streak of green below, constitutes the Stott formula for a work of genius" (quoted by Alice Corkran in the *Scottish Arts Review*, April 1889, p. 322).

The only feature of interest is the hedge, which provides a single diagonal leading the eye up and over the hillside. The gorse gives a reference to the foreground and creates the impression of a snapshot taken by a walker on a stroll in the country. Stott says in his notebook of *Pastoral*, "Summer sky, sheep and gorse". As in the landscapes of his mentors Whistler and Degas, Stott is attempting to see the world through an innocent eye that challenges traditional ideas about composition and lets the subject determine its own design, much as it does to the photographer. However, Stott's finish is always much finer than that in Whistler's more 'impressionist' landscapes, perhaps owing partly to his strict training under Gérôme in Paris.

In *Pastoral* Stott has caught the atmosphere of a calm summer's afternoon with only the sound of the distant sea and the skylarks.

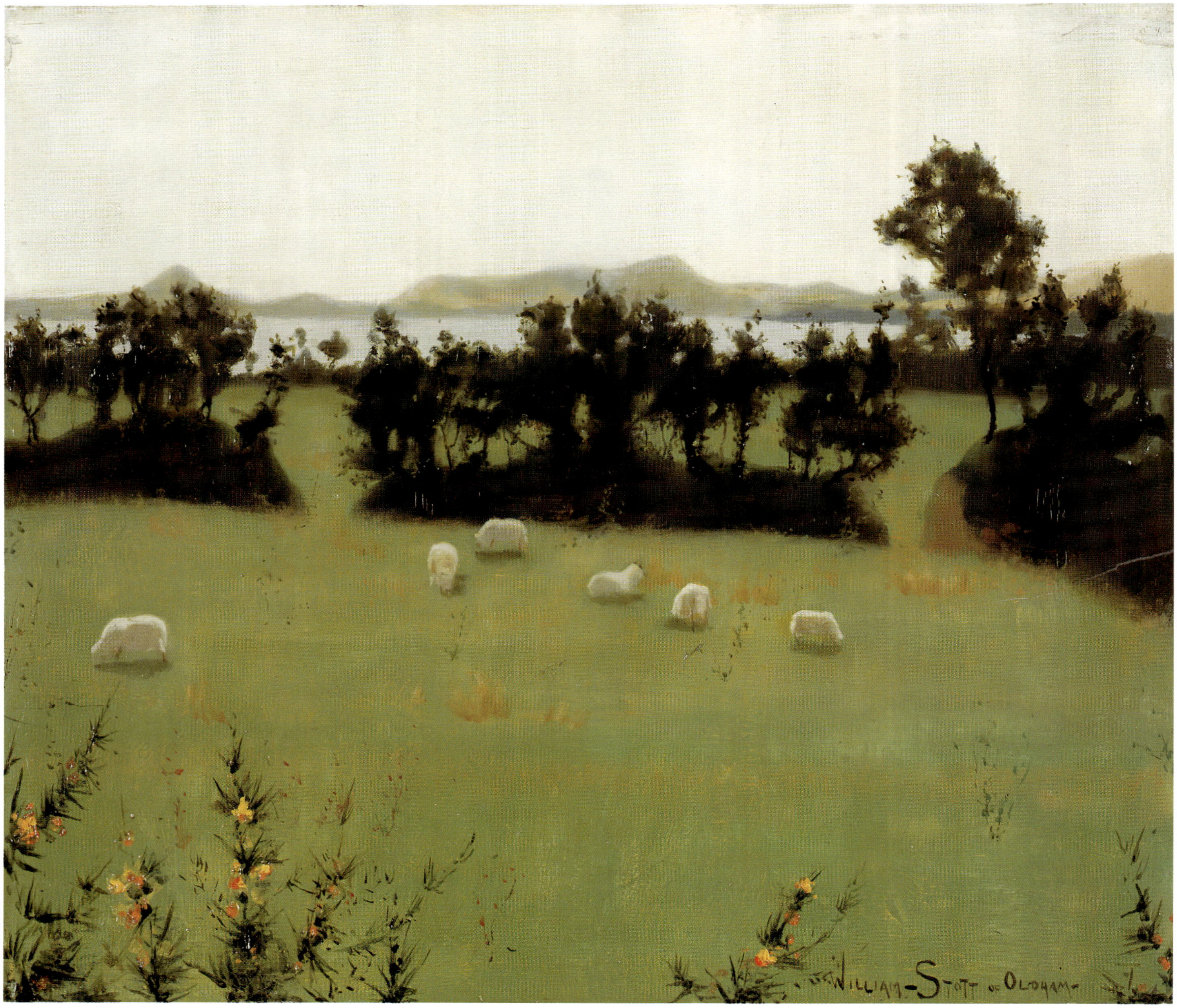

75 Ravenglass

ca. 1884
Signed *William Stott of Oldham*
Oil on panel 45.1 x 53.3 cm (17¾" x 21")
Manchester Art Gallery

In the summer of 1884 Stott completed a large number of landscapes in pastel and oils in and around Ravenglass, several of which were 'nocturnes' with titles such as *Waning Moon* (cat. 82) and *Starry Night*. This particular oil, which is painted on panel, he records in his note book as "Afternoon, sheep in greenfield, twilight seen through boughs of green partially – called 'Sheep Grazing'". The painting captures the quality of the light and atmosphere experienced on the Cumbrian coast between the sea and the mountains. It is not known when it became known as *Ravenglass*, although it quite clearly is in the environs of the village. It was exhibited at Stott's one-man show at the Goupil Gallery in London in 1896 as *Sheep Grazing*, but it did not appear in any of the memorial shows after his death and trace of it was lost until it was bequeathed in 1941 to the Manchester Art Gallery.

76 Corn at Hall Carleton

ca. 1895
Signed *William Stott of Oldham*
Pastel, 24.1 x 31.7 cm (9½" x 12½")
Private collection

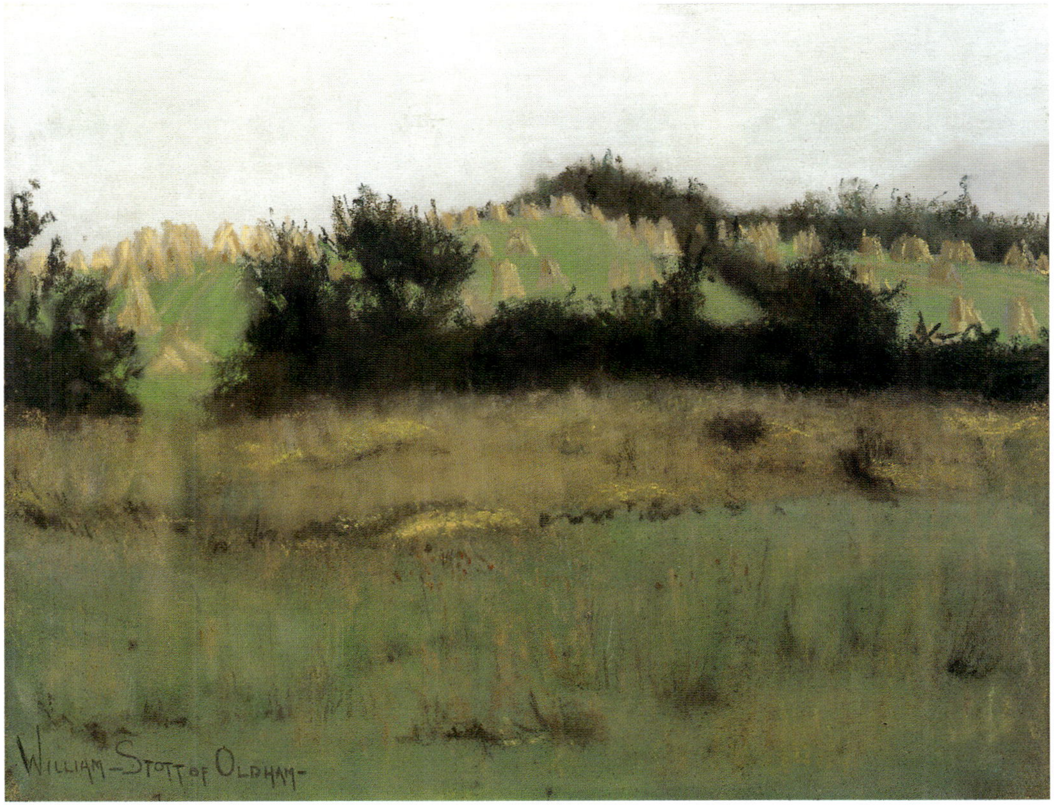

77 Barrow Farm (Home Farm)

ca. 1895
Signed *William Stott of Oldham*
Pastel, 24.1 x 31.7 cm (9½" x 12½")
Private collection

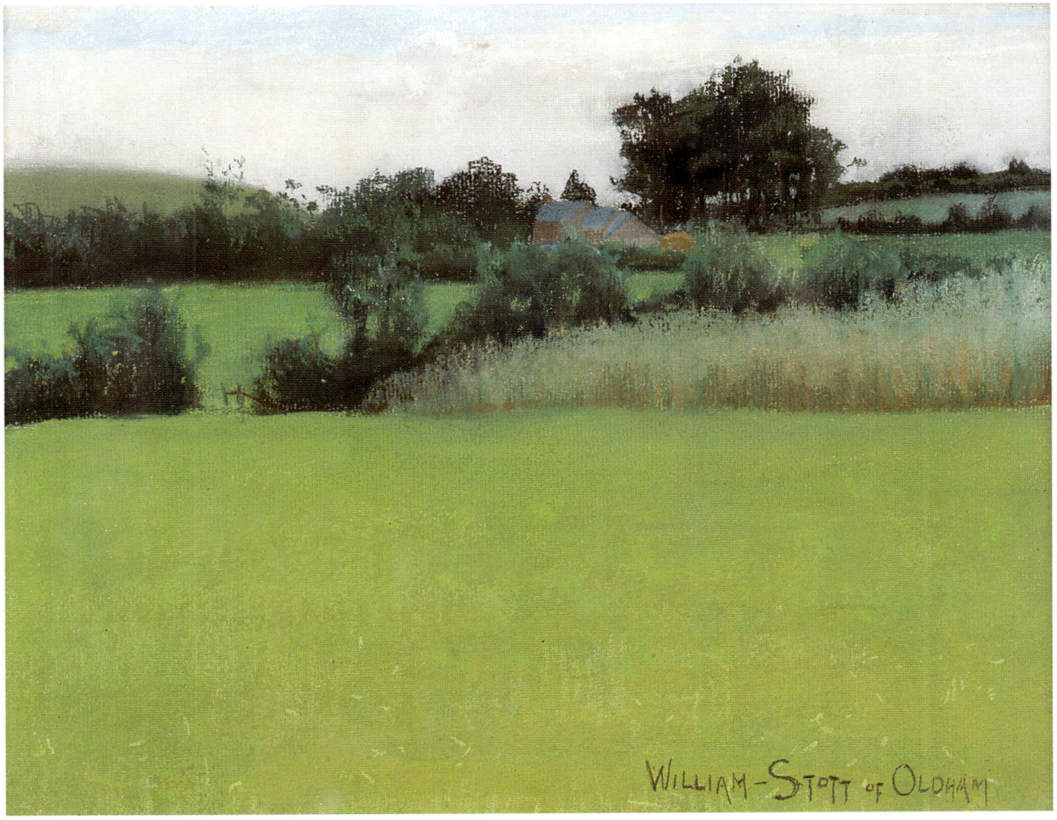

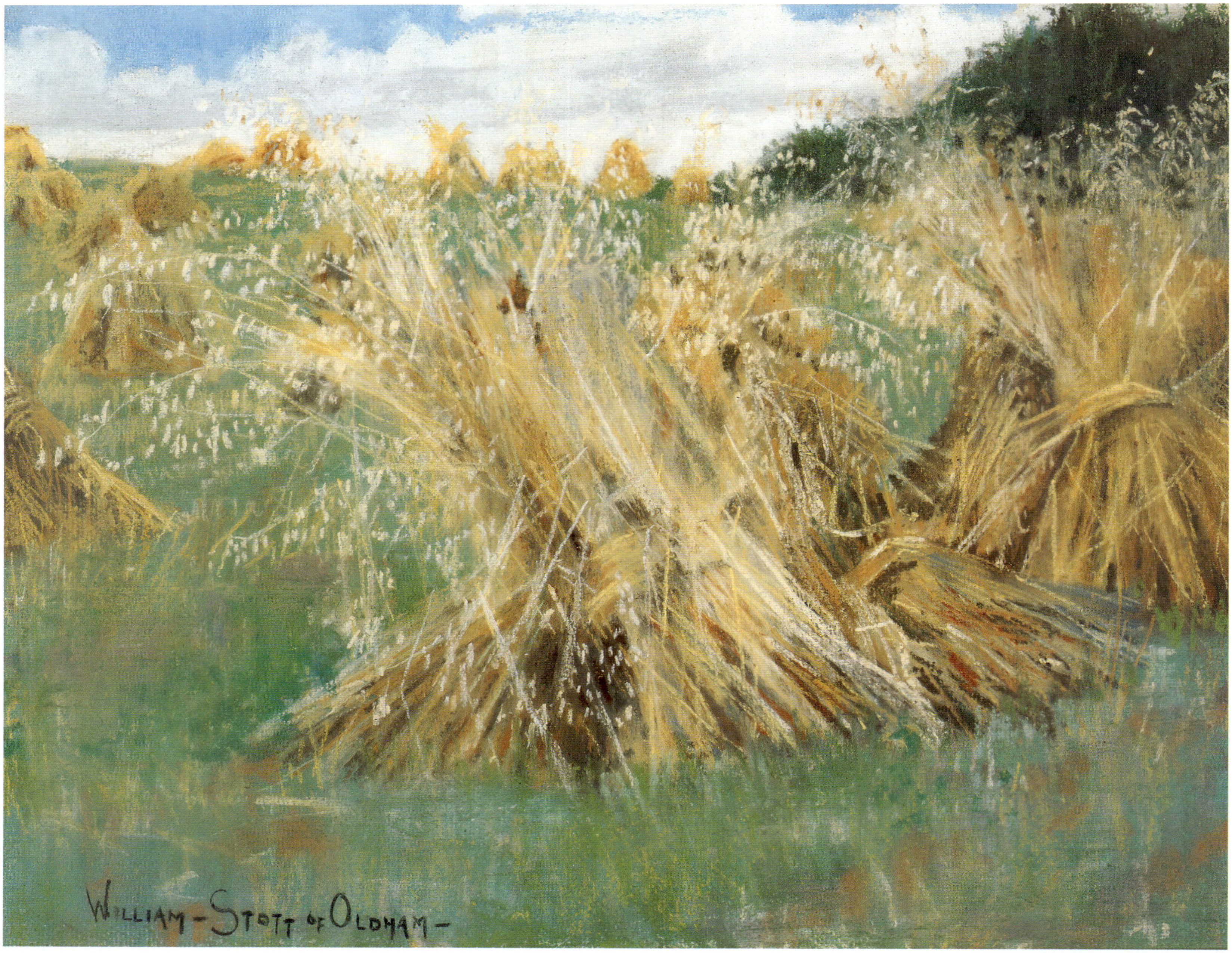

78 Wheat Sheaves

ca. 1895

Signed *William Stott of Oldham*

Pastel, 23.5 x 31.1 cm (9 1/4" x 12 1/4")

Private collection

79 The Cornfield

ca. 1895
Unsigned
Pastel, 23.5 x 31.1 cm (9¼" x 12¼")
Gallery Oldham

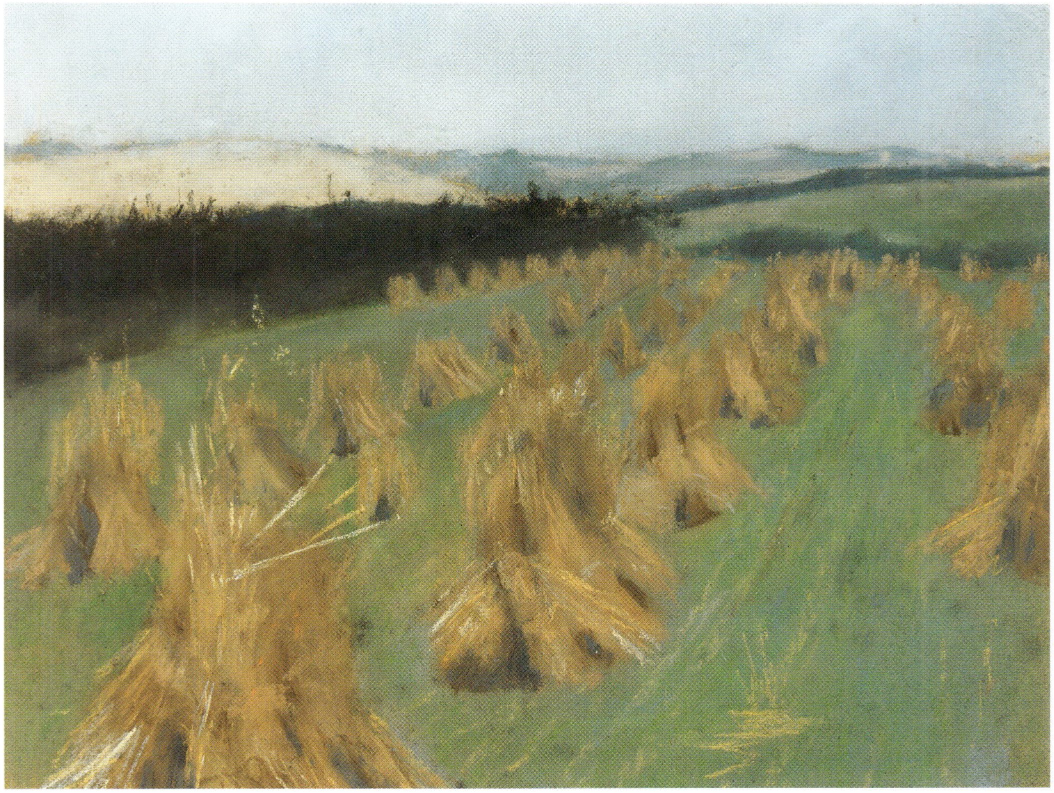

80 Haystacks

1887
Signed *William Stott of Oldham*
Watercolour, 11.4 x 20.3 cm (4½" x 8")
Bury Art Gallery

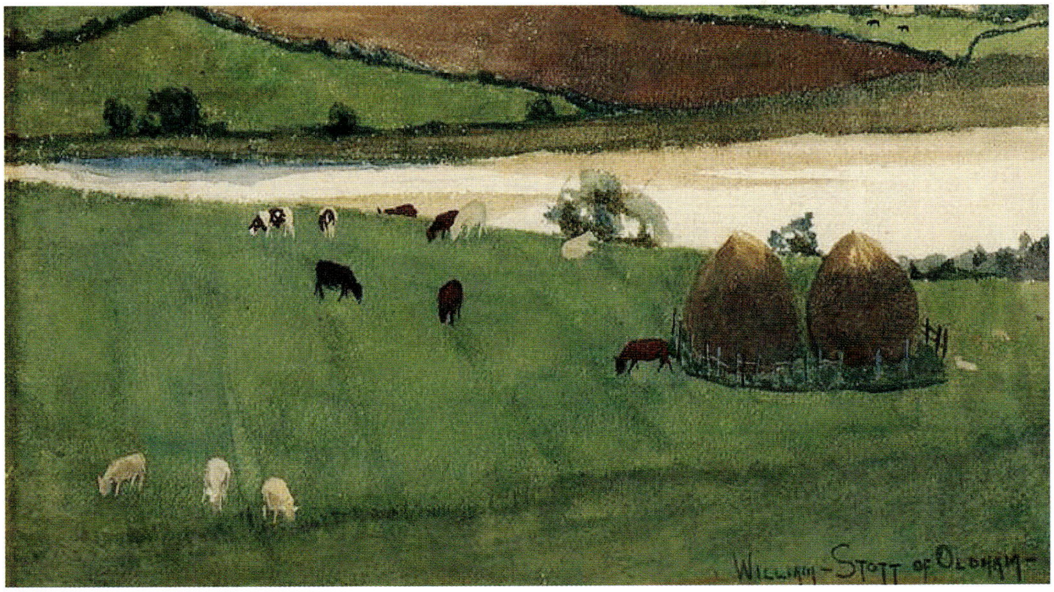

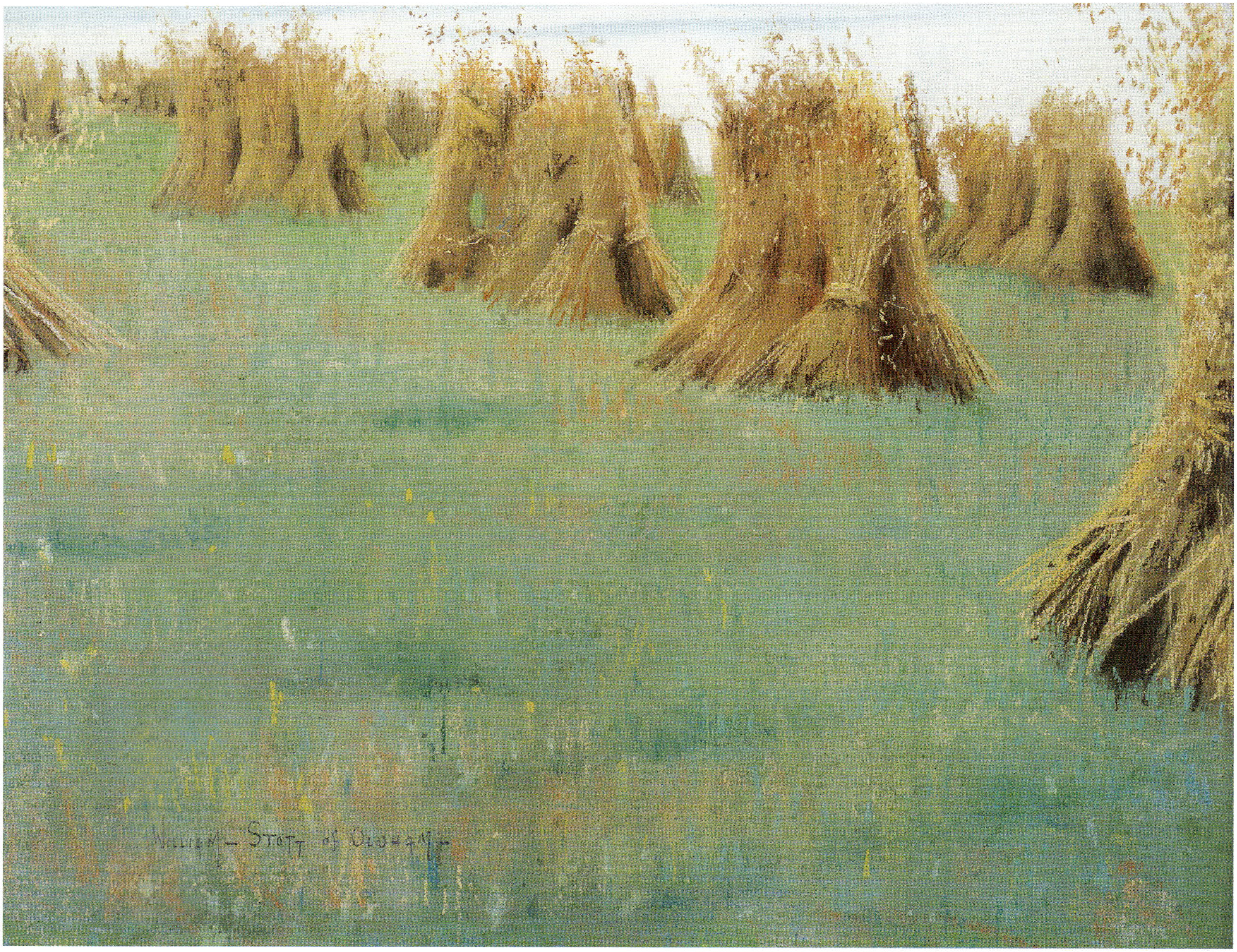

81 Stacked Corn

ca. 1895
Signed *William Stott of Oldham*
Pastel, 24.1 x 31.7 cm (9½" x 12½")
Private collection

82 Waning Moon

1885

Signed and dated *William Stott of Oldham 1885*

Pastel, 24.1 x 31.7 cm (9 3/4" x 12 1/2")

Private collection

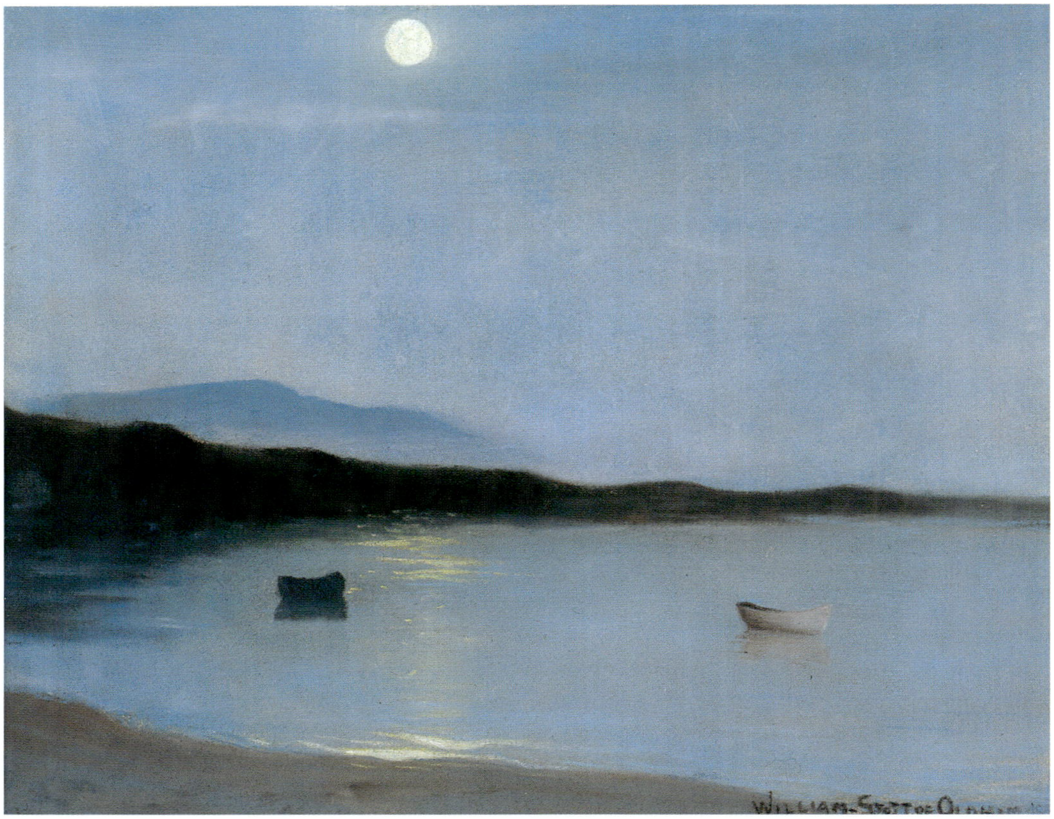

83 Summer Moonlight

1885

Signed *William Stott of Oldham*

Pastel, 23.5 x 31.7 cm ($9\frac{1}{4}$" x $12\frac{1}{2}$")

Private collection

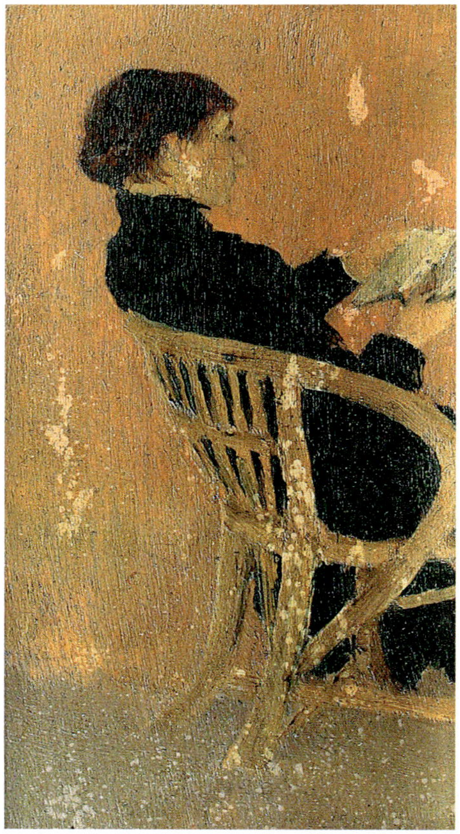

84 Seated Lady in Black (Mrs Butler)

ca. 1888

Unsigned

Oil on panel, 13.3 x 7 cm ($5\frac{1}{4}$" x $2\frac{3}{4}$")

Gallery Oldham

This little oil sketch is inscribed on the back *Mrs Butler*. In August 1888, on their way to the Swiss Alps, William Stott and his painting companion Tom Millie Dow stayed with the Butler family at Überlingen on Lake Constance. Butler had been a student with them in Paris. While staying with the family Stott painted a portrait of the son, Dickie 'Luck' Butler (untraced), which was exhibited at his one-man show at Durand-Ruel in Paris the following year. This sketch may have been a preliminary study for a portrait of Mrs Butler.

Appendix 1

Exhibition Record for William Stott of Oldham – The Royal Academy

4, Passage Dulac, Paris

1882 771 Return from Fishing

66, Adelaide Road, London

1891 239 The Bathing Place

1893 427 The Ferry

1894 584 The Awakening of the Spirit of the Rose
"See! Rosy in her bower;
Her floor is all thy flowers,
Her bed a rosy nest
By a bed of roses prest." *Lovelace.*
933 The Faerie Wood

1895 364 Morning in the Alps
679 Ophelia

1896 527 Memory of an Island
965 Idlers

1898 566 Autumn
"Who hath not seen thee
oft amid thy store?" *Keats.*
614 The Happy Valley

1899 675 Hide and Seek in the Garden of Epicurus; Leontion and Ternissa
1168 A Pebbly River: "Follow my leader"

Source: Algernon Graves, *The Royal Academy of Arts, A Complete Dictionary of Contributors, 1769–1904*, VII, London 1906, p. 286

Appendix 2

Exhibition Record for William Stott of Oldham – The Royal Society of British Artists

4, Passage Dulac, Rue de Vaugirard, Paris

Winter 1885
107 Portrait of my Father and Mother
292 Moonrise
.... By the Fireside (pastel)*

Spring 1886
.... Portrait of Tom Millie Dow*
.... The Kissing Ring*
.... Sandpools (pastel)*

Winter 1886
231 Portrait of Miss White
245 A Summer Day
272 A Village Street
438 Pastoral (pastel)

Spring 1887
62 Summer Moonlight (pastel)
64 Starry Night (pastel)
137 A Nymph
176 Silvery Day (pastel)
186 Souvenir de Plage

Winter 1887
162 The Purple Mountain (w/c)**
183 A Portrait (w/c)**
341 The Birth of Venus

Spring 1888
122 Pastoral:with Gorse
242 Endymion
467 The Blue River (pastel)

Source: Ed. Maurice Bradshaw, *RBA Exhibitors 1824–92*, 1973

Notes: * = Not in source document but added as they are recorded by Stott in his notebook
** = Catalogued as watercolours, but in fact pastels, as recorded in Stott's notebook. The portrait is the pastel of *Maud in a rocking chair*, executed when she visited Stott at Ravenglass in 1886 with Whistler.

Appendix 3

Exhibition Record for William Stott of Oldham – Paris Salon

1878 Stott (William) né à Oldham (Grande-Bretagne) élève de M. Gérôme
Chez M.Fatton, rue de Seine, 31
3860 – Un temps gris – acquarelle
3861 – L'apres-midi – acquarelle

1879 Stott (William) né à Oldham (Grande-Bretagne) élève de M. Gérôme
Rue de la Gaite, 27
4633 Vues de Morcambe [*sic*] (Grande-Bretagne); trois acquarelles
4634 Au bord de la mer - acquarelle

1880 Stott (William) né à Oldham (Grande-Bretagne) élève de M. Gérôme
Rue de la Gaite, 27
5874 Concarneau (Finistère)

1881 Stott (William) né à Oldham (Grande-Bretagne) élève de M. Gérôme
4, Passage Dulac, rue de Vaugirard
2205 Une Rêve de Midi [Daydream]
2206 La Tricoteuse [Girl Knitting]

1882 Stott (William) né à Oldham (Grande-Bretagne) élève de M. Gérôme
4, Passage Dulac, rue de Vaugirard
2496 Le Passeur [The Ferry]
2497 La Baignade [The Bathing Place] (3rd class medal)

1883 Stott (William) né à Oldham (Grande-Bretagne) élève de M. Gérôme
4, Passage Dulac, rue de Vaugirard
2255 Ronde d'enfants [The Kissing Ring]
2256 L'Atelier du grand-père [Grandfather's Workshop]

1884 Stott (William) né à Oldham (Grande-Bretagne) élève de M. Gérôme
4, Passage Dulac, rue de Vaugirard
2247 Portrait
[Portrait of Tom Millie Dow]
2248 Les Deux Sœurs [Two Sisters]

1885 Stott (William) né à Oldham (Grande-Bretagne) élève de M. Gérôme
à Ravenglass et à Paris, chez M. Blanchet, rue Bonaparte, 32
2283 Mon père et ma mère
[Portrait of My Father and Mother]
2284 Lever de lune [Moonrise]
3205 Au coin du feu (pastel)
3206 Portrait de M.W. (pastel)
(appartient a M. Whiteing)

1886 Stott (William) né à Oldham (Grande-Bretagne) élève de M. Gérôme
4, Passage Dulac, rue de Vaugiraud, et chez MM Durand-Ruel, rue de la Paix, 1
2238 Portrait de Miss White [Alice White playing the violin]
2239 Un jour d'été [Summer's day]
3362 Clair de lune d'été (pastel)
3363 Souvenir de plage (pastel)

1887

1888

1889

1890 Stott (William) né à Oldham (Grande-Bretagne) élève de M. Gérôme
Londres, 3, Wychcombe Studios.
2238 Endymion

This was the last time Stott exhibited with the Société des Artistes Francais, which had been formed out of the old Salon in 1881 by the artists themselves. From 1890 Carolus-Duran, Cazin, Puvis de Chavannes, Alfred Stevens, Sargent, Boldini and many other *juste milieu* artists moved over to the new rival Salon of the Société de la Nationale des Beaux-Arts, which was more liberal and did not award prizes.

After a gap of three years, from 1894, Stott began exhibiting again in Paris at the Société de la Nationale des Beaux- Arts, where he exhibited regularly until his death in 1900.

1894 Morning in the Alps

1895 [unknown]

1896 1179 Ophelia
1180 Portrait of Mme M
1181 Portrait of M. M

1897 1170 Pearl Clouds
1171 Idlers

1898 1187 The White Mountain
1188 Souvenir of an Island

1899 1364 The Happy Valley

Sources: *Catalogue of the Paris Salon, 1678–1881*, compiled by H.W. Janson, 60 vols., New York (Garland Publishing Inc.) 1977; Salon catalogues for 1881–90; 'Chronology', in *Post-Impressionism: Cross-Currents in European Painting*, exhibition catalogue, Royal Academy, London, 1979, pp. 280–97

Index